# The Optical Vacuum

# THE OPTICAL VACUUM

*Spectatorship and Modernized American Theater Architecture*

Jocelyn Szczepaniak-Gillece

OXFORD
UNIVERSITY PRESS

Oxford University Press is a department of the University of Oxford. It furthers
the University's objective of excellence in research, scholarship, and education
by publishing worldwide. Oxford is a registered trade mark of Oxford University
Press in the UK and certain other countries.

Published in the United States of America by Oxford University Press
198 Madison Avenue, New York, NY 10016, United States of America.

Library of Congress Cataloging-in-Publication Data
Names: Szczepaniak-Gillece, Jocelyn, author.
Title: The optical vacuum : spectatorship and modernized American theater architecture /
Jocelyn Szczepaniak-Gillece.
Description: New York : Oxford University Press, [2018] | Includes index.
Identifiers: LCCN 2017057748 (print) | LCCN 2018003140 (ebook) |
ISBN 9780190689377 (updf) | ISBN 9780190689384 (epub) |
ISBN 9780190689353 (cloth : alk. paper) | ISBN 9780190689360 (pbk. : alk. paper)
Subjects: LCSH: Motion pictures—Social aspects—United States. |
Motion picture audiences—United States—History—20th century. |
Motion picture theaters—United States—History—20th century. |
United States—Social life and customs—20th century.
Classification: LCC PN1995.9.S6 (ebook) | LCC PN1995.9.S6 S93 2018 (print) |
DDC 302.23/430973—dc23
LC record available at https://lccn.loc.gov/2017057748

9 8 7 6 5 4 3 2 1

Paperback printed by WebCom, Inc., Canada
Hardback printed by Bridgeport National Bindery, Inc., United States of America

For my father, James P. Gillece Jr.,
who believed in the possibility of a better world

# CONTENTS

# ACKNOWLEDGMENTS

A book is an object at once solitary and communal. Here, I celebrate those who helped make this—and me—what we are now.

I have been so lucky to work with my gracious and witty editor Norm Hirschy and with Oxford University Press. Every step of the way, Norm and editorial assistant Lauralee Yeary have been smart, efficient, and generous. I thank them and production editor Richa Jobin for taking this on and for treating my work with such care. I began this while a graduate student in Screen Cultures at Northwestern University. My thanks first go to Scott Curtis, whose brilliant historical mind and uncanny ability to realign an argument into something of elegance shaped my writing, thinking, and scholarship. Lynn Spigel is a model of historiographic wisdom and arch humor; Jeff Sconce is a favorite provocateur and fellow literary oddity. My thanks also go to Hamid Naficy, Jacqueline Stewart, Mimi White, Julia Stern, and the late Chuck Kleinhans, and a special thanks to Miriam Petty for her genius, kindness, and friendship. Early work on this book was supported by a Graduate Research Grant from The Graduate School at Northwestern.

At the University of Wisconsin-Milwaukee, my colleagues in the Film Studies Program have been supportive mentors and wonderful friends. Gilberto Blasini, Elena Gorfinkel (now at Kings College), Tasha Oren (now at Tufts), Tami Williams, Patrice Petro (now at USCB), and Andy Martin are the best colleagues and late-night conversationalists one could ever want. Thanks as well are due to Plan H (Stuart Moulthrop, Richard Grusin, and Lane Hall), the Department of English, and the Department of Art History. This work was supported at UWM by a Research and Creative Activities Support award as well as a fellowship at the Center for 21st Century Studies. I thank Kennan Ferguson, previous director, and the fellows with whom I shared a productive year: Erica Bornstein, Ann Mattis, Nan Kim, Nadine Kozack, and Tanya Tiffany.

My thanks to those who have helped me during my years of research, including the Colonial Williamsburg Foundation, especially Richard McCluney; the archivists at the Avery Architectural and Fine Arts Library at Columbia University and at the Billy Rose Collection at the New York Public Library;

the Museum of Modern Art; the Aldo Tambellini Art Foundation; the Manning Brothers Historic Photographic Collection; the Eberly Family Special Collections Library at Penn State University Libraries; and the Theatre Historical Society of America and their generous provision of a Dubuque Research Fellowship for my work. I am indebted to Sue Isman and Ken Isman, Benjamin Schlanger's grandchildren, who found me and opened up their family history to a stranger. I hope I have done them and their grandfather proud.

I am lucky to have had an array of friendships that have honed my thought and my appreciation for the world. I cannot imagine life without the endlessly brilliant Daniel Bashara, who is an irreplaceable presence in my thinking and my heart; his spirit speaks directly to mine. Winter Jade Werner has been a part of this—and of me—since we met our first year of graduate school. The incomparable and uncompromising Jill Godmilow's impact can never be overstated. Thanks to my true and dear friends, both in and out of this profession: (in no specific order) Annie McClanahan and Ted Martin, Andrew Philip and John Nolan, Catherine Clepper, Beth and Veronica Corzo-Duchardt, Christine Evans, Jill and Dave Baum, Ann Mattis and Bill Malcuit, Alex Thimons and Dustin Mays, Stephen Groening and Andrea Christy, Flora Chen, Elizabeth Petinga and Christopher Weakland, Matthew Kotar and Juan Lopez, Zachary Campbell, Kara Zuaro, Dave Sagehorn, Lisa Mahoney and Sean Kirkland, Jennifer Hasso, Cary Elza, Alex Bevan, Amy Oberlin and Rob Patterson, Elena Gorfinkel and Alex Pickett, Erica Bornstein, Jennifer Jordan, Jasmine Alinder, Ittai Weinryb, Darran White Tilghman and Ben Tilghman, Lesley Harvey, Laura Loos, Mollie Lohinski, Carrie Adams, Tony Jones, Meghan Bassman, and the Durels.

Thanks to my siblings Jessica Gillece Macpherson, Jillian Szczepaniak-Gillece, James Szczepaniak-Gillece, Juliette Szczepaniak-Gillece, and John Michael Szczepaniak-Gillece, and all of their partners; to my mother, Jane Szczepaniak; to my in-laws, Jeannie and Joel Leson; and to virtual family members Laurie Katz and the McLaughlins. It is a palpable sadness that my father, James P. Gillece Jr., is not alive to see this book, and so I dedicate it to his memory.

Finally, there are never enough things to say about Richard Leson, nor is any of it sufficient. None of this would have happened without him. He is the best part of my life, and I am eternally grateful for this love that is, like all the most precious things, inexpressible.

# Introduction

*The Theater, the Film, and the Spectator*

## MOVIES DREAM OF THE NEUTRAL

In William Wyler's 1935 film *The Good Fairy*, young innocent Luisa Ginglebusher (Margaret Sullavan) is recruited by Maurice Schlapkohl (Alan Hale) from a municipal orphanage to work as an usherette in Budapest's largest movie theater (Figure 0.1). At first, Luisa is dressed in a sequined cape and tight pants (how tight they are depends upon the girl, Schlapkohl informs the head of the orphanage; all the pants are the same size) and flourishes an electric pointer to show viewers to their seats—her costume and pointer sparkle with a splendor that matches the sumptuousness of the three-thousand-seat palace in which she works. But once inside the auditorium, she finds herself enraptured by the screen. There, screenwriter Preston Sturges's parodic film-within-a-film shows a glamorous lead actress melodramatically leaving her beau, Meredith. Moved to tears alongside her soon-to-be friend Detlaff (Reginald Owen), Luisa is rendered unaware of the impact of extraneous objects like her flashlight, absorbed completely in the screen.

Toward the end of the film, Luisa tries on a "genuine Foxine" stole and blissfully admires herself in a succession of mirrors (Figure 0.2). Six years prior to Gregg Toland's famous hall of mirrors shot in *Citizen Kane*, the protagonist gazes upon her image reflected ad infinitum. Yet both Sullavan's acting and the mise-en-scène in cinematographer Norbert Brodine's mirror shot suggest something other than Charles Foster Kane's egotistic paranoia; here, Luisa's mirror repetition fills the entirety of the image. Not only is there no additional furniture or wall space surrounding the mirror, but also there is no defined border between mirror frame and frame edge: both reach out to touch the end of the image. At first, Luisa replicates her usherette march, delighted at the multiplied

**Figure 0.1:** Still from *The Good Fairy* (William Wyler, 1935).

**Figure 0.2:** Still from *The Good Fairy* (William Wyler, 1935).

efficiency of the female body bookending her earlier experience in the theater with her coworkers. But then, Luisa removes her hat and wraps the stole more rakishly across her shoulders. "Oh Meredith," she drawls, lengthening her face in a Garbo approximation. The mirror into which she gazes is now a metonym for the screen. She has moved from worker to spectator to character, a trajectory effected by the removal of the glittering objects that might otherwise surround the frame.

In part, Luisa's transformation ably demonstrates the dream of wealth and fame promised for Depression-era audiences attending the movies. But in addition to this rags-to-riches orphan trope, the beginning and end of Luisa's story also unveil transformations in the American movie theater and its spectator. At the outset, Luisa discovers the movies through the luxury of the palace and all its accoutrements, of which she is undoubtedly one: another decoration framing the image and encouraging repeat attendance. Yet by the conclusion of the film, Brodine's mirror shot illustrates how a removal of extraneous visual information—chandeliers, elaborate furniture, or gilt frames around mirrors or screens—facilitates deeper immersion. Luisa, in effect, becomes an ideal spectator of the mid-1930s: no longer in need of distractions either visual or vaudevillian, Luisa requires only the primal connection between image and spectator to be completely entranced by the movies. Her surroundings fall away, neutralized in order to privilege the central relation between viewer and screen.

Alongside the rapidly proliferating product streaming out of Hollywood's studios, the 1910s and 1920s saw an explosion of theater building throughout the United States. While the size and style differed significantly depending on population density, location, and funding, our iconic image of this moment in exhibition undoubtedly remains the movie palace: jaw-dropping, majestic, sparkling, magical. This, we think, was when attending the movies *meant* something. Little surprise, maybe, that contemporary art house chain Landmark Theatres has made it a canny business practice to take over rundown palaces in cities like Milwaukee, showing Oscar bait in elaborate and lush surroundings with a hint of opulence gone pleasantly rancid. Perhaps it is also unsurprising that many of the most striking images from the *Ruins of Detroit* photography series by Yves Marchand and Romain Meffre are of the decaying grandeur of abandoned palaces: flaking gilt and dusty velvet, ripped curtains and eroded carpets evoking a lost fantasy moment made all the more precious by its slow disappearing act. When we attend the black box theater of today, its floors sticky, its decor utilitarian, its lobby dominated by massive concession stands and cardboard advertisements, we suspect that cinephilic spectatorship has similarly evaporated alongside the movie palace's arcane and romantic style.

But the palace was not built by cinephiles. In fact, its function was in many ways diametrically opposed to the kinds of immersive contemplation that acolytes of *Cahiers du Cinéma* would later espouse. Cinephilia's spatial attributes can instead be traced to a different moment and a louder voice: the late 1920s and the work of New Yorker Benjamin (Ben) Schlanger, theater designer, architect, and engineer for nearly half a century. Schlanger, the youngest of eleven children, was born in New York City in 1904 to parents who emigrated from Austria and Poland in 1891; his father, Eleazer, was an Orthodox rabbi who owned a Hebrew bookstore in Harlem.[1] Schlanger studied at Columbia and then the National Institute for Architectural Education (Beaux-Arts Institute of Design), and in 1929, he married his first wife, Sadie Meltz, with whom he had his only child, Dorothy. Schlanger went on to marry three more times; his final marriage in 1967 was to Marion, who would be widowed upon his death in 1971.[2]

Following his graduation from Columbia in the 1920s, Schlanger moved to Florida in the hopes of obtaining profitable assignments during the building boom. After the crash routed the Sunshine State's dreams of construction wealth, Schlanger moved back to the mid-Atlantic and began advising on and eventually building New York theaters during the largest Hollywood boom. Immediately, and perhaps surprisingly given his stylistic training in the Beaux-Arts method, Schlanger saw the necessity of introducing function-alism into theatrical structures. While modernist architecture had begun to infiltrate American building, theater owners and investors were notoriously slow to respond; their assumption that audiences required glistening, over-the-top spaces to get their money's worth remained rigid for much of the ensuing few decades. But Schlanger crusaded relentlessly, urging exhibitors to rid their buildings of unnecessary gingerbread and focus instead on pro-viding optimal viewing conditions—to create, as he described his 1957 mas-terpiece at Colonial Williamsburg, an "optical vacuum," an altar to attention that negated itself in order to celebrate and foreground the film. His calls for change would lead him to construct and advise on dozens of theaters around the country and the world, and to write hundreds of pages of editorializing material for multiple industry magazines that shaped the course of exhibi-tion practice.

Schlanger was, by all surviving family accounts, a humble and serious man who poured himself wholeheartedly into his work—sometimes to the point of undercharging clients. Unfortunately, he left no cohesive group of archival materials. Instead, in addition to what few theaters still stand, his legacy consists of a vast array of essays, designs, and columns in leading trade journals

---

1. I am indebted to conversations with Sue Isman, Ben Schlanger's granddaughter, for this information.
2. "Ben Schlanger, Theater Architect, Is Dead at 66," *New York Times*, May 4, 1971.

of the time, namely, the *Journal of the Society of Motion Picture and Television Engineers*, *Architectural Record*, and most prominently the *Better Theatres* section of *Motion Picture Herald*, as well as several patents. In this book, I look frequently to his writings in *Better Theatres* for several reasons. First, *Better Theatres* allotted significantly more space—and significantly more speculative writing—for exhibition leaders. Schlanger shared many of his perspectives on theatrical architecture with George Schutz, the section's editor, meaning that the publication was quite amenable to his ideas and to allowing him space to theorize ideal theaters of the future. Second, *Better Theatres* was the leading industry journal of the time—and also the only one that provided in-depth material about theater construction. *Boxoffice* published a contemporaneous section on *Modern Theatres* that frequently provided information on theater building (especially on drive-ins during the 1950s), but tended to have shorter, more straightforward writing. Finally, the main reason for relying so significantly on *Better Theatres* is that it is the closest object to a Schlanger archive that we now have. Given that he published there with such frequency over a period of several decades, tracing his consistencies and changes over time becomes a possibility with the use of *Better Theatres*.

Reconstructing Schlanger's pathway to neutralization requires a cobbling together of the preponderance of publications he left, his theater designs and the few that still stand, scattered portions of archival materials in other architects' papers and in corporate files, and conversations with the few family members that remember him. Beyond just architectural plans, however, these materials reveal not just the *practice* of Schlanger's work, as might be evident in early designs, but the *theory* behind his buildings. The goals and ideals that might not be visible in a final concrete product that is necessarily a compromise between architect and funder crystallize in publications that operate in the realm of the possible. And these possibilities espoused by Schlanger reveal an investment in high modernist ideals—contemplation, neutralization—within an industrial context. They offer a rejoinder to the assumption that only iconic buildings created by the most celebrated architects have weight, urgency, and historical merit. They demonstrate instead that the ideals that shape and sharpen larger cultural discourses are percolating even in the most single-purpose and readily replicable of public spaces—in this case, the movie theater. And they uncover the value in studying such places not merely as illustrations, but as defining of cultural currents, as necessary objects of discourse that demonstrate the multiplicities of spectatorship's coalescence.

What Schlanger advocated from early on in his career was not merely a new architectural style based on the work of European modernists. Indeed, what Schlanger sought was a new form of spectatorship that would upend the more chaotic traditions of the movie palace and maintain a silent, stilled, and attentive audience of viewers. Schlanger's ideal theaters would be places of both bodily passivity and contemplation, yet also of immersion in the sense that the local environment and fellow viewers would fall away in service of the screen. His work, then, bridged gaps between Benjaminian viewing patterns of contemplation and the disciplinary benefits of immersion: his theaters were designed so that spectators would engage with film's high art dimensions via careful observation, and remain docile, untroubled creatures held silently by comfortable chairs. Here, then, are the disciplinary aspects of cinephilia: awe, silence, and stillness are beneficial both for filmic observation and for keeping an audience in place. When we look to Schlanger as a model for cinephilia's patterns of watching, we similarly uncover the work of cinephilia not only as a mode of engagement, but of pedagogy and discipline, especially in a Foucaultian sense. A cinephilic viewer is the viewer any exhibitor would welcome into his theater: one who never talks, never causes trouble, and never makes herself an annoyance to other patrons. The neutralized theater therefore demands greater attention to cinephilia's function not just as a club of adoration, but as a means of integration into acceptable social behavior and a way of making film into a kind of social good. Cinephilia here is less concerned with auteur worship, and more with the shadow forces that might deploy its weapons for the purposes of good citizenship. Cinephilia, in short, was a useful industrial tool, something made clearer during the transition from the palace to the neutralized theater form. Hence the neutralized theater is a space where cinephilic attributes serve spectatorial governance.

Where the palace was a noisy, even at times brightened building based in large part on the stage theater, Schlanger's interests lay in a space designed specifically for the viewing of *film*. His theaters aided in ushering in the separation of film from the stage—a linkage, William Paul elucidates, that was maintained far past the coalescing of narrative film form into a distinct code.[3] For most historians of exhibition, the shift from the movie palace's grandiosity in the 1920s—its use of excessive sculptural detail, massive space, vaulted ceilings, chandeliers, lush fabrics, and rich jewel tones—to the stripped-down auditorium familiar to today's audiences was a result of Depression-era economics, the dramatic impact of which on exhibition has long been established. Few link the burgeoning austere filmic space of the 1930s to a new interest in attention, directed vision, proper film viewing, modernism, and optical science, yet economic pressures do not tell the entire story. In 1931, the editors of the predominant mainstream exhibition journal *Motion Picture Herald*'s architectural *Better Theatres* section observed that "theatre designers studying the function of the motion picture theatre with its special relationships to

3. William Paul, *When Movies Were Theater: Architecture, Exhibition, and the Evolution of American Film* (New York: Columbia University Press, 2016).

architecture, are adopting the attitude that interiors, particularly the auditorium, should contribute through their very lines and appointments to the focusing of all the patron's interest upon the screen."[4] Rather than a smaller auditorium simply for the sake of increasing Hollywood's lessened profits, exhibitors suggested the efficacy of architectural remodeling for the purpose of better-directed attention. By the late 1920s, the massive scale of the movie palace's size and decorative elements had overwhelmed the American exhibition scene. Calls for a transformed theater were in effect by 1928, partially due to the influence of modernism on American literature, art, and architecture. In July of 1928, George Schutz, editor for decades of *Motion Picture Herald's Better Theatres* section, explained that "Art Moderne may be called design based on the simple line. Immoderate embellishment—ornate figures, scrolls, floral excrescences, what is popularly referred to as 'lovely,' what we have been used to associating with the feminine—are ruled out, the more completely as the treatment is more severe, more purely Art Moderne."[5] In contrast to Victorian art, Art Moderne should operate not in mere harmony, but, like much modernist architecture, should express psychologically the purpose of the room.

Alongside Schlanger, Schutz would be a dominant figure calling repeatedly for a "new" art of cinema and architecture. Together, he intimated, the two disciplines could develop monumental aesthetic achievements. Schutz's ideas were far from unique. In 1928, Thomas E. Tallmadge described architecture as the noblest of the arts, but one that remained consistently misused in the movie theater given the continuing prominence of proscenia, ceiling decorations, and other remnants of vaudeville; instead, the theater should push architecture toward more idealistic heights.[6] John W. Root and Wallace Rice similarly argued that the movie palace relied too strongly on ornamentation from the past; to make it fully an art of the twentieth century, it should divorce itself from antiquated and grotesque forms, allowing contemporary exhibitors to create their own ancestral heritage:

> Once given an unobstructed view of the picture, the treatment of the theatre interior would be rather *neutral*, quite simple, and primarily arranged for the proper presentation of pictures only, with the various wall surfaces, the undersides of the balconies, the ceiling, the arch about the picture plain in character and undiverting, and treated acoustically for the voices to be heard in the movietone and the like. . . . While the conception and evolution of modern ideas

4. "Why Remodel?," *Motion Picture Herald*, April 11, 1931, *Better Theatres* section, 11.
5. George Schutz, "Modernizing the Interior," *Exhibitors' Herald and Moving Picture World*, July 7, 1928, *Better Theatres* section, 13.
6. Thomas E. Tallmadge, "The Screen, a New Art, Should Pave the Way to a New Architecture," *Motion Picture Herald*, March 17, 1928, *Better Theatres* section, 9.

in building should remain in control of the architect, he in turn should call upon the sculptor, the mural painter, and all other artists.[7]

By 1935, modernism in the movie theater had become relatively widespread practice. For Robert O. Boller, modernism for exhibition meant a "partially imported fashion in building lines and designs variously known as 'moderné,' 'the international style,' 'organic architecture,' and by other aliases. . . . We will, for convenience sake, adopt the term *modern* when speaking of the style under discussion."[8] Taking an increasingly common stance, Boller explained that modern design "stressing economy and simplicity in building construction" was a necessity post–World War I, resulting in what he termed "working class architecture," where

> Functionalism [was] their god. To these architects, utility meant beauty, and the old forms and designs were impatiently swept away as relics of a past dominated by an arrogant aristocracy. America, always too eager to grasp at anything with an imported label or flavor, tried the new design in her skyscraper. . . . Our factories, built with an eye for the maximum possibilities of air, light, and efficiency, to their great surprise found themselves hailed by Europeans as shining examples of the new architecture! . . . [Yet] Motion picture theatre architects . . . have been in a state of hibernation during these quiet years. . . . But this period of quiet and reflection helped many of us to study more deeply into various theories of motion picture theatre design. . . . The motion picture theatre, not the European factory or the American chain store or commercial building, should set the gait in up-to-date architectural design.[9]

As a result, American exhibitors in the 1930s, according to Boller, were ready to celebrate the "truly working class architecture" already embraced by Europe. Yet given the arguably instantaneous middle-class nature of America compared to Europe's history of peasantry and aristocracy, Boller argued that "modern" meant something different in the United States. For this reason, Boller proposed not an imitation of the European approach to modernism, but rather using "the simplicity and honesty of the new style and blend[ing] it with the tradition and folk lore of our own native land."[10] In this sense, the movie theater should celebrate the efficiencies and benefits of European modernism, standing as a shining beacon for the rest of the country's architecture, yet also develop its own quintessentially American approach. The movie

7. John W. Root and Wallace Rice, "The Taj Mahal, Mr. Coolidge, and the Motion Picture," *Exhibitors' Herald and Moving Picture World*, November 24, 1928, *Better Theatres* section, 7–9 (emphasis added).
8. Robert O. Boller, "Modernism: Its Meaning in Practical Remodeling," *Motion Picture Herald*, March 9, 1935, *Better Theatres* section, 14.
9. Ibid., 14–34.
10. Ibid., 34.

theater therefore should become the standard-bearer for middle-class modernism, the possibilities of the new art paired with the new architecture, and a machine-like, utopian American approach to meticulous environment and calibrated seeing.[11] Schlanger proposed to answer these calls via the neutralization of cinema space.

The relative lack of attention to Schlanger and to neutralization, as opposed to analysis of the films shown within a neutralized cinema's walls, combined with its substantial impact on the history of American moviegoing, affirms a current need to reopen pathways in exhibition studies to consider the impact of industry and space on conceptions of the ideal spectator. Anne Friedberg's work on the gaze that connects arcade, shop window, and movie screen in modernity provides an essential framework for understanding Schlanger's architectural approach. For Friedberg, the imbrication of capital, visuality, and urban experience combine to constitute a mobilized and virtual gaze as well as a new spectatorship shaped by space and temporality.[12] While Friedberg does not discuss the neutralized cinema, her modern spectator is a companion to Schlanger's. Giuliana Bruno's work on motion, emotion, film, and architecture similarly evokes a modern cinematic spectator whose experience pivots on the dualities of sensing and contemplating, and of stillness and movement.[13] In addition, Vanessa R. Schwartz insists on the importance of mass visual culture for the development of cinema's relationship to space.[14] Crowds that massed around museums, panoramas, and early film exhibition drew particular kinds of pleasure from both image and environment, paving the way for later film form. For all of these scholars, a consideration of architectural space is, simply, necessary to trace the development of a cinematic spectator; the spectator as we know her cannot exist without her built environment.

More recently, scholars including Richard Maltby and Kathryn Fuller-Seely have advocated for "new cinema histories" that incorporate global, economic, and material discourses into the study of film industry.[15] These arguments encourage consideration of the entirety of filmic practice to better assess film's place through a wider lens. Haidee Wasson and Charles Acland have engaged with this model in their examinations of useful cinema, global film exhibition,

11. Corresponding to Miriam Hansen's notion of "vernacular modernism" in the cinema, yet in this case through the architecture of the theater itself. See Miriam Hansen, "The Mass Production of the Senses: Classical Cinema as Vernacular Modernism," *Modernism/Modernity* 6, no. 2 (April 1999): 59–77.

12. Anne Friedberg, *Window Shopping: Cinema and the Postmodern* (Berkeley: University of California Press, 1993).

13. Giuliana Bruno, *Atlas of Emotion: Journeys in Art, Architecture, and Film* (New York: Verso, 2007).

14. Vanessa R. Schwartz, *Spectacular Realities: Early Mass Culture in Fin-de-Siècle Paris* (Berkeley: University of California Press, 1999).

15. See Richard Maltby, Daniel Biltereyst, and Philippe Meers, eds., *Explorations in New Cinema History: Approaches and Case Studies* (West Sussex: Wiley-Blackwell, 2011).

portable projectors and screens, and archiving practice at the Museum of Modern Art.[16] Along similar lines, Alison Griffiths's work on panoramas, museum display, IMAX, and prison screenings insists that the space of spectatorship must be considered alongside film form; especially in her work on prisoners and cinema, Griffiths describes the structures of authority that ultimately constitute the jailed spectator.[17] Stephen Groening's examination of exhibition patterns in in-flight entertainment considers another imprisoned spectator; in this case, one confined by travel requirements as opposed to criminality, yet one who also lacks choice in terms of what is viewed.[18] This call has been taken up as well by Brian Jacobson, whose examination of Thomas Edison's Black Maria and other studio spaces of early film urges recognition of the qualities of "luminosity, plasticity, and precision" in studio buildings that eventually found echo in film's form and place in culture.[19] In keeping with the work of these scholars, this book argues that extratextual filmic space must be included in a fuller definition of film spectatorship—yet rather than through the image of the studio, through that of the theater. Cinema's learned behaviors can be traced not only through the ideological qualities of continuity editing and representation, but also through the structures underpinning the creation of theater style. As cinema transformed, so did theatrical space—though not necessarily in tandem.

All of these recent scholars of new media histories affirm, then, that space constructs us as spectators, but also that spectatorial space shapes cinema's role in the larger cultural imaginary. Griffiths, for example, positions "carceral spectatorship" as a mutually constitutive process; prisoners in Sing Sing arranged their cells "cinematically" with wall images reminiscent of the constantly shifting advertising in theatrical lobbies, while films shot within prison walls in the 1920s and 1930s suggested a responsive gaze both inside and outside the American penitentiary system. Wasson's work on MoMA argues for the importance of placing film within a gallery context for contemplative film viewing. But if these spaces of viewing redefine our understandings of where exhibition takes place, and therefore how spectatorship is a far more

16. See Charles Acland, *Screen Traffic: Movies, Multiplexes, and Global Cinema* (Durham, NC: Duke University Press, 2003); Charles Acland and Haidee Wasson, eds., *Useful Cinema* (Durham, NC: Duke University Press, 2011); Haidee Wasson, *Museum Movies: The Museum of Modern Art and the Birth of Art Cinema* (Berkeley: University of California Press, 2005); and "Protocols of Portability," *Film History* 25, no. 1–2 (2013): 236–247.

17. See Alison Griffiths, *Shivers Down Your Spine: Cinemas, Museums, and the Immersive View* (New York: Columbia University Press, 2013); and *Carceral Fantasies: Cinema and Prison in Early Twentieth-Century America* (New York: Columbia University Press, 2016).

18. Stephen Groening, *Cinema beyond Territory: Inflight Cinema in Global Context* (London: BFI, 2014).

19. Brian Jacobson, *Studios Before the System* (New York: Columbia University Press, 2015), 11.

multifaceted process than once assumed, and insist on cinema's surroundings as indicative of how it will be consumed, how shall we place an idealized but empty box for viewing? What might it mean to dream of a space that is no space at all? How do we position the strange desire to "neutralize" cinematic space? And is there then an argument to be made that earlier architects of the moving image already recognized the impact that space had upon spectatorship—and that new cinema histories are, in a way, a return to what was already intimated by Schlanger?

For Schlanger, it is precisely because the space of viewing is mutually constitutive of spectatorship that the theater must be as visually and aurally flattened as possible. If this is an impossible desire, it also accounts for the constancy of cinema's structures of disavowal: its borders and unboundedness, its duration and atemporality, its volumetric weightlessness. The history of the neutralized cinema speaks, then, to an understanding that spectatorship is an environmental and bodily process, and therefore to a movie dream of negation where the walls surrounding film fall away into an immersive screen abyss: an optical vacuum.

## THE NEUTRAL AND THE APPARATUS

What constitutes the neutral? To engage with "neutrality" is to examine the stakes of idealism and its debt to ideology; a country's neutrality crumbles readily under scrutiny, while the modernist neutrality of white walls now signifies not only emptiness but erasure.[20] In order to neutralize an enemy, an assassin might commit a violent act of blind justice. To neutralize is to remake into nothing, to efface, to pacify, and to control. To be neutral is to be in a place of nothingness, akin to idealized versions of what Marc Augé describes as "non-places" in supermodernity, such as the airport lounge or the chain megastore repeated ad nauseam.[21] The neutral is a neither here nor there that masks impulse and desire. Yet the neutral also allows for projection; consider the home seller, urged by their agent to remove personal effects from rooms and repaint brightly colored walls a "neutral" gray or beige so that potential buyers might better imagine their own belongings fitting within the space. To neutralize is also to eliminate signifiers of individuality so that new images might blossom from nothing, and to erase environmental clues in service of a space more conducive to imaginative thought.

Tracing a concept of the neutral in the early parts of the twentieth century leads to two significant places. There is the neutralization impulse of

20. Mark Wigley, *White Walls, Designer Dresses: The Fashioning of Modern Architecture* (Cambridge, MA: MIT Press, 1996).
21. Marc Augé, *Non-Places: An Introduction to Supermodernity* (New York: Verso, 2009).

modernist architecture, where Adolf Loos decried the use of ornament in favor of purely smooth and functionalist surfaces and Le Corbusier reduced buildings to their barest forms and mechanics. And at around the same time, there is Bertrand Russell and burgeoning interest in the relevance of neutral monism for philosophy. In 1914, four years after Loos gave his lecture on ornament and crime in Vienna and a year after the essay was published in French, Russell first explained "neutral monism" in the pages of *The Monist*. While he was not the first to define the term, "neutral monism" would soon become one of Russell's central tenets. As Russell noted, unlike idealistic monism and materialistic monism, "neutral monism" argued that things understood as the physical and the mental are not inherently different. Instead, only "arrangement and context" separate one category from the other.[22] In the context of neutral monism, duality is erroneous; instead, "there is only one kind of *stuff* out of which the world is made, and this stuff is called mental in one arrangement, physical in the other."[23] While Russell had not yet ascribed to the theory in 1914, he eventually began to advocate for neutral monism in 1918, in the process asserting that it required a rejection of ego in favor of sensation. As Joanne A. Wood argues in her work on modernist literature and neutral monism, sensation insists on a bodily experience that is not permanent, but constantly renewed; "the body," Wood explains, "does not experience sensations, it is constituted by the sensations it experiences."[24] This, for Wood, proves necessary for understanding modernism after World War I, when a generation of literary figures epitomized by Virginia Woolf looked to ways to explain the fragmentation and realignment of the body in the wake of horrifying global violence. Neutral monism, and therefore theories of the neutral painted in broad strokes, retains essential links to modernist thought.

In *My Philosophical Development* (1959), Russell looks to an array of technological analogies to explain the constitution through sensation upon which neutral monism insists. In one, he imagines a "rich cynic," frustrated by the idiocy of theater-goers, who pays for a play to be performed in a theater populated with "cine-cameras" in the place of spectators. Each "cine-camera" observes the proceedings from its own angle and records each action, thereby illustrating how, at any moment, "a vast assemblage of overlapping events is taking place," all of which add up to the primacy of experiential sensation in constructing the world.[25] It is, Russell admits, an imperfect analogy. For one, the cine-cameras do not possess consciousness or minds. Still, if Russell quickly

22. Bertrand Russell, "On the Nature of Acquaintance," *The Monist* 24, no. 2 (April 1914): 161.

23. Ibid., 162 (emphasis original).

24. Joanne A. Wood, "Lighthouse Bodies: The Neutral Monism of Virginia Woolf and Bertrand Russell," *Journal of the History of Ideas* 55, no. 3 (July 1994): 491.

25. Bertrand Russell, *My Philosophical Development* (New York: Simon and Schuster, 1959; reprint, New York: Routledge, 1993), 14–15.

abandons the cine-cameras and the theater of the rich cynic, his curious reliance on the usefulness of visual technologies suggests an equivocation between neutrality and mechanical image production. In light of photography's claims to truth, such an association is hardly revelatory. Yet if neutral monism depends upon sensation to bridge the contextual and artificial separation between matter and the mind, visual technology seems a strange metaphorical avenue. For Russell, visual technology produces sensations that enter the mind through organs attuned to the outside world—a way that privileges neutral monism's relationship to the body and its constitution through events. In this sense, we could consider Russell's "cine-cameras" not only as the unusual aptitudes of a "rich cynic," but as indicative of a certain brand of ideal spectatorship that began to coalesce just after Russell's full adherence to neutral monism in the middle part of the 1920s. An audience of "cine-cameras," perfectly constructed and repeated mechanisms recording in silence, upright and still, have no history outside of the events they are observing within the confines of the theater. They are neutralized spectators acted upon by the sensations offered within the auditorium; they do not speak, but exist solely as objects of the theatrical experience. They are witnesses, anesthetized and prepared to be opened up by cinema's surgical drama.

In Russell's odd and seemingly inconsequential analogy, then, a history of mid-century spectatorship begins to unfold, one that valorizes the impact of theatrical sensation and that insists on the primacy of sensory experience. If Russell's analogy explained neutral monism, it also demonstrated the value of neutrality for a new generation of theater designers seeking out methods to encourage spectators' reconstitution by the multitude of events experienced via the screen. Indeed, neutral monism's spectator resembles Schlanger's: a figure of neither— yet both—body and mind, without memory beyond the picture show, silent but for the whirr and click of the camera motor, constituted by the images unspooling in front of them, and in possession of technological organs of perception that mimic and ultimately replace human vision. This is in many ways the spectator envisioned by Schlanger—one made by the movies and readied for event impact by the neutralization of the auditorium. Neutral monism and neutralization share root meanings, but also share an investment in an ideal spectator. Schlanger's choice of "neutral" to describe the new cinema auditorium enacts exactly the process its word implies: a meeting of body and mind in search of sensation, a legacy of modernist design and thought, and the surface effacement of these histories and components in order to privilege the work of projection.

There is another place where we might find hints of Schlanger's ideal spectator, yet one who is prepared by the movies for integration into ideology, and who appears in English in 1974, three years after Schlanger's death. Jean-Louis Baudry, along with Christian Metz, Jean-Louis Comolli, and Laura Mulvey, among others, led the charge in the 1970s to define cinema as a psychoanalytic and semiotic apparatus designed to incorporate the spectator into capitalist ideology. While apparatus theory has, by and large, dissipated from film theory in the wake of poststructuralist discourse, recent interest in its historiographic dimensions has shown the value of reconsidering its place in the study of cinema.

In "Ideological Effects of the Basic Cinematographic Apparatus," published in French in 1970 and in English in 1974, Baudry describes the process whereby cinema integrates its spectator into a fine-tuned web of intimations. Visual technology, he asserts, has proposed a kind of filmic objectivity that obfuscates the manner in which cinema operates upon us: "Does the technical nature of optical instruments, directly attached to scientific practice, serve to conceal not only their use in ideological products but also the ideological effects which they may provoke themselves?"[26] There is, Baudry explains, a kind of work that is done between the "objective reality" that is presented in front of the camera and the eventual shot; there is also a work, or transformation, done in the space between the film and its consumption, where "projector and screen restore the light lost in the shooting process," and the images unfold in front of captive spectators.[27] Such work enables the concealment of the instruments that create film—concealments that then enable ideological inscription of the viewer, who, Baudry reminds us, is so entranced that a rupture in projection brings about a disturbing stutter when he is brought back to "the body, to the technical apparatus which he had *forgotten.*"[28] For the cinematic apparatus to work effectively, a "formal continuity" must be established "through a system of negated differences and narrative continuity" with the utmost preservation of the "synthetic unity of the locus where meaning originates"—a symbolic reiteration of the Lacanian mirror stage and an equivocation of spectators by way of the elimination of personal detail and the suturing of viewer into unified screen reality, space, and subjecthood.[29] Of course, by the conclusion of the essay, we are to understand such concealments as the masking of capital and the economic forces underpinning our supposedly transcendent cinema experiences.

There may be little, at first, that seems to connect the apparatus to neutralization. After all, Baudry was writing his theory in the 1970s, long after the transformation of the movie theater into a silenced, stilled auditorium with little decoration beyond horizontal lines stretching toward the screen. The expansion of the screen in the 1950s was complete—even Academy ratio was no longer the standard, given the encroachment of widescreen into exhibition and television's poaching of a width of 1.33 to a height of 1—and had been for close to twenty years. Apparatus theory is a radical Marxist proposition that seems at odds with

26. Jean-Louis Baudry "Ideological Effects of the Basic Cinematographic Apparatus," trans. Alan Williams, *Film Quarterly* 28, no. 2 (Winter 1974–1975): 40.
27. Ibid.
28. Ibid., 42.
29. Ibid., 45.

industrial discourse. And certainly, Baudry pays little attention to the specific ways that movie theaters look. Yet what he cites as a kind of primal scene of cinema—"the darkened room and the screen bordered with black like a letter of condolences," "a closed space and those who remain there . . . find themselves chained, captured, or captivated"—is not what Miriam Hansen, for example, reconstructs as a messier, more uncontainable audience experience of silent cinema.[30] Instead, it is much closer to the viewer of the first and second waves of cinephilia, held in place and enraptured in a proper and civil mode of contemplation, and closer still to the ideal spectator that Schlanger sought to establish. "Unity," which Baudry called essential to the function of the apparatus, is a term returned to again and again by Schlanger and later neutralization advocates, who insisted that the theater should serve to visually unify auditorium space with the screen by virtue of self-negation. Relaxing the body in order to forget it was a notion also returned to again and again by Schlanger in seating plans and charts as well as larger theatrical designs. To forget the body is, as Laura Mulvey argued in her seminal essay, to default to the (white) male body; Hollywood's apparatus therefore insists upon a unified male, white, heteronormative spectator.[31] In short, while Baudry appeared to be defining *the* cinematic spectator, he was more precisely defining *a* cinematic spectator, one of particular historical context, one that emerged in the wake of the palace, and one that was constructed in large part by industry professionals, exhibitors, and particularly architects of the movie theater in addition to filmmakers. Baudry's spectator, cowed by the ideological drama unfolding in front of him, is neutralized by the image.

I am not proposing here that film bears no connection to economic ideologies, nor that Baudry was right to ignore the vast array of evidence for transgressive or disruptive or unruly spectatorship, nor even that the apparatus always works the way that Baudry (or, for that matter, Schlanger) claims it does. What I do want to propose is that Baudry, as well as the larger group of apparatus or screen theorists of the 1970s, was at once theorizing and historically describing a process that Schlanger had been attempting to enact in the theater from the late 1920s until his death. Within the very bones of neutralized theatrical architecture can be found deliberate attempts to negate spectatorial difference, to enforce immersion and bodily forgetfulness, and to construct a transcendent subject more able to project himself into the screen. The neutralized theater, in essence, should be considered the fourth limb of the apparatus: camera—projector—screen—and auditorium.

For Baudry, the major goal of the apparatus is conveyance: into market-centered ideology, gendered norms, and structured narratives that elide other modes of being. Neutralization adheres to this sense of passage, in that

30. Ibid., 44; Hansen, *Babel and Babylon*.
31. Laura Mulvey, "Visual Pleasure and Narrative Cinema," *Screen* 16, no. 3 (1975): 6–18.

it promotes total immersion into film's (and, generally, Hollywood's) hegemonic detail. Movement toward ideology—of capital, of American democracy, of the Hollywood system—undoubtedly constitutes a major aspect of Schlanger's work. Neutralization's promise was to effectively and efficiently funnel spectators from one part of the theater to the next, and from seat into screen; audiences could thus be cowed and enraptured, untroubled, still, and disciplined, prepared to purchase and to absorb. Yet the neutralized theater also emphasizes another aspect of spectatorship's history, which is the visualization of modern forms of transportation. Certainly, film has long been figured alongside the train and the car; from Hale's Tours to IMAX, novelty moviegoing experience is a complementary entity to the ways in which we see and traverse the country or the world. Sometimes, as in the RKO Roxy Theatre (New York, 1932), these connections between exhibition, movement, and photography were made explicit via direct reference to figures such as Peary, Lindbergh, Edison, and Muybridge (Figures 0.3 and 0.4). Neutralization highlights how the mainstream, as opposed to amusement-centric or drive-in, theater similarly evokes contemporaneous modes of vision and transportation, from the train to the window to the car to, finally, the spaceship. But it does so via paradox: physical stillness that determines visual movement.

**Figure 0.3:** Roxy, R.K.O. Theatre, Radio City, New York (N.Y.), 1932, Fay S. Lincoln photograph collection, Historical Collections and Labor Archives, Special Collections Library, Penn State University Libraries. Used with permission from the Eberly Family Special Collections Library.

**Figure 0.4:** Roxy, R.K.O. Theatre, Radio City, New York (N.Y.), 1932, Fay S. Lincoln photograph collection, Historical Collections and Labor Archives, Special Collections Library, Penn State University Libraries. Used with permission from the Eberly Family Special Collections Library.

Film therefore becomes an object of both seeing and transcendence, while illustrating the historical horizons of what transcendence means. In other words, at the very moment that neutralized theaters are linked to of-the-moment ways of moving, they evoke longstanding traditions of bodily transcendence. They are objects of impossibility that mandate both total passive immersion and high-art contemplation, both subjugation and attention. They unveil how transcendence itself is never operative in a vacuum; rather, the ways in which we configure transcendence are inexorably shaped by histories and ideologies. While the apparatus demands utter stillness, it also requires its contradiction: forward motion, even if metaphorical, into the screen. Similarly, while immersion and contemplation may seem opposed modes of watching, neutralization's slippage between them reinforces spectatorship's discursive formulations in at times oppositional ways. Schlanger's published words and built theaters are dynamic calls for a release into total aesthetic experience. Yet they function within a massive and exploitative industry, bound to hegemonic ideology and to capitalism. Schlanger can be—and was—both an architect and a theorist, both a profiteer and an idealist. His prose and his designs are pristine contradictions, all the more fascinating for their incommensurable natures. So, too, is film, and so, too, is spectatorship. The history of the neutralized theater is the history of a particular form of American spectatorship elegized by Baudry *and* Bazin, and Schlanger is one of its essential protagonists. Both approaches can—and do—exist simultaneously in Schlanger's ideal cinematic space.

In this history, I look to moments in Schlanger's career vis-à-vis crucial developments in theatrical form. Chapter 1 traces the beginnings of neutralization in the late 1920s and early 1930s via modernism, the machine age, and the changing values of darkness and light in the theater, from the grandiose chandeliers of the palace era to debates about proper levels of light for immersion in the modernized movie house. Schlanger's writings from the early 1930s are of particular import here, as the elusive structure of cinematic experience proves to be theoretically engaged since early attempts to divorce the film theater from the stage. Chapter 2 examines optics and the gradual decline of screen masking in the context of the shifting relationship between the screen and the spectator from early theories of the close-up through the expanded screen of the 1950s. Schlanger's Sychro-Vision Screen, eventually the RCA Synchro-Screen, constitutes one major moment of analysis. Chapter 3 considers the widescreen era and the aphysical attributes of widescreen exhibition through the lens of transportation: American seeing via the windshield of the car is a metaphor for the new goals of the enormous screen. The transcineum auditorium structures at Colonial Williamsburg, completed by Schlanger in 1957, constitute the chapter's central case study as culminations of an American form of democratic spectatorship. Schlanger described the overall structure as a "floating void" and "optical vacuum," the zenith of his lifelong work toward architectural neutralization and visual acuity. Chapter 4 discusses the aftermath of the neutralized cinema in the art house and underground theaters of the 1960s. Schlanger and Abraham Geller's Cinema I & II in New York and Aldo Tambellini's Black Gate Theater are two examples of the ruins of neutralization: both exemplify the failure of cinematic architecture's great vision of utopia.

For Luisa in *The Good Fairy*, work as an usherette is the pathway into the movie dream—but entering the movie theater is only the first step. She is sutured only when she looks upon herself in the expanse of the mirror/screen. There, she is fully seeing and seen, projected into the image with no visual distractions to draw her attention away. She is an ideal spectator of Baudry and his insistence on the mirror stage's repetition in the theater, and of Schlanger, who sought the neutralization of architectural space in order that viewers might lose their bodies through projection into the cinema. With Luisa's seemingly slight but surprisingly illustrative journey in mind, then, the story of Ben Schlanger and the neutralized cinema beckons to be unraveled: a history vital for comprehending the development of the twentieth- and twenty-first-century American filmic spectator and therefore film's position in cultural discourse of the last hundred years.

CHAPTER 1

# Nostalgia for the Dark

*Ben Schlanger and the Beginning of Neutralization,*

*1920–1932*

## GLAMOR AND FAILURE

Beginning in the late 1920s, the American movie industry underwent tremendous upheaval. From rapidly increasing ticket sales to multiformat extravaganzas combining vaudeville and cinema to dramatic new special effects to the establishment of the Hollywood studio oligopoly to the revolutionary introduction of sound, the film industry was on an unsteady, unsure, but undeniably upward path. Weekly ticket sales in 1929 topped 90 million—the largest attendance Hollywood would ever see—fueled not only by an increasingly regimented and genre-oriented product but also, as many exhibitors saw it, the luxurious escapism of the massive urban movie palace seating thousands of spectators.[1] The public purchased not only a ticket to the movies, but admission into extravagances such as those delivered by architects S. Charles Lee and Thomas Lamb: orientalist theaters with miniature minarets, atmospheric theaters replete with twinkling ceiling "stars," or any number of similar signifiers of wealth and wonder extending from Hollywood screen fantasy into ornamental glitz.

---

1. As Miriam Hansen has noted, the picture palaces were a relatively small portion of American movie theaters—5 percent between 1915 and 1933. But for exhibitors, they functioned as flagships: the glamorous ideal of motion picture exhibition. See Miriam Hansen, *Babel and Babylon: Spectatorship in American Silent Film* (Cambridge, MA: Harvard University Press, 1991), 100.

Yet by the 1930s, the effects of the Great Depression had winnowed Hollywood's profits by half. Accordingly, the picture palace of the Roaring Twenties not only began to fall out of favor, but became increasingly impossible to build; disappearing investment from the stock market coupled with ticket sales in freefall and expensive transitions to sound meant less and less money to spend on useless decoration. As a direct result of economic necessity, from the Depression onward, theaters slowly transformed into the black boxes we know today: minimal, significantly more intimate, darkened, and quiet. This is the familiar story of American twentieth-century exhibition: a fall from splendor, magic, and true cinephilia into our contemporary Spartan houses devoid of wonder.

This story, however, neglects a panoply of discourses from exhibition and, the history of theatrical architecture to tell a tidy narrative that concludes in the realm of nostalgia. If the authentic house of cinema—the grandeur of the movie palace, regardless of how widely accessible it actually was—is something relegated to pastness, then it aids in the now well-worn canard of the "death of cinema." Film and its proper house can both be situated conveniently in decades gone by, replaced by digitality and the sticky, chilly, and gloomy mall multiplex. The disappearance of the movie palace corresponds neatly to the disappearance of a *Cahiers du Cinéma* mode of cinephilia and the concurrent fracturing of the spectator into a multitude of discourses, figures, and identities.

But assuming that cinephilia and an idealized spectator are icons of the picture palace not only ignores the history of exhibition—it also ignores the ways in which the ideal filmic spectator has been carefully constructed via narratological, visual, and aural structures as well as architectural ones. Recent film theory has returned again to the 1970s with renewed interest in the *dispositif* and the apparatus. Apparatus theory, popularized first in English by Alan Williams's translation of Jean-Louis Baudry's "Ideological Effects of the Basic Cinematographic Apparatus" in *Film Quarterly* in 1974, posited a revolutionary notion of spectatorship for film theory.[2] For Baudry, the spectator enters into an ideological contract with the classical Hollywood system, wherein camera, screen, and projector serve to suture the audience member into the psychodrama of film viewing. While Baudry as well as his contemporary Christian Metz never theorized the impact of architectural space on the spectator, their highly influential work on spectatorial integration and its recent contemporary resurgence finds considerable illumination in the experience of theatrical space.[3] After the apparatus was discarded in postmodern theory, so

2. Jean-Louis Baudry, "Ideological Effects of the Basic Cinematographic Apparatus," trans. Alan Williams, *Film Quarterly* 28, no. 2 (Winter 1974): 39–47.

3. For examples of recent approaches to the apparatus, see "Cinéma & Technologie/ Cinema & Technology," *Recherches Sémiotiques/Semiotic Inquiry* 31, nos. 1–3 (2011).

too was the singular, universalized spectator—a figure of cinephilia, of the palace, of nostalgia. If this spectator was rightly decried as an at best impossible, at worst politically corrupt figure of reduction, to argue for its position in a particular historical context is not to suggest its inherent value. Rather, tracing the rationale for its emergence adds to our larger understandings of film's historiographic dimensions: how film form, film aesthetics, and indeed film theory arise within particular temporal horizons shaped by technologies, spaces, and cultural discourses.

In this chapter, I tell the story of the modernized or "neutralized" movie theater's emergence at the end of the 1920s and beginning of the 1930s. While economic reasons related to the Great Depression had an impact on theatrical architecture, a return to the exhibition archive proves that the rumblings of modernization—what I term "neutralization" based on its usage by architects—began prior to economic collapse, while Hollywood was still enjoying significant investment from the stock market. A singular focus on movie industry economics elides the specificity of discourses surrounding film theory, which had just as much if not more impact on the transformation of the theater as a new financial environment. By the mid-1920s, film's position in the United States was increasingly complicated; the movies were both a denigrated low and burgeoning high art, both mass spectacle and mass aesthetic, both a fully silent tradition and a form moving toward the mainstreaming of sound, and both ensconced in stage theatrical traditions and finding their own footing as a unique medium. Alongside these disruptions, theatrical architecture was similarly undergoing dramatic revisions—revisions that would affect the trajectory of twentieth-century spectatorship, the shape of film theory and its placement of the body, and film's position in the larger cultural sphere. To properly define the massive impact of these changes, we must first go back to the era of the palace and the ways in which its glamor and failures paved the way for Ben Schlanger to sound the charge against the palace and its particular structuring of American spectatorship.


## THE MOVIE PALACE IN 1920S AMERICA

Although the movie palace is still identified today as the pinnacle in theatrical achievement, by mid-century it was an object solidly of the past. In 1948, William Riseman, who designed many modern theaters over the course of his career, detailed over two decades worth of changes to the American movie theater and attributed the palace's end to a thoroughly modernist assumption: that

> materials did not have to be ornamented to be beautiful. Color was discovered as color, form as form, texture as texture, and the great medium for welding

together these components became Space rather than Mass. Solidarity gave way to lightness, and that which was *not* there became as important as that which *was* there.[4]

In looking back, Riseman observed a definitive shift from ornament to utility—yet this shift was neither cut-and-dry nor immediate. Instead, exhibitors argued for years over whether the elaborate nature of the palace or the efficiencies of Art Moderne and European functionalism represented the more modern path for the theater or the best way to show films.

From about 1915 until the early 1930s, movie palaces dominated the urban theater building scene (Figures 1.1, 1.2, and 1.3). While palaces required considerable economic investment and implied urbane taste distinctions, and therefore tended to be located within wealthier city locales, the exuberance of their designs and the grandeur of their settings meant that their overall impact outsized their national presence. Typically, these massive structures evoked lush scenarios such as a "magic carpet" or a "king's palace," trading in references to exotic lands and fairy tales.[5] Plush seats encouraged a lavish experience of "maximum comfort" that resonated through elaborate draping, gilding, and decoration.[6] Air conditioning provided another extravagance for audiences, but one economically and spatially affordable only by owners of palaces seating more than two thousand patrons; Balaban and Katz's Tivoli and Chicago Theatres (1921), "marvels of modern-day engineering and comfort," required a basement room with 15,000 feet of pipe, a 240-horsepower electric motor, and a dedicated engineer.[7] While in many ways the ultimate example of theatrical opulence, air conditioning was not without its aesthetic drawbacks. As one example, state-of-the-art down-draft systems of the early 1920s made architects queasy with their required eyesores: massive trumpet-shape distributors.[8] After the debut of Willis Carrier's smaller, cheaper system in the 1930s, however, smaller theaters gained additional access to air conditioning; even the more intimate theater could therefore extend the comforts of cooled air to a mixture of high-, working-, and lower-class patrons.[9] But the palace's main goal was an entirety of spectacle rather than straightforward focus on the film itself. At the height of the palace's popularity in 1925,

4. William Riseman, "The New Look for Theatres 1923 and Now," *Motion Picture Herald*, July 3, 1948, *Better Theatres* section, 38 (emphasis original).

5. E. C. A. Bullock, "Theater Entrances and Lobbies," *Architectural Forum* 42, no. 6 (June 1925): 369.

6. Heywood-Wakefield advertisement, *Exhibitors Herald and Moving Picture World*, March 10, 1928, 8.

7. Douglas Gomery, *Shared Pleasures: A History of Movie Presentation in the United States* (Madison: University of Wisconsin Press, 1992), 54.

8. See Gail Cooper, *Air-Conditioning America: Engineers and the Controlled Environment, 1900–1960* (Baltimore, MD: Johns Hopkins University Press, 1998), 100.

9. Gomery, *Shared Pleasures*, 76.

**Figure 1.1:** Fox Theater, Detroit, MI. From the Manning Brothers Historic Photographs Collection.

Samuel L. "Roxy" Rothafel stated that while he agreed that " 'The picture is the thing' . . . Of course the picture is important, and we could not do without it; but what we have tried to do is to build around it an atmospheric program that is colorful, entertaining and interesting."[10] For Roxy, music supplied the "body and foundation of the presentation. . . . It will become so integral a

10. Samuel L. Rothafel, "What the Public Wants in the Picture Theater," *Architectural Forum* 42, no. 6 (June 1925): 362.

**Figure 1.2:** Fox Theater, Detroit, MI. From the Manning Brothers Historic Photographs Collection.

part of the picture that the lines of confluence will hardly be distinguishable . . . reach[ing] the standard of grand opera."[11] Like the bombastic palace decorations, music strengthened an entirety of spatial rather than screen coherence. While Roxy mentioned that the theater of tomorrow would have a "neutral" decorative character, the eventual result would transform from movies as a "fusion of varied abilities" toward the "highest expression of art."[12]

11. Ibid., 363.
12. Ibid., 364.

**Figure 1.3:** Tivoli Theater, Chicago, IL. Theatre Historical Society of America, Chicago Architectural Photographing Company.

Roxy's suggestion of a "neutral" theater was far from in keeping with his typical designs, filled as they were with atmospheric conditions and spatial indulgence. For others, such as Prairie and Chicago School advocate Thomas Tallmadge, Roxy's approach was at best antiquated and at worst dangerous for film's potential abilities to promote citizenship, democracy, and uplift. In a controversial 1928 article that would be debated for months, Tallmadge decried the predominance of "prostituted" theaters. The palace, for Tallmadge, represented the "blare and din of an architectural circus," enhanced by the slapping-on of vaudeville and comedy acts that detracted from rather than encouraged focus upon the film. "Divorce the motion picture from vaudeville and jazz," Tallmadge insisted, "from tawdry decoration and vulgar architecture and it will yet take its place not only among the educational and moral forces of this country, but with the arts as well."[13] With a modernized and neutralized theatrical space, Tallmadge argued in rhetoric somewhat aligning with Roxy's, the movies could fulfill their educational, moral, and aesthetic ideals. To be sure, Tallmadge's rhetoric fits neatly alongside much Progressive-era reform discourse of the first decades of the twentieth century. As Lee Grieveson has explained, the stuttering consolidation of narrative film from the early 1900s through the 1910s evoked the uneasy status of a nascent form: as educational tool, as vulgar amusement, as press document, or as artistic expression.[14] In their contemporary consideration alongside cultural uplift movements, both film and the movie theater represented a risky potential intermingling of race, gender, and class differentials. Yet it was more commonly the nickelodeon, with its cheap gaudiness and immigrant clientele, that constituted the dangerous space; as Kathy Peiss has demonstrated, exhibition's search for a middle-class audience in part led to the construction of aspirational palaces.[15] Tallmadge's unusual movement here was not in associating the movies with vice, but in claiming that opulent theater space and not the nickelodeon was, in fact, the "prostituted" architectural form preventing film from rising to its true high-culture throne. Instead, modern film form should look to another option—a neutralization of its surroundings—in order to soar. Such modernist elevation reached across racial, class, and gender divides; while segregation continued in most theaters through the 1930s, the decade also saw the opening of over eight hundred theaters for African-American audiences, and modernist theaters tended to appear where workers were clustered.[16] If neutralization was not a progressive force per se, it was aligned with theater architecture's uplift potential.

Like Roxy and Tallmadge, many exhibitors were beginning to realize that this thoroughly modern art of film required similarly modern approaches to its display: it should be shown under the most precise conditions possible to maximize its effects. For them, the movie palace, with its myriad problems

13. Thomas E. Tallmadge, "The Screen, a New Art, Should Pave Road to a New Architecture," *Exhibitors Herald and Moving Picture World*, March 17, 1928, *Better Theatres* section, 9.

14. Lee Grieveson, *Policing Cinema: Movies and Censorship in Early-Twentieth-Century America* (Berkeley: University of California Press, 2004).

15. Kathy Peiss, *Cheap Amusements: Working Women and Leisure in Turn-of-the-Century New York* (Philadelphia: Temple University Press, 1986), 161–162.

16. Lary May, *The Big Tomorrow: Hollywood and the Politics of the American Way* (Chicago: The University of Chicago Press, 2000), 124.

including seating designs based on stage theater conditions, sinned not only in terms of its visual excess, but also its inability to provide a scientifically calibrated approach to seeing. This is not to say that palace designers entirely ignored the benefits of good sightlines, but rather that new voices in exhibition accused the palaces of sacrificing visual acuity for the sake of embellishment. In addition, during the Depression, several-thousand-seat movie palaces seemed examples of conspicuous consumption; worse, their substantial size resulted frequently in wasted space unfilled by eager consumers. As Lary May describes, the stock market crash of 1929 brought calls for a revolution in cinematic architecture, for the lavish displays of the palaces suggested to a poverty-stricken public rampant capitalism's terrible fall from grace.[17] Palaces were no longer interchangeable with exhibition, nor was their immensity a necessary apparatus for showing a film. In 1931, the editors of *Motion Picture Herald*'s *Better Theatres* section observed that "theatre designers studying the function of the motion picture theatre with its special relationships to architecture, are adopting the attitude that interiors, particularly the auditorium, should contribute through their very lines and appointments to the focusing of all the patron's interest upon the screen."[18]

The following year, architect and designer Ben Schlanger stated that "the large deluxe, lavishly treated theatre is no longer a symbol or agent of the motion picture. As a matter of fact, the motion picture was only an accompanying attraction in them at their inception . . . an unnecessary addition to the motion picture itself."[19] What was "unnecessary" were the decorative trappings glimmering throughout the palace; "necessary" theatrical touches focused on seating comfort, lessened eye strain, and continually improved viewing angles, all of which provided enhanced consumer value and a more directed cinematic experience. Here, Schlanger put forward an early version of his view on the necessity of neutralizing theatrical architecture: calibrating it into an unornamented, sparse, and efficient black box with horizontal lines converging at the screen, concentrated solely on visual and aural experience.

Schlanger's stance on neutralizing the decorative effects of the palace was in large part a response to discourses of modernism percolating throughout the United States and Europe. His functional approach to the theater recalled both Adolf Loos's dismissal of ornament in 1910 and Le Corbusier's insistence that "the house is a machine for living in."[20] As Beatriz Colomina has demonstrated, the occupants of Le Corbusier's houses are comparable to

17. Ibid., 110.
18. "Why Remodel?," *Motion Picture Herald*, April 11, 1931, *Better Theatres* section, 11.
19. Ben Schlanger, "Vision in the Motion Picture Theatre," *Motion Picture Herald*, July 30, 1932, *Better Theatres* section, 8.
20. Le Corbusier, *Towards a New Architecture*, trans. Frederick Etchells (London: J. Rodker, 1931), 89.

**Figure 1.4:** Villa Savoye, photo by Renato Saboya, Creative Commons.

movie viewers in that they are unable to "fix (arrest) the image."[21] In keeping with Le Corbusier's words and Colomina's analysis, we might then refer to Schlanger's stripped-down theater as a "cinema that is a machine for seeing." Le Corbusier's Villa Savoye, completed in 1929 to much fanfare, exemplified many of the tenets of the new architecture on which early modernized and, eventually, Schlanger's theaters would be based (Figure 1.4). Like the automobile, the Villa Savoye signified an advanced standardized construction delimiting a singular purpose: where the car transports, the house encloses. Yet the automobile, that most modern of movable objects, was first designed on "old lines"—those better suited to carriages, trains, or other, prior methods of locomotion.[22] So too had houses been built on "old lines" less amenable to the rhythms of modern life, and so too, at the end of the 1920s, had movie theaters. If cars were unavoidably at first considered through existing objects of transportation, the movie theater was similarly first considered through existing models of spectatorship, most particularly the theater. Like Le Corbusier, Schlanger insisted on discarding the "old lines" of the stage in favor of the new directionality demanded by cinematic viewing.

The neutralized theater, then, was undoubtedly a product of modernist architecture and ideological incitement, of demands like those of Le Corbusier's

21. Beatriz Colomina, *Privacy and Publicity: Modern Architecture as Mass Media* (Boston: MIT Press, 1996), 6.

22. Le Corbusier, *Towards a New Architecture,* 137. See also Adolf Loos, *Ornament and Crime*, trans. Michael Mitchell (Riverside: Ariadne Press, 1997).

to discard the remnants of the past for the sake of the efficiencies of the machine age, and of frustrations with the failures of obsolescent product exemplified by the palace. But as much as the functionalism and style of the neutralized theater were unavoidably modern, modernized theaters also relied on older aesthetic models of immersion in order to spur cinema toward its ideal state. If film was to provide a revelatory vision, the typical experience of the movie theater, filled as it was with distractions, noise, socialization, and conversation, was simply unsuitable for the possibilities of this new aesthetic object. The movie palace reflected this state of inattention that was the reality of the theater; its decorative gilt and frippery gave visual credence to the generalized cacophony of the auditorium experience. Indeed, such dynamic and confusing visual stimulation might even *encourage* a spectatorship of distraction—yet this was no way to treat the potentially religious experience the movies might offer. Instead, theatrical architecture should still the audience into an experience of the sublime.

For Schlanger and other early proponents of modernization, cinema was both *the* modern art and an opportunity to more fully realize aesthetic categories defined by Kant and Burke, in particular Kant's "dynamically sublime."[23] In the experience of the sublime—cliffs, the ocean, innumerable masses of stars—man is awed at his powerlessness over nature. The sublime's ability to strike one dumb stems in part from its overturning of established orders of magnitude. While the telescope makes the cosmos seem contained, or the microscope enhances the tiniest objects, there remains within us a striving toward an infinite that exists outside the realm of sensory judgment; there, the sublime is opposed to everything that is small or contained. This experience of endlessness and incomprehensible power awakens our minds into feeling moved compared to the calm that the beautiful evokes.

Kant's description of sublime experience was, by this point, nearly 150 years old. Yet Schlanger's insistence on film's latent potential realized by the perpetuation of visual endlessness echoed Kant's sublime aesthetics. By Schlanger's estimation, even thirty years past the Lumières' first public exhibition at the Grand Café in 1895, film's enormous capacities had not yet been fully awakened. While film could transform human concepts of scale—in the 1920s, the close-up was considered by many to be the most cinematic of all shots—its guardians persisted in showing it on a bounded screen in a cluttered auditorium that served to create defined borders between image and audience.[24] But neutralization's propositions—the elimination of proscenia, the expansion of the screen, and the darkening of audience space—sought

23. Immanuel Kant, *Critique of the Power of Judgment*, ed. and trans. Paul Guyer and Eric Matthews (Cambridge: Cambridge University Press, 2000), 143–144.
24. Jean Epstein in particular harbored intense affection for the close-up; see chapter 2 of this book.

to create an experience of the perceptual infinite. Removing markers of the external world and focusing attention on the screen would serve, in short, to condition spectators into entering a silent, encompassing world where vision expanded into endlessness. A modern auditorium was thus a Corbusian structure that defied the "old lines" of the stage—quite literally by substituting the verticality of the palace's wall decorations and light sconces for the horizontality of directional lines that merged at the screen. Simultaneously, its streamlined visual motion shuttled its spectators both backward into the Kantian sublime and forward toward the image unspooling into perceptual infinity. Both Le Corbusier's automobile and Kant's dynamic sublime meet in the figure of the theater: an efficient object of transportation that "moves" its spectators into revelation.

## NEUTRALIZATION, SPECTATORSHIP, AND THE MACHINE

In addition to models indebted to both modernity and modern aesthetics, the post-palace functional and intimate filmic space illuminated burgeoning interest in the efficacy of attention, directed vision, and a proper film viewing indebted to the talkies and their concurrent model of quieter watching. Such trends found expression in both the style and purpose of the movie house, where modernist design heralded an aesthetic of the machine, of efficiency, and of holistic attention. George Schutz, editor of *Motion Picture Herald*'s *Better Theatres* section, argued in 1928 for the more extensive use of Art Moderne and its use of "design based on the simple line" that could express the psychological purpose of the room. Like cinema itself, "Art Moderne is the child of the Machine," a form particularly relevant for a population told "more and more every day that we are machines ourselves, a part, like the steel machines, of another, merely bigger machine."[25] Later that year, Schutz reinforced the movies' connection to the industrial world and mechanization. Movies are a thoroughly modern art, and there is "a natural affinity between modernistic art and the photoplay theater which, it would seem, the architect and the exhibitor cannot ignore."[26] In this sense, modern design's purity of form was another tool for exhibition's rhetoric of uplift—for Schutz it shared

25. George Schutz, "Modernizing the Interior," *Exhibitors Herald and Moving Picture World*, July 7, 1928, *Better Theatres* section, 13–27.

26. George Schutz, "Modernistic Art, Its Significance to America and the Photoplay," *Exhibitors Herald and Moving Picture World*, October 27, 1928, *Better Theatres* section, 38; see also John W. Root and Wallace Rice, "The Taj Mahal, Mr. Coolidge, and the Motion Picture," *Exhibitors Herald and Moving Picture World*, November 24, 1928, *Better Theatres* section, 7–9; and Tallmadge, "The Screen, a New Art, Should Pave Road to a New Architecture," 9.

an affinity not only with modern film but with the modern theater, where viewers could be reduced to their components of shape, eye, and ear, metaphorical machines elevated through efficiency to a higher cinematic experience. Schutz's editorial influence would help shape a movement toward black box theaters through the 1930s.

Schutz's interest in the new photoplay theater and its properties of spectatorial unification hardly sprang from a void; instead, his investment in the new modern form bore conceptual linkages with theories of film and film space circulating in both industry and non-industry circles, both inside and outside the United States. Frederick Kiesler's innovative, if not entirely functional, Film Arts Guild Cinema, which opened in 1929, offered a rather extreme model. Alongside a modernist design that echoed the architect's strong links to the Bauhaus, Kiesler deployed his concept of "endlessness" to ensure the spectator would be granted access to her "spiritual and physical position in the universe."[27] While there is no evidence that American industry professionals were consuming European film theory, parallel developments in Germany suggested a larger formal investment in filmic architecture's effects. In 1926, Frankfurt theorist Siegfried Kracauer described Berlin's massive movie houses as "palaces of distraction," where "elegant *surface splendor* is the hallmark of these mass theaters."[28] These theaters, although large and ornate, adapted to a kind of tasteful grandiosity; accordingly, they showcased an array of entertainments, from the film to production numbers, songs, and other performances, so that a "glittering, revue-like creature . . . crawled out of the movies: *the total art work [Gesamtkunstwerk] of effects.*"[29] For Kracauer, Berlin's palaces traded in an outdated, luxurious, and giddy architectural aesthetic, and they presented a spectacle of modernity interwoven with capital; yet in addition, their spaces confused artistic disciplines. Berlin's theaters showcased far more than the movies, bringing together stage acts, music, and dance into a monstrous whole. Borrowing from Wagner, Kracauer described the picture palace as a perversion of utopia: a chaotic mingling of glitter and surface texture that elided all potential politics and insight in favor of a shimmering collaged façade. The problem with Berlin's movie theaters was their attempt to contain everything in a jewel box of delights at the cost of the potentially radical benefit that the movies might also promise.

27. Laura McGuire, "A Movie House in Time and Space: Frederick Kiesler's Film Arts Guild Cinema, New York, 1929," *Studies in the Decorative Arts* 14, no. 2 (Spring/ Summer 2007): 76.

28. Siegfried Kracauer, "The Cult of Distraction," in *The Mass Ornament*, ed./trans. Thomas Y. Levin (Cambridge, MA: Harvard University Press, 1995), 323 (emphasis original).

29. Ibid., 324 (emphasis original). Here, Kracauer references Wagner's concept of bringing all arts together so that the spectator might empathically project herself into the whole.

For Kracauer, distraction might prove valuable by enabling the spectator to break free of the bonds of unified illusion, ultimately experiencing the void at the center of modern capitalism. Indeed, Kracauer's distaste for the *Gesamtkunstwerk* belied the appeal he found in an engaged spectator who experiences communal revelation in a public space. Although he claimed that the total work of art was a flawed concept, Kracauer's belief that environment helped shape spectatorship suggested a trajectory of aesthetic development from Wagner rather than an irreparable gulf between them. If the film itself becomes the focus rather than the panoply of events and wonders that surround moving imagery, if the theater is scoured of "all trappings that deprive film of its rights" and the movie becomes the center of theatrical architecture, then and only then might be achieved a "kind of distraction that exposes disintegration instead of masking it."[30] In short, film might enable spectators to slough off the false consciousness that envelops the modern subject in capitalism. The theater might become the site of dawning awareness that, once bared, could be a functional structure surrounding a central vacuum that revealed to the modern spectator the emptiness at the core of her experience. To do so, the theater must first and foremost operate at the service of the moving imagery it holds inside. Kracauer's ideal theater would act as both a way of reconfiguring film as art and a display of modern experience, worthy of its own extended gaze and its own dedicated house. For Rachel Moore, Kracauer's essays on the Berlin picture palaces and on the mass ornament illustrate the tension between modernity's potential for dawning consciousness and the culture industry's dogged machine—a tension that has hardly disappeared in the wake of postmodernism.[31] Granted, Kracauer's stance on film was avowedly Marxist; compared to American cinematic architects, his relationship to the capitalist mode of film production was ambivalent at best. Yet comparing his arguments to those of exhibitors uncovers a spatial value: both sought to move film and its place of viewing into a more dynamic and sober space. To be sure, the profitable aspects of filmic spectacle cemented the impossibility of constructing film as a truly liberatory art. It is in these very contradictions— Kracauer's investment in distraction paired with his belief in film's redemptive potential, or Schutz's interest in the comfortable machine for seeing paired with an implied yearning toward cinematic release—that we might unveil the ambivalences of film viewing and the changes in ideal spectatorship over time. Film is not one thing or another, purely capitalist imbrication or purely source of liberation, and one essential way we might trace these continued fluctuations is through the development of its architectural space.

30. Ibid., 328.
31. Rachel O. Moore, *Savage Theory: Cinema as Modern Magic* (Durham, NC: Duke University Press, 1999), 91.

By the late 1920s, American writers and architects were likewise taking up calls for a purified, modernized, undecorated movie theater for the spectator demanded by the severe pleasures of the Hollywood system—one far different from the 1910s Coney Island and amusement park spectatorship of bodily jouissance.[32] Seymour Stern's 1927 essay "An Aesthetic of the Cinema House" proposed that the cinema house had yet to actually be built, partially because proper lighting conditions had not yet been fully achieved:

> Historically, the nickelodeon should be considered the only *actual* theatre cinema has possessed, for, while it was by no means the *ideal* theatre for this new art, it embraced the cardinal points of a house constructed, architecturally and psychologically, for and by the screen. It had pitch darkness, unbroken by ceiling lights or illuminatory distractions in the walls. It was small. It had very little ornamentation. Simplicity was its most distinguishing characteristic.[33]

Describing film as one of the "religious" rather than "aesthetic" arts, Stern saw cinema's potential as a mass call to action and a source of intellectual liberation—achievable specifically because of its immersive qualities.[34] The ego-projection possible in film would allow the spectator to fully encounter her radical individuality paired with communal experience; much like Kracauer, Stern hoped that the veil of modernity's and mass culture's illusions could be lifted by the power of the moving image. Cinema must "show us the way to freedom. . . . The shackles of mechanical reality must be broken; and cinema must break them!"[35] To this end, the cinema house must operate at the level of the individual, as opposed to in the palaces where the "mass" is the "unit of reaction."[36] Stern here resisted common associations of film with the

32. See Lauren Rabinovitz, *Electric Dreamland: Amusement Parks, Movies, and American Modernity* (New York: Columbia University Press, 2012), 161.

33. Seymour Stern, "An Aesthetic of the Cinema House: A Statement of the Principles Which Constitute the Philosophy and the Format of the Ideal Film Theatre," *The National Board of Review Magazine* 2.5 (May 1927); reprinted in *Spectator* 18, no. 2 (Spring/Summer 1998): 26 (emphasis original).

34. Ibid., 28–30. By "religious," Stern refers to a kind of auratic experience, akin to what Kracauer describes in the cathedral as opposed to the hotel lobby ("The congregation . . . is a *collectedness* and a unification of this directed life of the community," whereas "togetherness in the hotel lobby has no meaning"), or to what Benjamin describes in his "Work of Art" essay. See Kracauer, "The Hotel Lobby," in *The Mass Ornament*, 176; and Walter Benjamin, *The Work of Art in the Age of its Technological Reproducibility, and Other Writings on Media*, ed./trans. Michael W. Jennings, Brigid Doherty, and Thomas Y. Levin (Cambridge: Belknap, 2008). For a further discussion of this tension between attention and distraction, see Jonathan Crary, *Suspensions of Perception: Attention, Spectacle, and Modern Culture* (Cambridge, MA: MIT Press, 1999).

35. Stern, "Aesthetic," 28.

36. Ibid., 29.

mass, configuring it instead as an object potentially productive of an ecstatic state of individual consciousness.

Stern therefore exemplified one side of a debate that would continue throughout twentieth-century exhibition: whether film was an art object or a mass cultural spectacle. Although he considered cinema a "religious" art, for him it was, importantly, an art, and thus deserving of its own dedicated museum: the idealized film-theater of the future where the spectator is induced into a contemplative exchange between film and herself. Aesthetic contemplation therefore owns a privileged position as the instrument through which intellectual liberation might be achieved. Space is an integral aspect of the contemplative relationship; if the individual is to recognize cinema's artistic and aspirational attributes, she must receive environmental clues to this effect. And the first avenue for signaling the moment of contemplation was darkness:

> The initial requisite is darkness: complete, solid, unbroken. Whatever lights are found legally necessary should be properly diffused and softened, and under no circumstances should the decorative lights one gets in the "palaces," be allowed in the ceiling above the orchestra, just above the audience, for those prove detrimental to the eyes but positively impedimentary to the spectatorial focus on the screen.[37]

Despite Stern's confidence, ideal levels of lighting in the auditorium were subject to debate throughout the next several decades; although light diffusion was generally agreed upon, designers and engineers argued over whether dim lights, total darkness, or the brightest auditorium possible provided for a more optimal viewing experience based on camera and projection technologies currently available.

For Stern, calibrated optics were not the entire story. Rather, he demonstrated interest in bending the power of darkness toward a kind of primal response of awe: the light of hope, the spark of truth in the darkness of ignorance moves chronologically from the flickering fire of the ancients, to the candle flame of the enlightened philosopher, to the directed beam of projected light striking out against the darkened auditorium and the dumbstruck masses. "Above all, however," Stern argued, "the screen itself must be set off in an area of darkness designed to give it the utmost lucidity of appearance. It should be like the vision of another world, like some hallucinatory sphere, passing uncannily before our eyes."[38] Cinema could offer Aristotelian catharsis and its accompanying "balm," perfected for the needs of spectators in modernity—a linkage with the ancient past and an illuminated pathway toward

37. Ibid., 29.
38. Ibid.

a brighter future. The authority that Stern afforded cinema stemmed from its placement in a trajectory of important art forms and its status as world-maker. But cinema could not work miracles on its own; it must be framed by its location, set apart from the turbidity and falsity of the contemporary world, demarcated as worthy of undivided attention. By clothing itself in darkness, cinema could more effectively put on display its light-filled majesty: it could, quite simply, use invisibility to all the more powerfully reveal its own eminent visibility. In this way, Stern's desire for a perfected and darkened auditorium linked light, environment, and spectatorship, and elucidated the dramatic theoretical and historical crossroads at which the American movie theater found itself at the end of the movie palace era. American post-palace theatrical architects did not solely focus on the economics of the cinema system; they sought also to define their craft against rather than in tandem with the stage, to realize the promise of revelation, and to display how the medium of film depended upon the usage of darkness and light in the auditorium. Although, in contrast to Kracauer, profits and good business models remained consistent goals, their writings (and buildings) illustrated a powerful engagement in on-going aesthetic debates concerning the productivity of efficiency or ornamentation, modernism's relative validity, what made for an ideal spectator, and the power of art to induce mass revelation. Darkness and light could achieve these goals because, on the one hand, they were tools manipulated by modernist architects and artists, and, on the other, they enjoyed a particularly extensive philosophical status.[39] If Plato's allegory of the cave would later become an icon of Baudry's apparatus theory, its play on the power of darkness and light was foreshadowed in the 1920s and early 1930s in discourses surrounding the modernized movie theater.

## BEN SCHLANGER: ARCHITECT OF NEUTRALIZATION

During the very early years of the 1930s, Hollywood had begun to experience the shattering effects of the Depression: Wall Street investors were unable to continue aiding in the transition to sound, audiences on newly restricted incomes could not attend the movies as regularly, and expenses for elaborate theater materials were far more insurmountable. At this moment, the theater seemed an ideal place to cut costs; smaller, less obtrusive theaters therefore appeared quite fiscally appealing. Yet not only economic necessity contributed to a moment of transformation; so, too, did the urgency of rhetoric, both from writers such as Stern and Kracauer, and from Ben Schlanger (Insert 1,

39. See, for example, Hans Blumenberg, "Light as a Metaphor for Truth," in *Modernity and the Hegemony of Vision*, ed. David Michael Levin (Berkeley: University of California Press, 1993), 30–62.

**Figure 1.5:** Ben Schlanger and his daughter, Dorothy Schlanger, 1954. Courtesy Sue Isman.

Figure 1.5).[40] The impact Schlanger had on the movie house—in addition to his effects on the world of live theater, including stints as a consultant on the Kennedy Center, the Metropolitan Opera House at Lincoln Center, and the Sydney Opera House—has often been overlooked in favor of focus on palace designers such as S. Charles Lee.[41] Yet Schlanger's technical and theoretical

40. Schlanger was widely recognized for his architectural contributions at the time of his death, described as a "leader in contemporary theater design." "Ben Schlanger, Theater Architect, Is Dead at 66," *New York Times*, May 4, 1971.

41. R. R. Bowker, LLC, *American Architects Directory*, 3rd ed., s.v. "Schlanger, Ben," 1970, accessed June 7, 2011, http://public.aia.org/sites/hdoaa/wiki/Wiki%20Pages/ahd1039566.aspx. Those who have written on Schlanger include Amir Ameri, William Paul, and Lary May. See Amir Ameri, "The Architecture of the Illusive Distance," *Screen*

innovations dramatically influenced film exhibition for much of the twentieth century. His efforts, although not always completely successful, shaped pre- and postwar changes wrought in the American theatrical system—even if at times indirectly. His work toward total visual immersion in the picture through a rigorous approach to modern architectural form won him, along with Abraham Geller, recognition from the New York Municipal Arts Society for Cinema I & II in 1963, in addition to other national and international awards.[42] In the early 1930s, Schlanger began publishing articles in industry journals; in 1952, he was the first architect to be granted a fellowship at the Society for Motion Picture and Television Engineers.[43]

After a failed attempt to cash in on the Florida real estate boom in 1925, Schlanger returned to New York, where a friend asked him to help with designs for a new theater. Although the project remained unfinished, he was hired on by the architectural team; in 1926 he was assigned to complete work left unfinished on the Guard Theatre in New London, CT. From that moment on, Schlanger developed an expertise in theatrical architecture, particularly interior/auditorium space. Even in 1926, at the height of the palace style, Schlanger pushed for minimized decoration and attention to optical calibration; his interest in neutralization could be seen as early as 1927 in his work on the St. George Playhouse in Brooklyn. While Schlanger was not alone in his attention to minimalism, he seemed an outlier for exhibitors accustomed to the pomp and majesty of the palace. After finishing one of his new theaters in the late 1920s, where, like his other buildings, he omitted superficial decor, Schlanger brought in a prospective client to show him what he considered an excellent example of his work. After looking around, the exhibitor inquired, "When will the theatre be finished?"[44]

In 1931, Schlanger published his first of countless articles and columns in *Motion Picture Herald*; "Motion Picture Theatres of Tomorrow" appeared in the *Better Theatres* supplement of the February issue. *Motion Picture Herald* was the leading industry publication at the time and for several decades to come; similarly, its monthly supplement on theatrical innovations, edited by

54, no. 4 (Winter 2013): 439–462; William Paul, "Screening Space: Architecture, Technology, and the Motion Picture Screen," *Michigan Quarterly Review* 35, no. 1 (1996): 143–173; "The Aesthetics of Emergence," *Film History* 5, no. 3 (Winter 1993): 321–355; and May, *The Big Tomorrow*, 126.

42. "Architectural Award for Motion Picture Theatre Design," *Motion Picture Herald*, June 12, 1963, *Better Theatres* section, 41. Acoustics were also important for Schlanger, and he often worked with acoustic engineer C. C. Potwin in designing auditoriums for proper vision and hearing. Yet, consistently, Schlanger's main focus throughout his career was on sightlines and vision.

43. George Schutz, "Recognition," *Motion Picture Herald*, November 15, 1952, *Better Theatres* section, 16.

44. "Editorial Feature: The Accomplishments of Ben Schlanger, Architect," *Theatre Catalog* (Philadelphia, PA: Jay Emanuel Publications, 1953–1954), xii.

George Schutz, was an invaluable resource for exhibitors across the country. What Schutz chose to publish was an important standard for both exhibition style and even theory; blending practical advice, targeted advertising, and suggestions for future directions, *Better Theatres* provided an unequaled microcosm of trends in the larger exhibition sphere.

Schlanger's debut article immediately established what would become a tireless and aggressive tone; the essay's subtitle questioned "What Are the Faults of Today to Be Corrected?" Clearly a polemic guaranteed to raise many exhibitors' hackles, the article's placement at the beginning of the section reflected its assured controversial attributes, as did its announcement via a long introduction by the publication's editorial board. Schlanger, the editors mused, "sees the cinematic performance as an activity housed in a building— and a building which must, in turn, contribute to the performance. . . . Ben Schlanger, who has thus looked into the future in *Motion Picture Theatres of Tomorrow*, sees the present effort of the structure to contribute to the performance as false effort, being, as he insists, not adapted to the business of presenting motion picture entertainment, but, as he implies, *seeking to make the structure a show in itself.*"[45] Such a dilemma, however, was not restricted to the present moment; instead, the editors note, this controversy circling the palace versus a smaller, less decorated theater "has been going on for some time and which, it may be said in its favor, has not been without desirable results."[46] This observation begs to be highlighted: in very early 1931, less than two years after Black Tuesday, the leading industry publication referred to an ongoing discussion around the failures of the palace. To assert that the stripped-down theater was purely a product of the Depression is, quite simply, incorrect. Instead, its appearance was inextricably tied to larger theoretical trends around film, its proper place, and its proper spectatorship.

In this article, Schlanger gives a brief overview of the development and portents of decline for the palace. According to his short history, although fewer audience members lived near massive theaters, the appeal of live performances alongside the film caused many to travel to them; the smaller theater thus suffered in terms of attendance. Yet by 1931, alongside the full introduction of sound, the trend had reversed: audiences switched to the smaller theater, which could provide a better acoustical and visual experience than the caverns of the movie palace without the need for extensive travel. As Don Crafton has explained, the very early 1930s marked a moment when sound was no longer a novelty nor an icon of scientific progress; furthermore, Schlanger's explanation of the audience shift to the smaller theater was partially due to Depression-era efficiencies. Distributors gradually eliminated

45. "Notes on Writers and Subjects in This Issue," *Motion Picture Herald*, February 14, 1931, *Better Theatres* section, 9 (emphasis added).
46. Ibid.

the supply of silent film versions to smaller theaters, while independent theater owners found themselves forced to accept studios' sound requirements, even to their economic detriment.[47] Particularly given these trends, Amir H. Ameri has argued that the streamlined theater was essentially a response to the introduction of sound, where the sonic theater's balance of distance and proximity led to a newly immersed spectator and a newly immersive theatrical environment.[48] At the same time, new approaches to sound engineering and electroacoustics, put overtly into practice at the opening of Radio City Music Hall in 1932, set the stage for a modern sound design of virtuality and a pristine, controlled sonic space that mirrored Schlanger's precise visual calculations.[49] To be sure, sound aided in paving the way to the neutralized theater. Both hearing and vision constituted perceptions to be regulated by modernity's vicissitudes. Yet as Schlanger observed in 1931, the industry's shift over to sound was a curious one: why would a highly successful industry enjoying substantial financial stability undergo a hugely expensive transition to a relatively untested standard? For Schlanger, the answer lay in the needs of smaller theater owners for financial stimulation. Unable to provide the multitude of live attractions possible in the palace, smaller theater owners instead looked to the potential profits of sound technology to obtain new profit margins. Once synchronized sound took off there, larger theater owners found themselves forced to follow the trend.

Sound, then, certainly spurred the mainstream transition to more intimate theatrical space. But, Schlanger explained, sound accompaniment in the early 1930s was "not sufficient to demand the inadequacy of the theatre structure."[50] In other words, while sound's impact helped dictate new trends in theatrical scale, its emergence could not fully explain new trends in theatrical depth and decoration. Instead, the auditorium's image problem primarily affected other upcoming trends, including an enlarged screen, color, and three-dimensional effects, all of which would storm the industry over the following several decades. To fully adhere to such industrial innovations, the theater must follow suit by discarding the "trick" of decorative and romanticized architecture in the interest of becoming a *part* of the film. At that point, the viewer can "feel as little conscious of the surrounding walls and ceiling as possible" in order that he "completely envelop himself."[51] The proposed means of achieving the spectator's reduced consciousness included the use of bands of

47. Don Crafton, *History of American Cinema: The Talkies: American Cinema's Transition to Sound, 1926–1931* (New York: Scribner's and Sons, 1997), 16–18.

48. Ameri, "Illusive Distance."

49. See Emily Thompson, *The Soundscape of Modernity: Architectural Acoustics and the Culture of Listening in America, 1900–1933* (Cambridge, MA: MIT Press, 2004), 233.

50. Ben Schlanger, "Motion Picture Theatres of Tomorrow," *Motion Picture Herald*, February 14, 1931, *Better Theatres* section, 13.

51. Ibid.

light rather than sconces, elimination (or "slaughtering") of ornamental side walls and orientalist domes, usage of directional lines, reconsideration of balcony size, expansion of the screen, and removal of the proscenium arch, all of which Schlanger would continue to advocate throughout the course of the next several decades. All of these suggested methods of theatrical immersion would, of course, aid in sound film experience. Yet throughout this article, as well as in later publications, Schlanger insists primarily on screen dominance. While the undecorated theater would naturally increase acoustical excellence, it serves first and foremost as a directional aid into screen experience. Indeed, the "theatre of tomorrow" could result in the worthy return of the silent film—the enlarged screen, and the auditorium shaped around it, would, in fact, provide a new and better environment for silent film viewing. Thus, in Schlanger's first major intervention into theatrical architecture, two essential points can be inferred that add additional clarifying context to the historical record. First, the palace's architectural controversy began prior to the Depression, and therefore cannot be attributed entirely to Hollywood's ensuing financial crisis. Second, architectural neutralization led by Schlanger happened in tandem with but not completely due to the transition to sound; in fact, Schlanger's interest from 1931 on is first and foremost with screen integration. While sonic attributes of the auditorium were important, the film's visual component remained the primary locus of spectatorial immersion.

What Schlanger demonstrated, then, both early in and throughout his long career, was a tendency toward what Martin Jay has described as "ocularcentrism"—Western philosophy's reliance on vision as the most privileged and trustworthy of the senses.[52] In part, the camera and its suspicious claims to truth transformed the ubiquity of holy sight into anti-ocularcentric discourses around visual ideologies, such as the disciplinary structures of the modern panoptic prison described by Michel Foucault.[53] For Schlanger, architectural neutralization would promote the camera and screen's paired immersive qualities—an immersion that would ultimately cause the spectator to forget his or her body and move into a state of contemplative reverie that would, tellingly, discourage spectatorial movement and focus audience attention. Distance between spectator and screen would be purposely eroded through modern touches such as horizontal wall decorations and, eventually, downlighting that replaced exotically themed ornamentation and chandeliers. Although these attempts were naturally conducted with an ideal spectator in mind, curiously, as Robert Sklar has described, a larger transformation in audience behavior took place where "the talking audience for silent pictures

52. Martin Jay, *Downcast Eyes: The Denigration of Vision in Twentieth-Century French Thought* (Berkeley: University of California Press, 1993).
53. Michel Foucault, *Discipline & Punish: The Birth of the Prison*, trans. Alan Sheridan (New York: Vintage, 1995).

became a silent audience for talking pictures."[54] While it would be a speculative leap to argue that the neutralized theater imprisoned its spectators, perhaps what Sklar noted should not be credited solely to the regimented silence imposed on audiences so that others could comprehend synchronized dialogue. Schlanger's favored architectural forms, which visually elucidated the ways in which audiences should look—forward, toward the screen, undistracted by extravagant decor—served a similarly pedagogical function. An audience that is "completely enveloped" is unmoving, silent, still. An audience in contemplation is at once cinephilic and rigid, immersed and docile. To maintain ocularcentrality is to maintain behavioral standards that seek out the mental at the sake of the physical, the eye at the sake of the body. Schlanger's early ideal theater may not have been a prison, but it placed certain bodily demands upon its viewers in order to more fully suture them into the screen action. The neutralized theater, therefore, both offered a perfected house for a developing technological object and introduced an integrated, physically pacified spectator prophetically reminiscent of apparatus theory's inculcation.

## CHANGES IN THE 1930S: BENDING LIGHT AND DARKNESS

Historical factors thus aligned to usher in a new aesthetic moment for theatrical architecture: one of functionality, urbane sophistication, and low-cost options. By the early 1930s, debates around dramatic changes in film exhibition centered on the relative value of massive, several-thousand-seat movie palaces compared to the newer, intimate, and less opulent smaller houses of urban areas such as New York and Washington, DC. Certainly the movement toward smaller cinemas was partially dictated by the Depression, but as Barbara Wilinsky has argued, the "little cinema" movement began in the later 1920s just prior to the Depression with French ciné clubs that featured foreign and specialized art films.[55] "Little cinemas" were characterized by smaller size and lack of ornamentation compared to their massive mainstream competitors, and thus formulated an obvious model for modernist theatrical architects. By the mid-1930s, most "little cinemas" had begun to fail as foreign product dried up in the wake of burgeoning war in Europe, yet the strategies of smaller movie houses remained central to exhibitors seeking profits and new modes of attracting visitors. For Schlanger in particular, the little cinema movement promised a revolution in motion picture house design—one that did not depend, as the little cinemas did, on what was shown

54. Robert Sklar, *Movie-Made America: A Cultural History of American Movies* (New York: Vintage, 1994), 153.
55. Barbara Wilinsky, *Sure Seaters: The Emergence of Art House Cinema* (Minneapolis: University of Minnesota Press, 2001), 46.

inside, but rather on the display of the object in space. If each film shown was not pure art, at least its space of exhibition would demarcate it as such. And perhaps the most primary way that theaters could be effectively transformed was through the physical and conceptual deployment of light.

Prior to the late 1920s, light in the movie theater tended to be foregrounded by virtue of technology and ornament; giant chandeliers overwhelmed palace structures, or gleaming tiny points of light dotted the ceilings of atmospheric theaters. Ornate sconces drew spectators' eyes away from the screen and onto the multiple metallic nodes enclosing glowing bulbs. Many palaces also tended to leave colored lights on during the show, even at a minimum, in order to make the best use of expensive lighting decoration.[56] But as the building blocks for what it meant to be a modern spectator, issues surrounding darkness and light in the 1930s movie theater similarly brought into focus attitudes toward aesthetics, knowledge, and modernism as practice. In the theater, light served two additional, practical functions: its dampening was a cue to focus attention on the screen, while light itself could be used as a minimalist decorative element.

Through the middle of the century, advances in illumination technology and aesthetics brought light to the forefront as both a technique of and a metaphor for architecture's new ideals. In architectural modernism, in particular the utopian and formalist kind practiced by Le Corbusier, modernist architecture was often designed to appear as though made of light or at least permeable by it, in an example of what Beatriz Colomina describes as "Images as walls. Or as Le Corbusier puts it, 'walls of light.'"[57] As Colomina suggests, light's multivalent meanings—wisdom, divinity, truth, and futurity, but also human control over nature—were particularly relevant to the modernist movement's utopian leanings. Despite the American movie house's somewhat late, occasionally half-hearted acquiescence to modernist styles, light there took on additional meanings of narrative, form, behavioral control, and fantastic world creation. Especially in the cinema, light could be both transtemporal and of the moment, both ancient and modern, both elusive and clear, both immaterial and physical. Light not only created cinematic illusion but was also a visible and consistent symbol for the fluctuating experience of cinema in its space of containment; light's flexible metaphorical status extended from wisdom to modernism to the movies themselves.

Although theatrical lighting was not entirely useful as a model in other architectural settings, given that theaters could exercise complete control over the light and dark levels of their environment in ways often impossible in other buildings, the trend of using light in auditorium decor emerged early on

56. Gomery, *Shared Pleasures*, 148.
57. Colomina, *Privacy and Publicity*, 6.

in the debates over neutralization.[58] Film's status as a form essentially created from light and visible only in at least some darkness contributed significantly to its provocative, moment- and culture-defining attributes. In the cinema, light as a metaphor became light as an instrument of aesthetic experience; given cinema's reliance on light and dark, ways of lighting the auditorium as well as the theater on the whole were subject to nearly constant debate throughout the middle of the century. In 1928, Stanley McCandless, famed theatrical lighting designer and then assistant professor of lighting at Yale, argued that "lighting is no longer merely a means of illumination; it has color, pattern and movement," and is "something alive, with body and form."[59] Here, McCandless linked light in the theatrical space with both form and embodied experience; like film, it lacked volume, yet had weight, aesthetic power, and spirit. In a demonstration of light's malleability for multiple styles, in 1929 lighting technicians Francis Falge and Frank Cambria noted that theaters with utilitarian lighting tended not to be as successful as theaters such as those of Balaban and Katz with elaborate and colorful lighting schemes.[60] Falge and Cambria described the Brooklyn Paramount Theatre's lighting "as not an afterthought but [rather a case where] the architects, Messrs. Rapp and Rapp, ingeniously designed their artistry around the lighting. Agreeing upon a new and novel plan for lighting, the architect and the engineer worked as one to carry out the idea."[61]

While Falge and Cambria often fell on the side of theatrical showmanship here and in their other published writings, their concern with lighting as a necessary aspect of design points to the dawning importance of well-conceived lighting in the mid-century theater. Since the 1920s, theatrical lighting designers and architects were at least somewhat—and publicly, in the

58. A 1956 article in *Architectural Record* pointed to this design trend: "There are signs of increasing interest in lighting as well as a certain dissatisfaction. . . . Functional requirements have been pretty well emphasized, recognized and practiced, even though there is some disagreement between architects and engineers concerning the premises of certain existing standards. The desire is growing, however, to exploit the use of *light as a design material* rather than to provide merely for 'seeing.'" See "Light as a Design Material," *Architectural Record* 120, no. 5 (November 1956): 239 (emphasis original).

59. S. R. McCandless, "New Use of Light in the Theatre," *Exhibitors Herald and Moving Picture World*, June 9, 1928, *Better Theatres* section, 17.

60. As prominent lighting designers, Falge and Cambria often ascribed to the less subtle display of lighting techniques and tricks, perhaps to draw attention to the beauty and thus monetary worthiness of industrialized light. It should be noted, however, that elaborate lighting schemes were also a hallmark of neutralized theaters; but rather than highlight the fixtures or patterns themselves, their elaborate nature was focused more extensively on hiding light sources and manipulating light to privilege the screen.

61. Frank Cambria and Francis Falge, "Theatre Lighting: Its Tragedies, Its Virtues," *Exhibitors Herald and Moving Picture World*, September 18, 1929, *Better Theatres* section, 68.

press—working together to manipulate and control lighting as an architectural and decorative technique. While light in the theater was often targeted toward accurate vision—Falge and Cambria, among many others, pleaded with exhibitors to ensure that auditorium lighting did not interfere with that of the projector—from the movie palace era forward, light was considered both functional and mood-setting, atmospheric, and reflective of the performance of light and shadow about to take place in the auditorium setting. For professional lighting technicians such as Falge and Cambria, lighting's first duty was to create standardized viewing conditions in the house; efficiency and industriousness aided in developing the ideal optical environment. Yet given their professional affiliations, Falge and Cambria undoubtedly also saw ornamental lights as a way to foreground their trade and call attention to its beauty and power. Efficiency and ornamentation thus came into conflict in the domain of the professional: the best way to do one's job fluctuated between the invisibility of the perfectly oiled machine or pride in displaying ostentatious yet exquisitely produced grandeur. As in later debates surrounding minimalist art cinema versus bombastic Hollywood production, formalism and spectacle consistently formulated two potential avenues for successful work. For Schlanger, formalism was the obvious avenue for immersion: the intimacy of the little cinema paired with the tenets of architectural functionalism, ideally decorated via the ethereality of light.

At the time that he began publishing, Schlanger was hardly alone in looking toward smaller theaters as the wave of the future. In 1931, Falge and C. M. Cutler considered the smaller cinema movement important enough to dedicate an entire article to the proper illumination for this new kind of theater. "Theatrical circles," they mused, "have been buzzing in recent months with prophesies and ponderings regarding our latest addition to the theatre family—the little theatre of the movies. It is all the more startling because of the extreme contrast between our well-known ornate deluxe houses of four or five thousand seats, and this infant of a mere 150 or so."[62] While a new lack of availability of foreign and art house films affected what could be shown in the smaller movie house, a more intimate—and consequently less expensive—theatrical model had begun to filter into the rest of the exhibition scene. Even without the influence of the Great Depression, as Schlanger noted in 1932, lavish theaters detracted from the film; bigger, in other words, was not always necessarily more efficient, more effective, or better.[63] Smaller theaters also meant a movement toward the future away from the excesses of the past—and part of the way to achieve that was through modernization. As Falge and

62. Francis M. Falge and C.M. Cutler, "Illumination for the Intimate Cinema," *Motion Picture Herald*, November 21, 1931, *Better Theatres* section, 16.
63. Ben Schlanger, "Looking toward a Better Theatre," *Motion Picture Herald*, November 19, 1932, *Better Theatres* section, 8–9.

Cutler argued, light provided an ideal means of decorating both in the modern and fashionable mode and in terms of economic efficiency:

> Light in itself affords unlimited ways of providing novelty, beauty and decoration. . . . It is then obvious that our theatre requires a decidedly modern treatment. Light holds the key to the situation. Simplicity and efficiency go hand in hand with beauty and attractiveness. The recent little theatres as well as their forerunners have proved the desirability of simple but effective treatment.[64]

Here, Falge and Cutler state that theatrical modernization based on the cinephilic-oriented little cinema movement is both modern and appropriate; light offers an ideal means of achieving this style. Light is modern, attractive, and economically sound (among its other uses, it can make the ticket booth "stand out like a jewel," thereby highlighting the theatrical space of profit-making), and speaks to the privileging of the motion picture form.[65] Light's place in the exterior is to draw audiences into the theater; inside the auditorium, light's place is to be distributed at a "maximum amount" in order to prevent stumbling and produce a "cheerful and comfortable" environment where parents will not be concerned with the potential dangers of a dimly lit theater.

Somewhat paradoxically, then, light for Falge and Cutler both made film into a more aesthetic object *and* ensured a family-friendly atmosphere. In this way, Falge and Cutler's recommendations for theatrical illumination pinpointed many concerns regarding light's place both in the theater in general and in the new, smaller mid-century cinema. Prior to the 1930s and the movement from silent movies into talkies, live music performed much of the work of beautification; by the late 1920s and early 1930s, light began to be more commonly considered as a tool with multiple uses, a modular characteristic not just of the film but of the theater in general.[66] During the years of modernization taking place from the 1930s to the 1950s, the ways in which such a tool could and should be used involved not only pragmatic aspects of visibility, but also escapism, efficiency, beauty, and directing the focus of the spectator's eye. Illumination's "simple and effective treatment" was one of the best ways to attract the modern spectator seeking the aseptic standards promised by the machine age.

64. Falge and Cutler, "Illumination for the Intimate Cinema," 16.
65. Ibid., 132.
66. By the late 1920s, statements such as the following had become much more commonplace in exhibition journals: "[Today] in place of the tin pan piano, we have symphony orchestras, colored and speaking pictures, elaborate musical reviews, and, for our purposes most of all, an elaborate lighting equipment and an increased dependence upon the effects of lighting. . . . Motion picture theatres all over the country are devoting more attention to lighting every day. . . . Lighting is beginning to have quite as much appeal as music." See McCandless, "New Use of Light in the Theater," 17.

One of the more striking aspects of Falge and Cutler's practical plans for the small theater is their call for a brighter, more well-lit auditorium. Falge and Cutler were not alone; throughout the 1930s and even into the 1940s, exhibitors continuously debated the merits of a more darkened auditorium versus a brighter one.[67] Couching better illumination in veiled reference to the dangers of the darkened auditorium not only suggested a switch to a more family-oriented theatrical space, but a struggle between art and mass entertainment. For Schlanger, however, lighting's main purpose besides general illumination was to eliminate unnecessary physical architectural detail by providing subtle decoration that framed what was happening on screen. Where the older, larger theater of the 1910s and 1920s was draped in "costly ornamentation, affording poor aesthetic environment, besides being disturbing to restful screen exhibition," partially due to chandelier and elaborate sconce lighting that drew attention to itself, the new and smaller theater of the future offered "simplicity in decoration, accented by effective lighting complementing the screen performance."[68]

In Schlanger's view, light was efficient, effective, and, as in the case of Falge and Cutler, modern. Yet a major difference divided them: Schlanger's concept of the other less-than-serious theater-goer, a category that at times included women.[69] In this sense, the ideal spectator in the neutralized theater tended to occupy the default position of an adult white male. Although motivated in part by profit, Schlanger focused his cinemas' efforts on privileging a personal and intimate connection with the undeniable power of the moving image—in

67. By the late 1930s, the fully darkened auditorium was decidedly associated with the neutralized movement or an "extremely plain, functional design." See Eugene Clute, "Selecting Furnishings for Modern Foyers, Lounges, and Auditoriums," *Motion Picture Herald*, November 13, 1937, *Better Theatres* section, 32. Through the 1940s, most agreed that some level of dim lighting was required during projection, while a greater level of brightness was considered beneficial to certain immersive effects, such as the 3D illusion. See George Schutz, "Definite Guidance in Auditorium Lighting," *Motion Picture Herald*, May 8, 1948, *Better Theatres* section, 16–20. Low lighting was often also thought to be best for reducing eye strain. See, for example, George Schutz, "Modern Technique Urged to End Old Lighting Evils," *Motion Picture Herald*, November 15, 1947, *Better Theatres* section, 12. At the end of the 1940s, low lighting was frequently considered modern. See R. T. Dorsey, "Modernizing Your Lighting," *Motion Picture Herald*, August 6, 1949, *Better Theatres* section, 32–33. Yet other concerns existed with auditorium lighting, such as its potential to interfere with the picture. See, for example, Ben Schlanger, "How We Can Use Our New Lighting Tools to Best Advantage," *Motion Picture Herald*, August 18, 1945, *Better Theatres* section, 15; and "Specs & Speculations," *Motion Picture Herald*, October 12, 1945, *Better Theatres* section, 24.

68. Schlanger, "Looking toward a Better Theatre," 9.

69. Children disrupt seating plans by slumping, while women's tendency to wear hats or voluminous hairstyles have an impact upon sightlines; men, however, appear not to present any problems for necessary seating consideration. See Ben Schlanger, "How Viewing Conditions Form the Basis of the Theatre Plan," *Motion Picture Herald*, September 19, 1942, *Better Theatres* section, 7.

other words, an early cinephilic approach. Light, like other aspects of the theatrical auditorium, functioned as another architectural aspect that drew eyes toward the screen:

> Much of the effect desirable in the theatre interior must be obtained by the use and control of light. It is here that the mistake is often made. The walls and ceiling are usually designed as if they were going to be seen in broad daylight, neglecting the fact that the light in the auditorium of a theatre must be kept dim during most of a performance. Thus the architectural forms employed are blotted out and have little or no effect on the viewer during the performance. To correct this, most existing theatres light up the various separated architectural *motifs*, which only become annoying by their incoherent, spotty effect, and detract from the presentation. This same spotty effect is also caused by hanging bracketed lighting fixtures, the use of which would best be discarded. The very forms used to make up the character of the interior must carefully be thought of in terms of light found in a dark space. These forms, which should contain bands or areas of light, must compose, giving an effect, by varying the intensity of the different parts at different times which could be synchronized with the presentation, as well as the musical and sound accompaniments.[70]

Schlanger's description of synchronized forms, lights, music, and performance recall a Wagnerian *Gesamtkunstwerk*, where a multiplicity of artistic objects merge into an overwhelming nationalistic spectacle. Yet Schlanger's version does not equalize all art forms into parts of one work, but rather exists ultimately to celebrate one particulate: the film. In the space envisioned by Schlanger, light was an element of design and a reminder of the liminal dark space of the motion picture theater surrounding the audience. If it operated well as decoration, that was partially because it could negate itself and its surrounding environment, encouraging the eye to slide past it and onto the more important force of the screen.

In addition to its usefulness for highlighting and illumination, light could be harnessed in making theatrical surroundings vanish once the show began. Light's place in the auditorium also aids in the visual negation of other architectural motifs—motifs that are supposedly eliminated once the lights go down. Yet given a general tendency at the time to keep house lights at a minimal level, Schlanger's claim that the surrounding forms "are blotted out and have little to no effect on the viewer during the performance" appears strangely contradictory. In fact, Schlanger's argument that motifs disappear once the lights go down seems a thinly veiled attempt to circumvent his more typical argument: that architectural detail in the auditorium should be

70. Schlanger, "Motion Picture Theatres of Tomorrow," 13–56 .

minimized in order to prevent audience distraction from the projected film. Ornamental side walls, for example, cause

> a disturbing pull of the eye away from what should be the main focal point. These walls should have a gradual simplification and omission of forms as they recede to the rear of the auditorium; the forms used should have strong horizontal direction, instead of vertical emphasis, fastening the eye to the screen, the focal point, at the front of the auditorium. . . . While the viewer should not be conscious of the different walls and ceiling that enclose him, he should by all means be conscious of the effect of the unified surroundings, which should assist rather than compete with the presentation.[71]

If details such as the ornamental side wall actually did become invisible once the house lights went down, their presence in the auditorium would not have been such a point of contention for Schlanger and his crusade for auditorium unification. This insistence on muted light, preferably only coming from the screen during the time of projection, appeals less to Schlanger's calls for neutralized decoration and instead reveals the importance of retaining the enigma of darkness to the fullest possible extent. Cinema's contrast of dark space with illuminated screen would quickly demand attention to the one beam of light in the room—that of the projector—and bring to mind the singular brightness of revelation in the face of darkness. Light was a more fitting design element than most architectural decoration, especially given Schlanger's aesthetic of a blended International and Chicago Style, but also due to its ability to promote continual visual focus in the hallowed space of the auditorium, particularly when bathed in surrounding shadow. Evoking the ignorance of darkest night would, by contrast, allow the *film* to play the role of dawning enlightened wisdom; darkness and the ensuing cinematic light would signal the spectator to move from a state of physicality in the seats to the mental lucidity of a visually and to a lesser extent acoustically oriented film viewer. Unlike the potential obstacles and juxtapositions of physical built decoration, light's symbolic clarity signaled more efficient means of achieving attention and therefore revelation.

For Schlanger, lighting in the cinema was less concerned with attractive fixtures and more with the idealization of the filmic experience. "Effect lighting," as he described it, was the most important aspect of lighting the auditorium, followed by presentation (at screen area, during performance), emergency, and utility lighting. Proper effect lighting created the right atmosphere for viewers to "*transition* into the motion picture performance." For Schlanger, "effect lighting" was a more important lighting schema than

71. Ibid., 12–13.

lighting during projection because it minimized lighting besides screen illumination while the film was being shown. "Effect lighting" on prior to the
show potentially had the largest impact on spectators before the film began,
putting them in the proper frame of mind for the filmic encounter, making
them passive yet engaged viewers reduced to their opened eyes.[72] Yet "usually
this lighting is overdone and without taste, especially when used to silhou-
ette and panel-light poorly designed architectural features."[73] Effect lighting
too frequently drew attention either to itself or to the looming physicality of
the surrounding theatrical walls. Presentation lighting, on during projection
in order to eliminate the contrast between auditorium darkness and screen
illumination to make "the screen appear more natural," served, in Schlanger's
view, not to assuage fears of an overly darkened room nor to pacify the
worries of concerned parents, but to orient the auditorium specifically toward the aesthetic experience cradled within.[74] In fact, according to Schlanger,
presentation lighting should usually be extinguished (except when capacities
are fuller) and emergency lighting allowed to perform its job. So long as eye
strain—a consistent bugaboo for Schlanger and Society for Motion Picture
and Television Engineers (SMPTE) members—could be avoided, the space of
the auditorium should be as dark as possible.

Indeed, in order to minimize the space's impact on the spectator, even
emergency lights "must not compete with screen illumination"; the light of
the projector must be the strongest, the visual rationale for theater attendance.[75] Despite emergency lighting's functionality, Schlanger insisted that "its
effect must be considered part of the aesthetic character of the interior."[76]
Thus even lighting for practical purposes must not intrude on lines of vision
nor distract from the screen, and should be understood as part of the theater's
unity. Not only should lighting be considered part of the design of the space,
but it should also be the predominant characteristic of decoration; in April of
1937, Schlanger declared that the "light coming from, or falling upon, wall
or ceiling surface, should form the architectural pattern."[77] Such light ideally
emitted not from fixtures themselves, but from screen light reflected onto
carefully painted and colored auditorium surfaces:

> Here the designer must employ his ingenuity to create shapes and color
> intensities which will tend to increase the amount of light received from the

72. Ben Schlanger, "Lighting Equipment as Applied to Modern Auditorium Forms,"
*Motion Picture Herald*, January 9, 1937, *Better Theatres* section, 11.
73. Ibid.
74. Ibid.
75. Ibid.
76. Ibid., 33.
77. Ben Schlanger, "How Modern Lighting Serves the Functions of the Auditorium,"
*Motion Picture Herald*, April 3, 1937, *Better Theatres* section, 7.

screen, as the surface in question becomes farther away from the screen, by using lighter shades and making the surfaces face the screen to a greater extent as the surface is more distant from the screen. This utilization of screen light becomes the basis for the architectural treatment, and the number of decorative effects possible is almost unlimited.[78]

In this mysterious and perfected auditorium, the walls, as Le Corbusier had suggested only seven years earlier, appeared made of light.

While the most vocal and prolific among his contemporaries, Schlanger was not the only designer fixated on lighting design for its usefulness in developing seamlessness between picture and architecture. In 1937, John Eberson recommended relatively ornate fixtures compared to Schlanger, yet insisted that

> in planning lighting for the auditorium, this division of the theatre is to be considered as a great shadow-box, with the luminous screen as its focal point. There must be no interference with this shadow-box function, and properly designed fixtures can provide suitable ornamentation, create a warm, welcoming and stimulating environment, and supply a judicious amount of illumination to permit patrons to feel safe and find seats, without at the same time reducing the clarity of the picture or distracting patrons seated in certain sections of the house.[79]

The theater is a "great shadow-box" balanced by a "luminous screen"—a dramatic combination of the harnessed powers of darkness and light. In addition, both darkness and light must be properly contained and controlled in the cinema to contain and control the attention of its spectators. Safety through illumination was not the only reason for keeping a low level of light; a shaded rather than pitch-black auditorium contributed to a "warm, welcoming and stimulating" environment. Yet once in proper balance, the theater's combination of light and dark focused and retained its spectators' attention, encouraging their intellectual progress from the womb-like uncertainty of the darkened room to the slow dawning of wisdom through the projector's heady beam. The architecture of the cinema could instruct on how pristinely one could see.

The spectator who would best experience the heightened visual consciousness determined by the theater was, for Schlanger, as for other film theorists of the early mid-century, an adult rather than a child, a man rather than a woman, but also a spectator full of contradiction.[80] He would gaze

78. Ibid., 7–8.
79. John Eberson, "Modern Forms and Materials in Theatre Fixture Lighting," *Motion Picture Herald*, February 6, 1937, *Better Theatres* section, 9.
80. Here, I draw on a long tradition of understanding male aesthetic experience as contemplative and attentive, and women's and children's as less intellectual and distracted. For a more in-depth discussion of these themes and an argument for women's

silently and in stillness at the proper parts of the screen, yet also be engaged with the narrative force of the film.[81] Undistracted by petty forms of
attraction or beauty in the cinema house, this mythical viewer would attend
completely to the architect's carefully diagrammed spatial flow, gaining
wisdom from the authenticity of aesthetic experience in a state of passive
receptivity. Women, however, were a problem: in general, they were assumed
to be attracted to decorative flourishes more than the clean functional lines
of the International Style. Prior to the emergence of the neutralized theater,
women were often considered problematic spectators for many reasons,
most frequent among which was fashion. As Shelley Stamp, Kathy Peiss, and
Maggie Hennefeld have demonstrated, the height and breadth of women's
hats in the mid-1910s constituted a major threat to enjoyment of the picture by male audiences.[82] Women's pursuit of haute couture demonstrated
their slavish dedication to trend over cinephilic demands on attention. Their
attachment to ornament not only negated their own ideal spectatorship, but
allegedly disrupted men's cinematic immersion. Similarly, in the mid-1930s,
a Classic Modern style, influenced by Art Deco and Moderne streamlining,
was thought to be more enticing to women than the "plain," "simple,"
and cold modernism of neutralized theaters such as Schlanger's. "Classic
Modern's" appeal to femininity lay in its ability to be up to date, retain
some sense of domestic space, and possess "refinement, beauty and ultra-
smartness."[83] As opposed to the warmth of Classic Modern, the neutralized

experience in the theater, see, for example, Patrice Petro, "Modernity and Mass Culture
in Weimar: Contours of a Discourse on Sexuality in Early Theories of Perception and
Representation," *New German Critique*, no. 40 (Winter 1987): 115–146; and Hansen,
*Babel and Babylon*.

81. Despite the complications women posed to spectatorship, Schlanger tended
to consider them more serious patrons than children, whom he generally declined
to acknowledge as even possible attendees. In his proposal for a family-oriented
community center with a movie theater, no recreation or games are in place; rather,
the center "provides an atmosphere of leisure, with provisions for the care of children so that attendance may be convenient and unhurried." A nursery onsite
allowed more serious adult patrons to leave their children for the sake of better
filmgoing for themselves; service to the community, then, meant removing the distraction of children. See Ben Schlanger, "Plan for a Theatre to Serve Residents as
a Community Center," *Motion Picture Herald*, November 16, 1946, *Better Theatres*
section, 19.

82. See Shelley Stamp, *Movie-Struck Girls: Women and Motion Picture Culture after the
Nickelodeon* (Princeton, NJ: Princeton University Press, 2000); Peiss, *Cheap Amusements*;
and Maggie Hennefeld, "Women's Hats and Silent Film Spectatorship: Between Ostrich
Plume and Moving Image," *Film History* 28, no. 3 (Autumn 2016): 24–53.

83. See Eugene Clute, "New Schemes in Remodeling," *Motion Picture Herald*,
November 17, 1934, *Better Theatres* section, 19. The flourishes inherent to Classic
Modern were, however, more akin to theaters focused on showmanship; singular
Greek, floral, or other decorative elements were affixed to an otherwise streamlined

theater was cold, severe, and masculine. Along the same lines, the tendency to appreciate floridity and embodiment exemplified by clothing or hairstyle made women too aware of being within their surrounding space to act as ideal spectators; to work as a negated space, the cinema must be negated not only in design but in reception.[84] Women upended the careful efficiencies of neutralized theatrical space.

Schlanger's early 1930s theaters were also designed to provide maximum comfort, which meant seating patterns and chairs that guided spectators into positions as close to supine as possible while retaining maximum clarity of sightlines. Although a more comfortable theater would probably result in a re-turning audience, such planning was also intended to prevent spectators from moving during the film. Prior to the 1930s, aspects of the larger movie palaces included the use of either flattened floors or downward slopes toward the front of the auditorium, where patrons in the first few rows and the balcony were forced to shift their bodies into awkward positions in order to look downward at the screen. Schlanger's reverse floor slopes sought to rectify this situation by ending in a small slope toward the back rather than front of the auditorium. The screen was lifted slightly above the eyeline of spectators in the first rows for maximum clarity of sightlines, while front-row and balcony spectators could recline and look up in what Schlanger argued was a more natural position.[85] In this way, the spectator's relaxation could prepare him to be willingly and passively acted upon by the whims of the designer and the filmmaker. Indeed, Schlanger intended for his spectator never to need move during screenings, at once eliminating distractions for other audience members and shaping a totally inert viewer. Allowing as well for standardized theater chairs, the reverse slope implied a standardized audience, each member of whom fit properly into each identical seat. The neutralized movie house called for a similarly neutralized spectator: so comfortable as to be unaware of his body or his surrounding en-vironment, he remained totally aware of those aspects of aesthetic experience that the architect and director sought for him to observe. Through his gradual succumbing to passivity paired with visual stimuli, he learned from filmmaker and architect together how to move from the claustrophobic space of his body into the dynamic and revelatory space of the mind. This spectator was alive without action, eyes without a body, a brain with entirely regulated function;

interior, illustrating how women tended to be associated with showmanship, men with neutralization.

84. Thus advocates of neutralization had much in common with Kracauer; see Kracauer, "The Little Shopgirls Go to the Movies," in *The Mass Ornament*, 291–306.

85. The reverse floor slope continued to be used in some capacity through much of the 1940s. For a description of the slope, see, among other examples, George Schutz, "Reversing the Slope of the Main Floor: An Examination of the Schlanger Plan," *Motion Picture Herald*, July 4, 1931, *Better Theatres* section, 12–13.

the modernized theater's modernized spectator was a model of receptive efficiency, a machine-made man for a machine-like cinema.

By the middle part of the 1930s, Schlanger's preferred method of illumination was downlighting, a practice he advocated as soon as it showed the promise of wide adoption. With downlighting, the light's source was concealed, further rectifying the excessive ornamentation of the theater. In addition, downlighting allowed the projector's light to dominate and tamped down reflections ricocheting across the auditorium space. Downlighting therefore solved problems of surface and texture: eliminating light bounce both necessitated covered, and therefore minimally decorative, lighting, and smoothed auditorium surfaces that might otherwise be awash in clamorous disturbing patterns. Schlanger's problem with light was its potential for visual chaos; but to bend it to a directional will meant it could also formulate neutralization's perfect companion. Harnessed light promoted visual acuity, attention, and minimalism, all hallmarks of the neutralized theater. Light recalled the purpose of the theater by virtue of its necessity for production and projection; light linked the cinema to the quiet flame of wisdom and the eternal nature of aesthetic formalism.

What would this new theater look like, and how would it be lit? In 1935, the Pix Theatre, designed by Bianculli & Ghiani with Schlanger as architectural associate and consultant, opened in White Plains, New York (Figures 1.6 and 1.7). As the first of a series of theaters designed based on principles recommended by several writers in *Motion Picture Herald*, the Pix was intended to be a model for low overhead cost and high exhibition standards, while its functionality echoed the International Style's burgeoning popularity in the United States.[86] Seating only three hundred, the theater was an experiment in cost-cutting and exquisite visual presentation. The "eccentric" appearance of the theater's front section of white stucco with no decoration except for signage was described as part of the designers' desire to make "the architecture observe only the space requirements of the interior."[87] Inside its hushed auditorium, the Pix boasted a shell-like, sloping, and curved ceiling that glided toward a screen guarded by two metallic panels, the auditorium's grey curves echoing the rounded

86. In 1932, four years prior to the Pix, the recently opened Museum of Modern Art (MoMA) and curators Henry-Russell Hitchcock, Alfred Barr, and Philip Johnson introduced the United States to the International Style in "Modern Architecture: International Exhibition." The exhibition showed in New York from February 10 through March 23 and nearly immediately had a significant impact on the art and architectural world. As Helen Searing, among others, explains, American building types were nothing less than transformed by this new vision of purity, functionalism, and austerity. See Henry-Russell Hitchcock Jr., *The International Style: Architecture since 1922* (New York: W. W. Norton, 1932); and Helen Searing, *New American Art Museums* (New York: Whitney Museum of American Art, 1982).

87. "The Pix: An Experiment in Theatre Planning and Operation," *Motion Picture Herald*, January 11, 1936, *Better Theatres* section, 8.

**Figure 1.6:** The Pix Theatre, White Plains, N.Y., 1935, Fay S. Lincoln Photograph Collection, Historical Collections and Labor Archives, Special Collections Library, Penn State University Libraries. Used with permission from the Eberly Family Special Collections Library.

granite or concrete used for a mausoleum. The Pix's lighting trough shone hazily above the seat backs repeating and multiplying the ceiling's buoyant swells in miniature; the walls and ceiling were constructed of plaster, while two stepped metallic panels painted a "neutral" color flanked the screen platform.[88] Otherwise, the entirety of the auditorium's decoration came from a

88. Probably grey, beige, off-white, or dark cream, which, generally speaking, were the colors alluded to as "neutral" by designers in the 1930s through the 1950s.

**Figure 1.7:** The Pix Theatre, White Plains, N.Y., 1935, Fay S. Lincoln Photograph Collection, Historical Collections and Labor Archives, Special Collections Library, Penn State University Libraries. Used with permission from the Eberly Family Special Collections Library.

lighting trough running the length of the room and three bracket luminous elements on the two sidewalls. Especially given that the Pix's floor had a slight upward slope similar to Schlanger's more dramatic reverse floor slopes, the trough's location on the auditorium's ceiling created a streamlined visual momentum, intended to encourage the spectator's eye to forwardly traverse the room's length and focus on the screen dominating its front end. In an at-the-time radical development, light bouncing from the screen and reflected on the walls formed nearly all of the illumination during screenings; without the interference of extraneous light falling on the image, this assured that the true blacks and shadows onscreen did not appear grey. The entirety of the theater was geared, therefore, toward what Jean Epstein might describe as "maximum visual acuity"—a physical plant in the service of sharpened eyesight whereby space fell away to reveal magnified sight.[89] As exemplified by the Pix, Schlanger's neutral theater of the early 1930s shaped the viewer's

---

89. See Jean Epstein, "On Certain Characteristics of *Photogénie*," trans. Tom Milne, in *French Film Theory and Criticism, A History/Anthology, vol. 1, 1907–1929*, ed. Richard Abel (Princeton, NJ: Princeton University Press, 1988), 318.

perception via a rhetoric of emptiness—the auditorium would resemble in the closest way possible an optical vacuum, wherein vision pierced an architectural void to rest solely on the screen. Neutralizing the effects of the overwhelming and even absurd palace, the new modern theater sought to reaffirm the centrality of light and dark and thereby celebrate film and screen as the theater's focus.

## REVERIE, SPACE, AND THE APPARATUS

As practiced by Schlanger, neutralization in the 1930s promoted an early kind of apparatus: a spatial enclosure of the spectator in film's ideologies. In many ways, Schlanger's insistence on bodily and visual regulation made Baudry's theory physically manifest, and provided archival evidence for the apparatus beyond the filmic text. But, as Gabriele Pedullà elucidates, apparatus theory fails to account for the fact that spectators willingly give themselves over to the immersive properties of the movie theater.[90] In addition, then, to visual authoritarianism, Schlanger's form of neutralization may also be considered alongside Gaston Bachelard's permutation of reverie: the waking dream or daydream whereby we watch with eyes half open, untouched by the rigid boundaries of the psychoanalytic metaphorical dream, prepared to understand consciousness as unfettered and round.[91]

For Bachelard, close study of inhabited space unveils the poetic ways in which we dwell in the world. Spaces that at first glance seem empty or staid come alive through phenomenological experience; examining that experience uncovers the richness of spatiality. Bachelard explains that, for those who dream of corners and holes, "nothing is ever empty, the dialectics of full and empty only correspond to two geometrical non-realities. The function of inhabiting constitutes the link between full and empty."[92] By dwelling within a space, the subject balances fullness and emptiness. In much the same way, Schlanger's spectator in the neutralized theatrical space was never intended to experience the auditorium as empty—instead, spectatorial reverie activated the cinematic dialectic of volume and void, of presence and absence, of darkness and light. Schlanger's spectator was at once enraptured and disciplined, cinephilic and pedagogical, a product of designed space constituted for the purpose of a new filmic immersion where visual reverie trumped extravagance. By the middle part of the 1930s, as modernized theatrical space

90. Gabriele Pedullà, *In Broad Daylight: Movies and Spectators after the Cinema*, trans. Patricia Gaborik (London: Verso, 2012).
91. Gaston Bachelard, *The Poetics of Space: A Classic Look at How We Experience Intimate Places*, trans. Maria Jolas (Phoenix, AZ: Orion Press, 1964; reprint, Boston: Beacon Press, 1994).
92. Ibid., 140.

flourished into a more mainstream style, such a spectator was of larger importance not only for Schlanger, but other theatrical designers as well.

Increasingly, this spectator appeared like the imbricated viewer described by 1970s apparatus theory. While Baudry explained the apparatus via Hollywood's enclosed system, or Raymond Bellour looked to continuity editing to define cinema's ideological operations, the new cinematic architecture emerging at the end of the 1920s and beginning of the 1930s exemplified many of cinema's dogmatisms that Baudry and Bellour attached to film's formal elements.[93] In this way, study of the transformations in cinematic architecture and exhibition discourse uncovers an alternative history of film theory: one that reaches further back and into other territories than we normally assume. Yet such definition of the purpose of film remains ambivalent in its status. While Schlanger clearly sought a silenced, still audience prepared for film's suturing effects and thus demonstrated the development of the new spectator, his designs and rhetoric speak as well to the machine age, to the efficiencies and functionalisms that prevailed in many other buildings of the time, and to the older aesthetic models to which even the most modern art forms remained indebted. If, as Mary Ann Doane and Ben Singer, among many others, have explained, film's mechanized abilities to capture time and space represent modernity in its clearest artistic incarnation, Schlanger's interest in deploying the cinema for revelatory purposes simultaneously reveals its intrinsic connection to earlier modern and even ancient forms of aesthetic experience.[94] The Kantian sublime and the ancient power of bending light and dark find expression in the modern theater; intent on discarding its "old lines," the neutralized auditorium transported its audience both backward and forward into the perceptual infinite.

## THE THALIA AND THE MASK

Reporting in 1932 on the opening of Ben Schlanger and Raymond Irrera's Thalia Theatre at 95th and Broadway in New York City, George Schutz noted that, prior to the Thalia and other modernist theaters, "the motion picture has always taken second place when the principles of auditorium design have been under consideration. As a result of this, the suitable housing of motion picture exhibition has progressed very little in comparison with the attainments of

93. See Raymond Bellour, *The Analysis of Film*, ed. Constance Penley (Bloomington: Indiana University Press, 2001).

94. See Mary Ann Doane, *The Emergence of Cinematic Time: Modernity, Contingency, the Archive* (Cambridge, MA: Harvard University Press, 2002); and Ben Singer, *Melodrama and Modernity: Early Sensational Cinema and Its Contexts* (New York: Columbia University Press, 2001).

**Figure 1.8:** Ad for the Thalia, *Motion Picture Herald*, June 4, 1932.

the motion picture itself." (Figures 1.8 and 1.9)[95] Schutz here referenced the booming emergence of sound over the past several years, as well as the consolidation of narrative film form during the early golden age of the Hollywood

95. George Schutz, "The Reversed Floor Slope in Practice," *Motion Picture Herald*, April 9, 1932, *Better Theatres* section, 29.

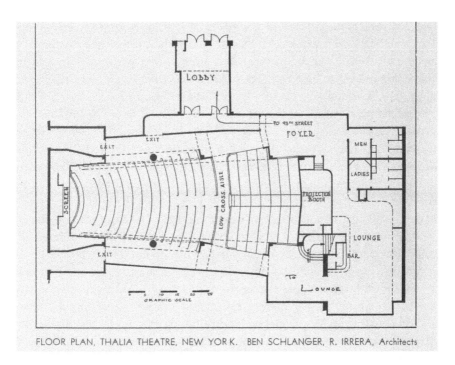

FLOOR PLAN, THALIA THEATRE, NEW YORK. BEN SCHLANGER, R. IRRERA, Architects

**Figure 1.9:** Floor plan for the Thalia, *Motion Picture Herald*, April 9, 1932.

studio system.[96] With the Thalia, Schlanger and Irrera sought also to bring the theater in line with advances in film technology. All parts of the auditorium were designed to support attention to the screen, including indirect lighting without visible fixtures. Nine front rows of seats flowed in single, uninterrupted lines in an early version of the continental seating plan that discouraged audience members from standing up during screenings. Sleek directional lines made the auditorium into a graphic, instructional rendition of potential eye movement; some vertical lines on the walls closer to the floor ended in horizontal lines slightly above eyeline that reconditioned spectators' vision toward the illuminated screen. The Thalia also unveiled the first usage of Schlanger's reverse floor slope for proper spectatorial posture and full view of the film from every angle; for Schutz, it was "as though the seats were placed in an ideal position for viewing the screen."[97]

Besides directional lighting, reduced aisles, and the reverse floor slope's influence on corrective visual conditioning and eye strain reduction, the Thalia included an even more significant advance: the black velour or velvet

96. For more on the studio system's golden age, see Thomas Schatz, *The Genius of the System: Hollywood Filmmaking in the Studio Era* (New York: Henry Holt and Company, 1988).
97. Schutz, "The Reversed Floor Slope," 29.

masking that typically covered the edges of motion picture screens in the 1920s and 1930s here was set back eighteen inches. While masking usually aided in stabilizing shaky images from substandard projectors, its use in the 1930s tended to be a result of habit rather than need; like the proscenium arch, masking was a vestige of earlier exhibition practice that had not yet caught up to advances in film form. The Thalia's screen maintained its mask, yet deepened the space between fabric and screen. In an evocation of Richard Wagner's *mystischer Abgrund* or mystical abyss at his Festspielhaus in Bayreuth (1876), the empty recession resulted in a "columnar effect of colored light on each side of the screen."[98] Schutz's understated description of the Thalia's "interesting idea in screen masking" belied the revolutionary impact of Schlanger's transformative design; up until the theater's opening in 1932, mainstream American moviegoers fully expected a screen with intense, solid black borders. In visual practice, beyond sharpening fuzzy screen edges and correcting problematic framing, this created a sharp separation between screen and auditorium space: the screen, in essence, framed an outsider's view on another world. Yet by softening the border between screen and masking, and demonstrating its volumetric fluidity by filling it with light and color, the Thalia's half-masked screen pointed to a new integration of screen and its surround. Not only would a neutrally and flexibly decorated theater such as the Thalia, with its modernist built-in lobby furniture and ornamentation motifs stemming solely from directional lines and lighting, focus attention on the screen, but it would visually transform the screen's place from a partitioned objective image into a window to be peered through, to be opened, and to be accessed via a newly integrative spectatorship. Into the later 1930s and 1940s, these impulses toward architectural change found new credence in screen transformation: from a focus on privileging the screen in the late 1920s through 1935, neutralization in the later part of the 1930s and 1940s moved toward expanding and demasking the screen itself.

98. Schutz, "The Reversed Floor Slope," 116.

# CHAPTER 2

# A Field of Light

*Optics and the Demasked Screen, 1932–1952*

## PROXIMAL SCREENS

On April 1, 1948, President José Bustamante y Rivero, actor Ray Milland, and Paramount International's Theatre Department Head Clement S. Crystal attended the opening of Paramount's deluxe Ciné Tacna (Schlanger, Hoffberg, Reisner & Urbahn; Florez & Costa), the first fully air-conditioned and fireproofed theater to open in Lima, Peru (Figure 2.1).[1] A combined 1,945 people could be seated on the main floor and two balconies, while each of the upper cantilevered levels were located in careful positions according to the height of the screen; this maintained clear viewing positions and allowed for flat balcony pitches. In keeping with Schlanger's insistence that doubled balconies result in better viewing angles and decreased viewing distance, no spectator was forced to lean forward or look down at the screen while seated. In part, these two levels represented what one observer called a "sociological innovation" departing from a South American tradition of cheap, uncomfortable balcony seating. Instead, the Tacna's floor design pivoted on an "American" notion that middle and lower classes are necessary for theater success:

> Once this idea is accepted as valid there follows no course but to give the balconyites a warm welcome instead of the cold shoulder. Accordingly, the balcony of the Tacna has been equipped with fully upholstered seats, given a well-furnished lounge, and had its floor carpeted. The aisles leading to the balcony have also been fully carpeted. As a crowning gesture, the new theatre makes available to balcony patrons for the first time in recorded South American

1. "Para. Int'l Previews Lima Theater Bow," *The Film Daily*, October 3, 1947, 7; "Coming and Going," *The Film Daily*, March 10, 1947, 2.

**Figure 2.1:** From Jay Emanuel's *Theatre Catalog*, 1948–1949.

theatrical history, beautifully tiled, completely equipped modern rest rooms. Here is an interesting example of a sociological reform based on a sound economic motive. The theory implicit in civilized treatment of the balcony world is simply this—that a theatre built to attract only the better classes can never be as successful a business venture as a theatre whose comfort, safety, and entertainment are bestowed equally upon the entire clientele, independently of the admission price.[2]

While the Tacna's balcony deserved acclaim from an architectural and optical perspective, it was also of note for its benevolent democratizing effects. Still, press coverage failed to note the United States' practice of racialized balconies; while all audience members might be worthwhile in terms of their ticket

2. "An Interesting Latin-American Theatre," *Theatre Catalog* (Philadelphia, PA: Jay Emanuel Publications, 1948–1949), 43–44.

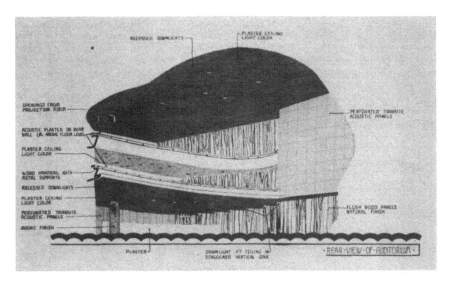

**Figure 2.2:** From "The Advantages of Balconies for Motion Picture Presentation," *Motion Picture Herald, Better Theatres* section, November 15, 1947.

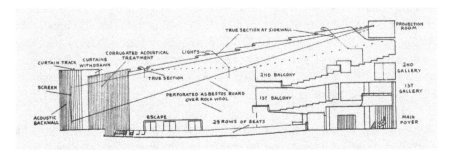

**Figure 2.3:** From "The Advantages of Balconies for Motion Picture Presentation," *Motion Picture Herald, Better Theatres* section, November 15, 1947.

prices, segregated American theaters typically restricted black audiences to balcony seats with views generally worse than the main level. The Tacna's dual balconies, with their surroundings as modernized and as optically perfected as the orchestra, might well have been even more radical in North America than in Peru.

Elsewhere in the auditorium, vertical battens of white oak lined the dado wall along the auditorium, a rear standing wall was covered in mahogany leather, metallic gold fabric draped the two structural columns, and a sliding coral curtain and gold stationary drape framed the transparent contour curtain (Figures 2.2 and 2.3). Downlighting, cove lights, and pocket lights ensured a total lack of exposed light fixtures as well as a soft, consistent pattern of illumination that avoided sharp angles or hotspots. One of the most striking aspects of the Tacna's design was the designers' approach to screen illumination, accomplished through two design characteristics related to both screen and wall decor. In years prior, auditorium walls required darker hues in order to prevent distracting reflections. At the Tacna, however, a corrugated texture laid on top of the auditorium walls and ceiling allowed for the use of lighter colored paint, at once preventing the reflection of projection light onto the walls and enabling the walls to pulse with a gentle luminosity. Even more strikingly, the Tacna's screen lacked the normal frame of black velvet masking that American movie theaters used almost without fail. Instead, Schlanger and his associates installed a screen with a border of synchronous light variation, where illumination fluctuated according to the levels of projected light during the screening. With these two advances, the Tacna's screen image was both revolutionary and mystifying. Ostensibly providing greater eye comfort to its attendees, the Tacna's screen surround also bathed the image in a wash of fluid light. Rather than being separated by a demarcated border and set at angles uncomfortable for the audience's bodily posture, the Tacna's screen floated straight ahead of its viewers, gleaming and glistening in a placid field of light, a liquid and radiant object that seemed close enough to touch.[3]

The Tacna's revolutionary properties, then, were twofold, and represented two intertwined areas of concern in the lead-up to the mainstream widescreen era: first, the auditorium's optical conditions, and second, its relationship to proximity and participation. In 1927, John Barry and Epes Sargent told theater managers that "the architect has mastered the psychology of the moviegoer," reiterating a common cry that cinema offers enrichment for one and all: "Here is a shrine of democracy where there are no privileged patrons."[4] By the mid-1930s and 1940s, the neutral theater was an object full of potential energy, a rallying point for a call to arms of theatrical transformation, and a symbol invested with the power to reconfigure the spectator's relationship to film. Yet many exhibitors were still reluctant to totally eliminate flourish in favor of functionalism. Frequently, theaters were slow to adopt larger architectural trends; notoriously conservative exhibitors assumed that audiences required elaborate surroundings to part with their hard-earned cash. One of the areas in which such lasting traditionalism could be most clearly observed was in the frame of black masking that remained around the screen.

When the Tacna was completed, demasked screens were still unusual enough to be remarked upon, yet not so experimental that Paramount would chance a massive investment failure. Sixteen years earlier in 1932, Schlanger's Thalia was at the forefront of this trend, replete with its significantly reduced

3. For further information on the Tacna, see "The TACNA," *Theatre Catalog* (Philadelphia, PA: Jay Emanuel Publications, 1953–1954), xxvi.

4. John F. Barry and Epes W. Sargent, *Building Theatre Patronage: Management and Merchandising* (1927), reprinted in *Moviegoing in America: A Sourcebook in the History of Film Exhibition*, ed. Gregory Waller (Malden, MA: Blackwell, 2002), 104.

and recessed masking. While the Thalia did not entirely discard the mask, its development in the early 1930s signaled a new strain in screen technology that would begin to account for similar shifts in film form. Throughout the 1930s, Schlanger experimented repeatedly with the reduction or elimination of the mask; while masking would remain a general exhibition practice through the mid-1940s and in use through the 1960s, more and more theaters installed Schlanger's various versions of a lessened mask or completely demasked screen. This was in keeping with exhibition's interest in screen brightness, masking, and projection's relationship to optics and eye strain. In 1937, the Projection Practice Committee of the Society of Motion Picture Engineers, a group that included Schlanger, began studying theater form in relation to projection; among the factors they assessed were screen size, screen brightness, and auditorium and screen border illumination, the latter of which related to masked versus demasked screens.[5] While the slow transformation of screen borders seemed minor on the surface, its impact resulted not only in the widescreen revolution of the 1950s, but, in tandem with neutralized theatrical architecture, a total reformulation of film spectatorship in the context of the window.

For Anne Friedberg, the "age of windows" encapsulates four centuries of fenestration that culminated in the 1950s widescreen revolution; with advances in both modernist architecture and media, movie and television screens and building windows were shifting metaphors for one another.[6] Friedberg details set design elements from William Cameron Menzies's 1936 science fiction film *Things to Come* and its depictions of a multiscreened future, where a "windows environment" bleeds into "window-walls" to evoke eventual movements toward wall-mounted screens as "virtual walls." While Menzies's film constitutes a textual side of the slow spectatorial shift beginning in 1930s film history, screen demasking is an undertheorized environmental other. If screens inside the film form provided models for new virtual windows, so too did the screen on which those multiplied images were projected; if spectatorship's changes were narrativized onscreen, spectators themselves were also subtly indoctrinated vis-à-vis architectural transformations within their auditorium space.

The Tacna, then, implied three categories for the changing American screen: the culmination of a general shift of exhibition's understanding of the screen from stilled frame to ever-expanding and mobile window; a reformulation of the debates surrounding the role of optics in film aesthetics; and an American approach to spectatorship within the mid-century widescreen

5. "Theatre Form Included in Projection Studies," *Motion Picture Herald*, March 6, 1937, *Better Theatres* section, 6.
6. See Anne Friedberg, *The Virtual Window: From Alberti to Microsoft* (Cambridge, MA: MIT Press, 2006), 101.

revolution. Compared to the smaller screen framed in black masking familiar from the 1910s, the screen in the later part of the American mid-century grew into an unbordered leviathan that promised greater immersive potential. A larger screen implied a consistently stronger position for cinema in American culture—especially an American culture in which television's potential threat to cinema attendance had become a reality. Yet widescreen's emergence reignited longstanding debates about embodiment and disembodiment, high and low art, and participation and immersion. Widescreen, so frequently cited primarily for its technological innovation and corporeal pleasures, proved to be a flashpoint for ongoing discussions about the role of the body in film viewing. The status of widescreen's immersive power was hardly unified; instead, tactics of immersion in widescreen also tended toward visceral individual experience and abstracted communal disembodiment as the purpose of an immense screen.

Although the widescreen revolution generally occurred in the early-to-mid-1950s, the 1930s saw multiple calls for screen expansion. In 1930, W. B. Rayton observed that "the employment of film wider than the standard 35 mm seems imminent," though the industry faced multiple difficulties in areas such as screen brightness and grain in achieving high-quality widescreen.[7] Schlanger in 1930 similarly advocated for increasing screen size, observing that "sound accompaniment with the film as developed to date is not sufficient to demand the inadequacy of the theatre structure. It is the enlargening of the screen, together with the three dimensional effects, that will substantiate the dire necessity for a complete new aspect of the problem."[8] Among the solutions proposed in the early 1930s were panoramic and revolving lenses, while in 1933, H. S. Newcomer suggested the benefits of the anamorphoser at two moments: during shooting and during projection.[9] Two decades later, anamorphic lenses would form the backbone of the major studios' widescreen systems, particularly with the introduction of CinemaScope, Panavision, and some later Todd-AO processes in the early 1950s.

But in the fall of 1937, Ben Schlanger bemoaned the fact that the spectator was still "picture conscious" while in the theater. The fault, for Schlanger, lay in the limited size of the screen and the "artificiality of the black border, which

7. W. B. Rayton, "The Optical Problems of Wide Film Motion Pictures," *Journal of the Society of Motion Picture Engineers* 14, no. 1 (January 1930): 50.

8. Ben Schlanger, "The Theatre of Tomorrow," in *American Theatres of Today*, ed. R.W. Sexton and B. F. Betts (New York: Architectural Book Publishing Co., 1930), 52.

9. See, for example, F. Altman, "A Revolving Lens for Panoramic Pictures," *Journal of the Society of Motion Picture Engineers* 24, no. 5 (May 1935): 393; and H. Dain, "Memorandum on Widening the Field of Camera Lenses and on the Use of Normal Films for the Panoramic Screen," *Journal of the Society of Motion Picture Engineers* 19, no. 6 (December 1932): 522; H. S. Newcomer, "Wide Screen Photography with Cylindrical Anamorphosing Systems and Characteristics of Motion Picture Lenses and Images," *Journal of the Society of Motion Picture Engineers* 20, no. 1 (January 1933): 31–53.

sharply cuts off edges of the picture."[10] A year earlier, Schlanger had already begun advocating a border of variable light that would self-adjust according to the levels of projected light; this would mimic what Hermann von Helmholtz had described as the transitional area of peripheral vision from the lightness at the front of the head to the darkness at the back, and thus decrease "picture consciousness."[11] Helmholtz's lasting influence on exhibition technicians and engineers in the 1930s illustrated a fixation on the optical impact of the motion picture screen and the physiological dimensions of the cinematic experience, both of which in turn signaled burgeoning interest in the theatrical impact of visual accoutrements such as masking. According to Schlanger, not only did masking prevent full psychological absorption, it also made cinematography inflexible and limited. Until the masking was removed, both the viewer *and* the filmmaker would be unable to realize their potentials. While other factors prevented widescreen's mainstream use in the 1930s, such as lack of funding due to the Depression, engineers and designers demonstrated significant interest in widescreen development throughout the 1930s. Why, then, did the revolution lie dormant until the 1950s? In addition to economic reasons, the screen in the 1930s was conceptually stunted: its frame of black masking prevented both exhibitors and Hollywood producers from expanding outward. Until black masking was challenged as an exhibition necessity, the screen would necessarily continue to resemble a framed picture on a wall.

In the ongoing examination of screens' rhetorical use in cinematic discourses, much attention has been paid to the 1950s; monumental in size, scope, and meaning, the newly immense screens of the mid-century reshaped film's cultural status and its spatial environment.[12] Exhibition histories generally agree that widescreen ushered in a moment of bodily immersion, where the spectator's entire physical form along with her eyes seemed swept up in the picture; consequently, this kind of embodied experience is assumed to

10. Ben Schlanger, "A Method of Enlarging the Visual Field of the Motion Picture," *Journal of the Society of Motion Picture Engineers* 30, no. 5 (May 1938): 508.

11. See, for example, E. M. Lowry, "Joint Discussions of Screen Brightness and the Visual Function," *Journal of the Society of Motion Picture Engineers* 25, no. 5 (May 1936): 518–521; and B. O'Brien and C. M. Tuttle, "An Experimental Investigation of Projection Screen Brightness," *Journal of the Society of Motion Picture Engineers* 25, no. 5 (May 1936): 505–517.

12. John Belton's *Widescreen Cinema* (Cambridge, MA: Harvard University Press, 1992) is the urtext of widescreen technology in the 1950s; other examples include sections in Alison Griffiths, *Shivers Down Your Spine: Cinema, Museums, and the Immersive View* (New York: Columbia University Press, 2008); Tim Recuber, "Immersion Cinema: The Rationalization and Reenchantment of Cinematic Space," *Space and Culture* 10, no. 2 (2007): 315–330; Harper Cossar, *Letterboxed: The Evolution of Widescreen Cinema* (Lexington: University Press of Kentucky, 2011); John Belton, Sheldon Hall, and Steven Neale, eds., *Widescreen Worldwide* (Bloomington: Indiana University Press, 2008); Pam Cook, ed., *The Cinema Book* (London: BFI, 2007); Steve Neale and Murray Smith, eds., *Contemporary Hollywood Cinema* (London: Routledge, 1998).

be the goal of all widescreen exhibition, akin to earlier modes of amusement park-esque cinema such as Hales tours, or later incarnations such as IMAX.[13] Yet rather than only echoing the cinema of attractions of its earliest days, widescreen highlighted continuing ontological questions regarding the differentiation between film and the other arts, between the necessity of the communal and the importance of the individual, and between the place of the body and the place of the mind. Debates surrounding widescreen's proper deployment—varied debates that deserve nuanced analysis—illuminate, therefore, exhibition's ambivalence toward thrill, thoughtfulness, immersion, corporeality, and vision. Rather than enumerating a singular ideal, widescreen debates in mainstream exhibition revealed a spectator who was alternately embodied or disembodied, of the elite or of the masses, either a participant or a witness—rather than a singular thrilled viewer embodied through the movies.

Spectatorship in the presence of the enlarging screen was an answer to the encroaching threat of the rise of television. Yet prior to the consolidation of television's status in the 1950s, earlier film theorists such as French avant-gardist Jean Epstein looked to the close-up as the emblem of cinema's affective power. For Epstein, writing in 1920, the close-up "is drama in high gear. . . . The close-up is an intensifying agent because of its size alone."[14] It is the cinematic icon par excellence, the blade that hones vision, and the source of proximity between screen and spectator. With television's arrival, the close-up was no longer relegated solely to the theatrical environment—but, in the era of widescreen, scale remained the domain of film and the rationale for a new closeness to the image. If television provided instantaneous, free entertainment at home, then cinema could still offer stunning size and shape in a communal, even sophisticated setting; moreover, where television was small, cinema could be enormous. To compensate for the impossibility of enormous theaters, exhibitors increased what some saw as the "participatory" effect of cinema, or, alternatively, its sense of presence: expanding and demasking the screen could remake the auditorium into an illusion of enormity. Enlarging the screen, therefore, served not just to encourage visceral sensation, but to provoke the awe, motionlessness, and fear that accompany an experience of the sublime. Television, on the other hand, was small, intimate, and domestic; with an ever-growing screen, theatrical space could challenge television's

13. See Lauren Rabinovitz, "More than the Movies: A History of Somatic Visual Culture through Hale's Tours, IMAX, and Motion Simulation Rides," in *Memory Bytes: History, Technology, and Digital Culture*, ed. Lauren Rabinovitz and Abraham Geil (Durham, NC: Duke University Press, 2004): 99–125.

14. Jean Epstein, "On Certain Characteristics of *Photogénie*," trans. Tom Milne, in *French Film Theory and Criticism*, ed. Richard Abel (Princeton, NJ: Princeton University Press, 1988), 318.

emerging primacy and reinforce cinema's status as the reigning technology of the sublime.

To maintain this status, cinema required an environmental apparatus that enhanced the vastness of the picture without prohibitively expensive theatrical construction. Sending the screen out into the space of spectatorship, as close to the seats as possible, meant a more encompassing image, but also the diminishment of theatrical space in favor of more visually important parts of the apparatus, most notably the screen. If the demasked screen promised the impression of an image bleeding into the audience, then it also proposed the masking of the theater itself. Here, then, the theater was a necessary component of ideological and psychological indoctrination. By the mid-1950s, widescreen cinema coupled with a more generally acceptable neutralized auditorium to introduce exhibition's new interpretation of a cinematic-architectural apparatus. In this sense, the success of the neutralized movement and its obsession with expanding the screen proposed both a filmic and a spatial identification where audiences were ideally sutured into moving imagery via manipulation of the spatiotemporal cinematic experience. The apparatus composed of the expanding screen and the invisible theater included experience as a category of reality effects.[15]

This chapter and the next will not retell the familiar narrative of bodily integration and immersion often attributed to widescreen, but attend to voices that called instead for large screen's use as a tactic of optical perfection and disembodied visual projection. Among their points of discussion were cinema's metaphorical shifts in the cultural imaginary, exhibition's suspicion and dread of domestic television, and the intertwining of American citizenship and modernism. Widescreen was not just a product of a cinema of distracted entertainment. Instead, theories regarding the body's place in aesthetic experience were expressed materially in mid-century widescreen exhibition; unsurprisingly, then, the voices that sought out a widescreen of disembodiment similarly argued for regarding film as high art rather than cheap amusement. To sustain film's upward momentum into the category of high art, Schlanger and other supporters of neutralization insisted on a disembodied contemplation achieved in tandem with architecture. Yet this also meant an ambivalence about film's status: while the borderless screen may have echoed the contemplative aspects of gallery and museum viewership, exhibition's general investment in filmic immersion meant that audience passivity also remained a consistent goal. Thus a neutralized cinema at once evoked modernist ideals of active and engaged watching (contemplation) as well as a more popular,

15. For examples of the phenomenology of widescreen and its techniques of embodiment, see William Paul, "Breaking the Fourth Wall: 'Belascoism,' Modernism, and a 3-D *Kiss Me Kate*," *Film History* 16, no. 3 (2004): 229–242; Griffiths, *Shivers Down Your Spine*; and Rabinovitz, "More than the Movies."

spectacular form of inactive entertainment (immersion). That both were seen as valuable—even if contradictory—highlighted the ways in which theater architecture continued to echo and shape the place of film texts in the larger cultural arena.

A focus on widescreen's visual techniques does not mean that advances in sound played no role in the larger field of tactics of immersion in the 1950s; surround sound was of particular merit at that time. Yet the legacy of the neutralized cinema from the 1930s and 1940s into the 1950s can be traced via demasking and subsequent widescreen movements, and this legacy resulted in a pathway of widescreen where vision is the strongest sense for spectatorial engagement. Screens as opposed to speakers were the primary technology of fascination for Schlanger's project—a project that, since its inception, was obsessed with transforming the auditorium into a machine for seeing.[16] As both trendsetter and innovator, Schlanger sought to replicate and enhance human vision; hearing was essential, but of secondary importance.[17] For Schlanger, sensory perception tended to focus on vision as the most intellectual and noble category of experience. Such interest in demasked and larger screens in decades prior to mainstream use of widescreen and stereophonic sound suggests that expansive screens were essential to modernist cinematic design *even before* the development of such systems as CinemaScope, VistaVision, and Todd-AO in the 1950s.[18] By eliminating peripheral detail and moving the screen farther and farther into the space of reception, some screen and cinema designers sought to freeze spectators into their seats, amazed by the enormity of the images filling their entire line of sight.

## THE CLOSE-UP, PROXIMITY, AND VISUAL IMMERSION

In the earliest days of exhibition, shaky machinery projected a jittery image; in response, theater owners began draping the edges of the screen in black

16. Stereophonic sound was thought to increase filmic "presence" (see George Schutz, "'Stereo' Sound Aids Realism in Any Theatre," *Motion Picture Herald*, August 1, 1953, *Better Theatres* section, 7), but widescreen had a larger significant impact on the physical footprint and design of the auditorium (see George Schutz, "Putting the Big Picture into Theatres," *Motion Picture Herald*, September 5, 1953, *Better Theatres* section, 11).

17. Stereophonic surround sound was an important aspect of the widescreen movement, particularly for Cinerama and CinemaScope exhibition practices. While Schlanger may have been in a vocal minority in terms of his obsessive fixation on vision, the general approach to widescreen did tend to center to a greater degree on the screen rather than the speaker.

18. This should come as no surprise, given experimentations in the 1920s such as Abel Gance's *Napoléon* (1927) and its famous three-screen Polyvision sequence. Here, however, I consider mainstream theatrical design rather than event status film form.

to stabilize the picture. Often, the mask consisted of a dark velour fabric laced in front of the screen.[19] Even once projection was more secure, masking tended to be used throughout American exhibition. To be sure, images were less likely to jump haphazardly across the screen. Yet inconsistent standard apertures for projection meant that theaters often had to account for a more rectangular image than their screens could provide; in addition, optical sound tracks running across the bottom of 35 mm film meant an "undesirable" frame proportion, leading exhibitors to mask the height of and magnify the image.[20] The quick and cheap response to both of these problems was reliance on an outdated technology: masking. Although the Academy first began standardizing the aperture in 1929 in Academy ratio, swift changes in the transition to sound meant that many theaters in the early 1930s had already abandoned the square image shape demanded by Movietone's sound-on-film system. Instead, they projected a reduced image in a 3 x 4 ratio, resulting in the loss of a good 20 percent of the frame at the top and bottom of the screen.[21] Recommendations from projection experts included such roundabout solutions as photographing action within a confined frame space, thereby allowing exhibitors to adjust their aspect ratios via masking as they saw fit for their space.[22] These debates saw echoes in Sergei Eisenstein's insistence in 1931 on the necessity of the square for film presentation; for Eisenstein, integration of the horizontal and the vertical was a fundamental component of film exhibition. It was, in fact, due to the limits of this one square that "every geometrically conceivable form" could be projected, and the interplay of new sound technologies and excellent optics fully achieved.[23] Such complications from the integration of sound—and therefore optical sound tracks—meant that masking's legitimacy remained relatively unscathed, despite its nascence in a much earlier moment. Masking certainly performed useful tasks in exhibition. It consistently stabilized the image—whether from fringing and movement, or from unsettling dimensions. But its deployment in the architecture of the theater also added to arguments regarding scale and proximity, particularly in terms of screen presence. Masking both contained the image by scaling it down into a smaller version of itself, and set it at a visible remove from the theatrical surround. While masking might offer a relatively

19. George Schutz, "The Reversed Floor Slope in Practice," *Motion Picture Herald*, April 9, 1932, *Better Theatres* section, 116.
20. "Banquet Speeches," *Journal of the Society of Motion Picture Engineers* 16, no. 2 (February 1931): 226.
21. "New 3 x 4 Standard Aperture for Projection," *International Projectionist* 6, no. 11 (November 1931): 16; "Ratio of 3 x 4 Three-to-Four Okayed by Producers," *Motion Picture Herald*, November 7, 1931, 10.
22. "Screen Brightness the Major Current Projection Problem," *International Projectionist* 2, no. 6 (June 1927): 28.
23. Sergei Eisenstein, "The Dynamic Square," in *Film Essays and a Lecture*, ed. Jay Leyda (Princeton, NJ: Princeton University Press, 1982), 52.

flexible and instantaneous solution to a number of technological problems, its visual impact impeded the very immersion promised by a stable, standardized screen. By separating the picture from the rest of the auditorium space, masking maintained the screen as something separate from the audience. It stabilized both screen image and spectatorial relations to the picture, rather than promoting absorption and effacement.

To reduce, remove, or rethink the mask and expand the screen was therefore not only a technical or architectural undertaking; it also implied the roles of scale, optics, and proximity in the creation of immersion. In this sense, Schlanger's calls for lessened eye strain, a larger picture, and maximum visual acuity echoed not only the words of fellow exhibition practitioners, but also the aims of film theorists such as Jean Epstein and Béla Balázs writing either just a few years prior or at the same moment as Schlanger was developing his new screen approaches. Their desires for scrutiny, careful visual observation, and enormity of scale read as blueprints for Schlanger's eventual screen demasking, particularly in revelatory film theory's obsession with the close-up.

Film theory contemporary with early interest in screen demasking called for an intimate cinematic experience where the camera's instantaneous visual information might awaken audiences to the underlying truths of daily existence. For utopian film theorists (and Schlanger), aesthetic proximity, scrutiny, and highly manipulated modes of seeing—whether through the place of display, a canted perspective, or both—induced states of higher spectatorial consciousness. In the emerging world of film theory, proximity and magnification proved to be useful, appropriate categories for defining aesthetic experience—in its own fashion, not completely distinct from the plays on scale which, for Kant, helped to define the "dynamically sublime."[24] Much as contemplation became a sibling to immersion in mid-century theatrical rhetoric, so proximity to the screen and its twin, enormity of image, were techniques for incorporating viewers into the cinematic object. These early-to-mid-century writers of filmic utopia, who include Dziga Vertov, Béla Balázs, Hugo Münsterberg, and Jean Epstein, celebrated the revelatory properties of the new visual medium, but in particular the uniquely cinematic property of scrutiny through plays on scale: large projected images, magnification, and close-ups.

The term "close-up" connotes multivalent meanings. Mary Ann Doane explains that while in French and Russian it implies an enormity of scale, in English it relates to intimacy and proximity. A central function of the expanding screen appears in all three of these languages: gigantic but close, awe-inspiring but personal. Invariably, the close-up strengthens links between the world of

24. Immanuel Kant, *Critique of the Power of Judgment*, ed. and trans. Paul Guyer and Eric Matthews (Cambridge: Cambridge University Press, 2000), 143.

the film and the world of spectatorship. For Doane, "three decades of film theory have insisted that the classical cinematic text works to annihilate this space of the spectator—to suggest that the only world is that on the screen. Hence, the embrace of the close-up as autonomous entity by Balázs, Deleuze, and especially Epstein, is an attempt to salvage spectatorial space, to reaffirm its existence and its relevance in the face of the closed, seamless space of the film."[25] The close-up is always torn between the enormous and the miniature, where "the cinema plays simultaneously with the desire for totalization and its impossibility."[26] Here, Doane argues that another aspect of cinema's privileged status is its reliance on categories that seem opposed; it depends upon inner contradictions and balances to maintain its philosophical structure. Fluctuating between totalization and impossibility, distance and immersion, and large and small, the cinema's confounding of categories made it an apt subject for film theorists seeking out strategies for interpreting a confusing and chaotic modern world. The close-up's miniature leviathan constituted an ideal object for analysis: the mystical contradictions of a three-inch-long eye engulfing an entire screen, worlds of meaning writ so small, the enormity of a miniscule movement, the universe as a gesture, the face as a void.

In addition to providing an opportunity for visual scrutiny, the close-up also represented cinema's role in the destruction of the aura in modern aesthetic experience. For Benjamin, the aura's decay is predicated on two circumstances: *"the desire of the present-day masses to 'get closer' to things, and their equally passionate concern for overcoming each thing's uniqueness [Überwindung des Einmaligen jeder Gegebenheit] by assimilating it as a reproduction."*[27] Both modern desires can be fulfilled by the cinematic close-up, an object that artificially induces intimacy through its nature as a reproduction. Indeed, the close-up cannot exist without the dual events of excessive proximity and technological reproducibility. While Benjamin does not draw on the close-up as such, its centrality to film theory, a discipline so dramatically defined by the "Work of Art" essay, is clearly illustrated by the two requirements for the aura's erosion. If the decay of the aura is located in an overcoming of distance—a "getting closer" to things—and things' reproducibility, then the close-up is the most salient example of a new, modern visual aesthetic. What the close-up might also offer, however, beyond an example of the loss of authenticity in modern experience, is both revelation through visual acuity and a linkage between cinema and science. Seeing things up close is, after all, also an

25. Mary Ann Doane, "The Close-Up: Scale and Detail in the Cinema," *differences: a Journal of Feminist Cultural Studies* 114, no. 3 (Fall 2003): 108.

26. Ibid., 109.

27. Walter Benjamin, "The Work of Art: Second Version," in *The Work of Art in the Age of Its Technological Reproducibility, and Other Writings on Media*, ed. Michael W. Jennings, Bridget Doherty, and Thomas Y. Levin (Cambridge: Belknap Press, 2008), 23 (emphasis original).

attribute of scientific experimentation—microscopy in particular—meaning that its usefulness extends from artistry into the realm of scientific advance. If the close-up evokes a cinematic promise of new knowledge, it is partially because its interest in scrutiny recalls the possibilities inherent in observing things closely. Visual revelation in the cinema, then, is not only a product of aesthetic tradition, but also of the scientific. In the close-up's seductive landscape, spectatorship is figured as a process both individuated and communal, both metaphysical and physical, both spiritual and scientific; the looming, tiny mysteries sprawled across the screen speak to what we now know, what we might discover, and what we hope to find through acute observation.

Among the revelationist film theorists, as Malcolm Turvey has named them, French writer and filmmaker Jean Epstein, who wrote during the silent era, was perhaps most entranced by new visions possible in the movie theater.[28] The cinema, as Epstein put it, was the most visual of all visual arts: "although sight is already recognized by everyone as the most developed sense, and even though the viewpoint of our intellect and our mores is visual, there has nevertheless never been an emotive process so homogenously, so exclusively optical as the cinema. Truly, the cinema creates a *particular system of consciousness limited to a single sense*."[29] Spectators in the cinema view "a cyclopean art, a unisensual art, an iconoscopic retina. All life and attention are in the eye. . . . Wrapped in darkness, ranged in the cell-like seats, directed toward the source of emotion by their softer side, the sensibilities of the entire auditorium converge, as if in a funnel, toward the film. Everything else is barred, excluded, no longer valid."[30] Observation of the moving image here depends not just on visual organization, but on the elimination of sensory distraction, that is, other senses at all. *Photogénie*, Epstein's concept of the photographically enhanced qualities of objects, thus depends in large part upon the objects being reproduced *as solely visible*. There, looking into "a new reality . . . a reality for a special occasion, which is untrue to everyday reality just as everyday reality is untrue to the heightened awareness of poetry," the viewer face to face with "the clear thread of thoughts and dreams, what might or should have been, what was, what never was or could have been, feelings in their secret guise, the startling face of love and beauty, in a word, the soul."[31]

For Epstein, it was not just simple vision that the cinema perfected, but a proximal gaze achieved through the camera lens's ability to home in on

28. Malcolm Turvey, *Doubting Vision: Film and the Revelationist Tradition* (Oxford: Oxford University Press, 2008); and "Jean Epstein's Cinema of Immanence: The Rehabilitation of the Corporeal Eye," *October* 83 (Winter 1998): 25–50.

29. Jean Epstein, "Magnification," trans. Stuart Liebman, in *French Film Theory and Criticism*, 240 (emphasis original).

30. Ibid., 239–240.

31. Epstein, "On Certain Characteristics of *Photogénie*," 318.

minute details in filmed objects. *Photogénie* appeared most saliently, was most intensely inherent, in the close-up:

> The close-up is drama in high gear. . . . The close-up is an intensifying agent because of its size alone. If the tenderness expressed by a face ten times as large is doubtlessly not ten times as moving, it is because in this case, ten, a thousand, or a hundred thousand would—erroneously—have a similar meaning. Merely being able to establish twice as much emotion would still have enormous consequences. But whatever its numerical value, this magnification acts on one's feelings more to transform than to confirm them, and personally, it makes me uneasy. Increasing or decreasing successions of events in the right proportions would obtain effects of an exceptional and fortunate elegance. The close-up modifies the drama by the impact of proximity. Pain is within reach. If I stretch out my arm I touch you, and that is intimacy . . . maximum visual acuity.[32]

Through the close-up, the spectator could inhabit the spatial, temporal, and affective world of the projected image. In addition, the cinema's unique ability to magnify small portions of the surrounding world makes it a particularly intense art—intense in that it could encourage a slow, incisive gaze, at once attentive ("The close-up limits and directs the attention"), supremely visual ("there has never been an emotive process so homogenously, so exclusively optical as the cinema"), and deliberately separate and superior to the stage ("The habit of strong sensations which the cinema is essentially capable of producing, blunts theatrical sensations which are, moreover, of a lesser order. Theater, watch out!").[33] What the theater is incapable of providing is precisely proximity; of necessity, live theater maintains a distance between spectator and actor, whereas the camera's lens shortens the distance between the two, transforming spatial separation and perspective into something instantly crossed and sharpened. While not a theorist of cinematic space per se, Epstein here makes the argument not only that film must be separated from the theater, but that it is automatically a completely different object via the close-up. It must therefore be treated differently, including in terms of space. Through the close-up, cinema provides a window into the visual systems that make up the spectator's surrounding environment: how something as seemingly inconsequential as a glance, a quivering lip, or a minute gesture can be decoded through careful study, and understood as part of a greater system of connection.

32. Epstein, "Magnification," 239.
33. Ibid., 239–240.

The close-up as the central component of cinema's visual potentialities was also espoused by Hungarian film theorist Béla Balázs, who exemplified what Tom Gunning has called cinema's new gnosis.[34] Akin to Epstein, Balázs saw film as a source of new knowledge, and in his view, a lack of attention to film in the academy and as a cultural product worthy of study was absurd given film's status as the great new art of the twentieth century. As Gertrude Koch describes, Balázs's interest lay in an "anthropocentric aesthetics of expression . . . anticipat[ing] many insights film theory has been elaborating over the past decade, for instance the inscription of the spectator into the film."[35] For Balázs, cinema's expressiveness is located in its visuality; specifically, film promised a return to embodied visual and physical culture from the conceptual and word-based nature of print culture. As a result of the new art of film, "the whole of mankind is now busy relearning the long-forgotten language of gestures and facial expressions. This language is not the substitute for words characteristic of the sign language of the deaf and dumb, but the visual corollary of human souls immediately made flesh. *Man will become visible once again.*"[36] Film's visuality predicates a return to embodied experience by reintroducing us to our own bodies, visible onscreen. And the close-up, the means by which the director guides the viewer's gaze, evokes the proximity necessary for bodily reawakening: "The magnifying glass of the cinematograph brings us closer to the individual cells of life, it allows us to feel the texture and substance of life in its concrete detail."[37] Looking closer, the spectator gains access to the details that make up life, the objects that fill what, from far away, seems to be empty space. The close-up thus suggests the endlessness of existence rendered visible; scrutiny provides revelation. Cinema thereby fulfills a condition of an endless architectonics, à la Frederick Kiesler: through protracted plays on scale, it introduces a world inside of the world, of cells, relationships, textures, and other precious miniature things that can only be accessible through human vision paired with mechanical vision. Cinema allows us to see, closer, through to the heart of the world.

It is this quality of cinema—this insistence on intimate vision—that separates film from other arts and permits its emergence as an embodied experience. In Balázs's final work of film criticism, 1948's *Theory of the Film*, he decried how "the scholars and academies let this opportunity pass, although

---

34. Tom Gunning, "In Your Face: Physiognomy, Photography, and the Gnostic Mission of Early Film," *Modernism/Modernity* 4, no. 1 (1997): 1.

35. Gertrude Koch, "Béla Balázs: The Physiognomy of Things," trans. Miriam Hansen, *New German Critique* no. 40 (Winter 1987): 171.

36. Béla Balázs, "Visible Man," in *Béla Balázs: Early Film Theory: Visible Man and the Spirit of the Film*, ed. Erica Carter, trans. Rodney Livingstone (New York: Berghahn Books, 2010), 10 (emphasis original).

37. Ibid., 38.

for many centuries it was the first chance to observe, with the naked eye so to speak, one of the rarest phenomena of the history of culture: the emergence of a new form of artistic expression, the only one born in our time, and in our society and therefore the only one with the material, intellectual and spiritual determinants of which we are entirely familiar."[38] Beyond the power of the close-up, what also made film so novel for Balázs was its means of immersion. Although mobility formulated one important aspect of the new art, cinema's most important characteristic was its ability to show "not other things, but the same things in a different way—that in the film the permanent distance from the work fades out of the consciousness of the spectator and with it that inner distance as well, which hitherto was a part of the experience of art. . . . In the cinema the camera carries the spectator into the film picture itself."[39] Whereas the spectator could not fully penetrate other art forms, "Hollywood invented an art which disregards the principle of self-contained composition and not only does away with the distance between the spectator and the work of art but deliberately creates the illusion in the spectator that he is in the middle of the action reproduced in the fictional space of the film."[40]

Of all of film's components, however, close-ups offer "the most hidden parts in our polyphonous life," "dramatic revelations of what is really happening under the surface of appearances."[41] They transform our sense of dimension and space, for "an isolated face takes us out of space, our consciousness of space is cut out and we find ourselves in another dimension: that of physiognomy."[42] For Balázs, the close-up is particularly useful in uncovering formerly unseen aspects of facial structure and therefore meaning; the close-up of the actor's face shows how, in its array of "microphysiognomics," "the invisible face behind the visible had made its appearance, the invisible face visible only to the one person to whom it addresses itself—and to the audience."[43] Balázs's investment in physiognomy illustrates the stakes of vision as both a sensory and signifying practice. In looking very closely at enlarged parts, the spectator allows the visible onscreen body to fall away into meaning; through visual acuity attained in close-up shots, the projected body becomes a signifier rather than a signified. Thus in addition to operating as sources of experience, pleasure, and sensory awareness, bodies in cinematic space are meaning-making entities, both founts of embodied vision and creators

38. Béla Balázs, *Theory of the Film: Character and Growth of a New Art*, trans. Edith Bone (Mineola: Dover Publications, 1970), 22.
39. Ibid., 47–48.
40. Ibid., 50.
41. Ibid., 55–56.
42. Ibid., 61.
43. Ibid., 76.

of signification past physical boundaries. Most importantly, the close-up and its implications for physiognomy immerse the spectator into an interior, endless state: by moving forward visually to engage in intimate scrutiny of the filmed object, the spectator gains access to a hermeneutic universe of mystical connections, aesthetic expressions, and purified experience. The webs between objects, audiences, and space reveal a world bound up in secret knots.[44]

In Balázs's view, access to this secret world could be partially explained by advances in both philosophy and science; for example, French phenomenologist Henri Bergson's analysis of melody, time, and duration clarified the microphysiognomics of the facial close-up.[45] Jean Epstein as well saw this window into mysterious new visual systems, undiscovered until the camera could contribute to human vision's revelatory qualities, as in part emergent due to scientific advances:

> If today, every modestly cultivated man can represent the universe as a four dimensional continuum in which all material accidents are situated by the interplay of four spatio-temporal variables; if this richer, more variable, perhaps truer figure is gradually supplanting itself for primitive flat schematizations of the earth and heavens; if the indivisible unity of the four factors of space-time is slowly acquiring evidence which modifies the inseparability of the three dimensions of pure space, the cinema is responsible for the wide fame and popularity of the theory with which Einstein and Minkowski have principally associated their names.[46]

Not only was cinematic visual immersion partially a product of the discovery of relativity, but relativity could find its most potent metaphor in the cinema. Space and time brought together in the cinema—duration, illusory space, and narrative wrapped into aesthetic experience—was a perfect testing ground for further artistic experimentation with the fourth dimension and with the general connectedness of space, objects, and human spectators.

How these disparate theories and experiences could be brought together in the cinema depended entirely on visual representation. Through the power of proximal vision, space, time, duration, and community might become an

44. Deleuze describes Balázs's close-up not as tearing away "its object from a set of which it would form part, of which it would be a part, but on the contrary *it abstracts itself from all spatio-temporal co-ordinates*, that is to say it raises it to the state of Entity." Gilles Deleuze, *Cinema 1: The Movement Image*, trans. Hugh Tomlinson and Barbara Habberjam (Minneapolis: University of Minnesota Press, 2006), 95–96 (emphasis original).

45. See Béla Balázs, *Theory of the Film*, 61–62.

46. Jean Epstein, "Timeless Time," in "Magnification and Other Writings," trans. Stuart Liebman, *October* 3 (Spring 1977): 18.

uninterrupted whole. Vision in the cinema must be perfected; once an ideal visual structure could be achieved, experimentation could come to fruition. Yet while advances in science were thrilling, for Epstein and Balázs they operated mainly as metaphors or as inspiration. Constructing or writing based on new scientific principles remained an elusive phenomenon. In the 1930s, however, the Society of Motion Picture Engineers was increasingly interested in optics, particularly in relation to eye strain or fatigue. Eye strain presented a serious problem for several reasons: first, it decreased the pleasurable and comfortable attributes of filmgoing, and second, it did so in a quite insidious fashion. Rather than blaming poor projection conditions for headaches and exhaustion, many in the industry surmised, audiences would simply blame "the movies" in general, and therefore stay home. In an attempt to combat this secret shame, the Society offered fellowships at the Institute of Advanced Optics (University of Rochester), one of which was obtained by Peter Snell, who published his findings in 1933.[47] Ultimately, Snell determined that the retina in particular is susceptible to contrast fatigue, of which flicker was a specific component. The eye, Snell found, responds to significant contrast by either accommodating and adjusting, or overexerting—both of which lead eventually to temporarily decreased retinal efficiency. Due to black and white film's strong contrasts, patrons were regularly at risk of developing eye fatigue at the movies. In order to avoid exhaustion and, eventually, pain, exhibitors and scientists had to work together to determine methods of maintaining filmic contrasts at an everyday, normal level. Following these findings, F. H. Richardson suggested practical ways to ensure movie houses and projection could avoid eye fatigue.[48] Maintenance issues such as oil and dirt in the projector lens and travel ghosts were obvious culprits. Yet Richardson also identified design flaws that could lead to eye strain: glare spots caused by unnecessarily exposed lighting, poor screen illumination, and extreme fluctuation of illumination levels. Sudden changes in screen illumination, Richardson speculated, meant wear and tear on the retina. If the screen instead could modulate these changes, whether in the moment of production and editing or, more realistically for exhibitors, in the moment of projection, eye fatigue could be relegated to the past, and maximal visual acuity and comfort could be achieved.

By this time, Schlanger had already developed significant ties to the SMPE—and in fact was the sole architect in the 1930s and early 1940s to attend their annual convention on theater engineering. In 1931 and 1932, he published his first articles on floor slopes, seating, and optical conditions

47. Peter Snell, "An Introduction to the Experimental Study of Visual Fatigue," *Journal of the Society of Motion Picture Engineers* 20, no. 5 (May 1933): 367–389.
48. F. H. Richardson, "Avoidance of Eye Fatigue," *Journal of the Society of Motion Picture Engineers* 20, no. 5 (May 1933): 391–395.

in their monthly journal. No other architects worked this closely with SMPE members at this time; Schlanger's interest in scientific calibration and in wedding technical conditions to aesthetic ones made him a singular force able to pivot from one end of the industry spectrum to the other. For Schlanger, advances in optical science could be harnessed to bring weight to metaphysical desires. By pinpointing exact detail in the movie house, optics could add to the proximal quality of filmic experience—not just the close-up, but the close-up seen in perfected conditions; not just the theory of space and time, but a better angle of vision to experience space and time as unified. Where Epstein insisted that theater should "watch out" due to its "blunted" experiences compared to film's sharpened ones, Schlanger demonstrated the specific manner in which subtended viewing angles differentiated one medium's psychological impact from the other. In the stage theater, staggered seating was simply not as essential, given that the area of action remains relatively small and centered. But in the film auditorium, the entirety of the screen width contains visual information and movement, necessitating a wider subtended visual angle for every spectator. This not only requires greater attention to viewing angles but also implies a wider field of vision– and therefore an experience closer to everyday vision.[49]

Early on, Schlanger advocated consideration of the peripheral areas of the screen to heighten viewer immersion. In order to make the spectator feel as though he inhabited the image, Schlanger argued that attention should turn from attempts at three-dimensional effects toward the viewer's psychological "projection" into the picture. But in the early 1930s, even the term "motion picture" had an effect on such thinking.[50] "Picture" implied stasis, or a feeling of looking "through a picture frame"; although "motion" combats such separation between object and spectator, too frequently the movies were thought of as akin to art hanging on a wall with a definitive shape and border. Instead, Schlanger argued, film should be redefined and represented as a "shapeless shape" that would "make the viewer least conscious of a limited boundary."[51] If, in the theater and on the screen, optical conditions that mimic how peripheral vision works are deployed in tandem with calibration of vision that mimics our day-to-day experience, projection into a "shapeless shape" comes within reach. Rather than the "dead black masking" still covering screen edges, "a supplementary border should be used, having a shape conforming to the natural vision contour," lit to merge with auditorium conditions and therefore serve "as

49. See Schlanger's subtended angle diagrams in Ben Schlanger, "Advancement of Motion Picture Theater Design," *Journal of the Society of Motion Picture Engineers* 50, no. 4 (April 1948): 309.

50. Ben Schlanger, "On the Relation between the Shape of the Projected Picture, the Areas of Vision, and Cinematographic Technique," *Journal of the Society of Motion Picture Engineers* 14, no. 5 (May 1935): 402–409.

51. Ibid., 404.

a transitional blending between the walls of the auditorium and the illuminated screen surface."[52] Here, Schlanger pointed to an early version of what would eventually become the RCA Synchro-Screen: a replacement for masking that, in keeping with recommendations voiced by Snell and Richardson, focused on lessening illumination and color contrast, and thereby relaxed the eye. Yet the fluctuating, illuminated screen surround served an additional purpose: it not only reduced contrast between density and brightness onscreen, but also visually blended screen edge into auditorium flow. Once the eye was liberated from stress, once it was free to gaze relaxed in an immediate natural angle of vision, the spectator could more smoothly "project" himself without distraction into the "shapeless shape" floating in a field of gently pulsing light.

In a 1935 presentation to the SMPE, Schlanger proposed an auditorium promoting precise visual acuity—"maximum visual acuity," per Epstein—through reduced distance from the screen and concentration of seats in the path of least visual distortion. Noting shifts in ideal acuity ratios determined by Helmholtz, Weber, Luckiesh, Moss, and Freeman, Schlanger also observed that one of the most "valuable features of the motion picture lies in the fact that the spectator can, at will, be placed exceedingly close to, or at any desired position in relation to the action upon, the screen, thus transplanting him from the theater to the actual time and locale of the story that is unfolding."[53] Although Schlanger argued for "realism" in the movie theater, his assertions on what constitutes "real" experience are tenuously real at best; "real" experience hardly allows for perfected close positioning in relation to the world. Thus at the heart of this goal was not reality per se, but transplantation into wonder, strangeness, other worlds—the combination of the space of spectatorship with cinematic space for immersion. Drawing closer to the screen and the images on it, peering as though through a window, the spectator might better experience not necessarily reality but temporal and spatial intimacy, connections that either hint at some universal truths or are impossible to grasp otherwise in the distancing effects of the American twentieth century. Immersion regains tenderness, a vulnerability forgotten in the perpetual shock of modern life. Where Freud's tiny cellular organism builds perceptual defenses against the outside world's incessant annoyance, the cinema might also take us beyond the pleasure principle, outside our bodies, closer to something sweeter.[54] Proximity, therefore, as a tool of revelatory immersion was not unique to film theorists, but was also embraced by exhibition practitioners. Distinguishing Schlanger from Epstein was not a difference in goal—both sought spectatorial immersion into the artistic object through a manipulation of its space of presentation—but

52. Ibid., 409.
53. Ben Schlanger, "The Motion Picture Theater Shape and Effective Visual Reception," *Journal of the Society of Motion Picture Engineers* 26, no. 2 (February 1936): 128.
54. Sigmund Freud, *Beyond the Pleasure Principle*, trans. C. J. M. Hubback (1922; reprint Eastford, CT: Martino Fine Books, 2010).

rather the ways in which it could be most effectively achieved. For Epstein, relativity and metaphysics broke ground toward immersion; for Schlanger, optical science. For both, however, cinema functioned as a radical possibility for showing the spectator the path toward aesthetic immersion. In Schlanger's view, proximity must be paired with an understanding of human perception as subject to optical laws. By working within those laws, better immersion could be achieved through a more efficient means of reaching toward the same goal: metaphysics as machine.

In concert with revelatory film theorists, Schlanger proposed another visual condition: not just the close-up, but the close-up in perfect focus at a perfect angle:

> It might be argued that close-up shots in cinematography circumvent the need for great acuity with more distant shots. This is not so, because with the increase in size of the close-up, there is a corresponding increase in the number of details to be discerned. . . . Ideal visual reception of motion pictures is not achieved merely by limiting the viewing distance for visual acuity only. The visual angle for the viewer, subtended by an image on the screen, and the 'visual' angle for the camera lens, subtended by the object being photographed, should, under ideal conditions, be the same.[55]

Although such an ideal was pragmatically impossible to achieve in the theater, Schlanger's point was that the industry must consider both camera angle and angle of vision by spectatorial position in the audience to create more effective immersion. By combining ideal visual acuity and angles, close-ups, and literal proximity to the screen, by intertwining cinema's dramatic possibilities with a perfected space of exhibition, Schlanger sought to unify human eye and camera eye into a roving, disembodied visual organ for a new modern spectator. His theatrical design therefore materialized concepts put forth by Epstein: a physical experiment for cinematic immersion both mimicking and expanding human vision into an extended sense of the relational world.

According to Schlanger, the risk of improperly directed vision and distortion was at the root of the movie industry's general woes in the 1930s; rather than the imminent economic distresses related to the stock market crash, imperfect exhibition constituted Hollywood's most pressing problem. As the pictures made significant technological advances, exemplified by the emergence of optical soundtracks in the 1920s, "real progress," Schlanger argued, "in the exhibition of motion pictures has been thwarted by ineffective means of exhibition in existing theatre structures."[56] Whereas in

55. Schlanger, "The Motion Picture Theater Shape and Effective Visual Reception," 131.
56. Ben Schlanger, "Vision in the Movie Theatre," *Motion Picture Herald*, July 30, 1932, *Better Theatres* section, 9.

the live theater three-dimensional forms are foreshortened and converged according to natural human perspective, the cinema complicates this by showing images already foreshortened by the camera's lens on a two-dimensional screen. Therefore, ill-positioned spectators in the movie theater encounter unpleasant distortion in too many of the available seats. The "human eye can not be placed arbitrarily in any position in order to view a two-dimensional surface of photographic images"; rather, to obtain "the full benefit of a great art like the motion picture, the problem of the position of the patron's eye while he is viewing the screen looms up as of great prominence. . . . When will the motion picture industry as a whole respect its own product sufficiently to insure effective delivery of their efforts to the patron?"[57] Comfort was also a rallying cry for Schlanger, who considered spectatorial stillness essential for promoting the illusion of immersion. He decried that while range of vision and comfort had been studied, "unfortunately, such research has not been carried to the relation between bodily comfort and vision of a fixed object, such as a motion picture screen, with motion appearing on it. The studies have been limited to eye comfort only."[58] Respecting the motion picture industry's product required solutions not only to general auditorium positioning to minimize visual distortion, but also position in theater chairs. If audience members were kept perfectly comfortable and perfectly still, the eye could forget its bodily encumbrances for the sake of a direct linear trajectory from camera/ screen apparatus to vision to liberated mind.[59]

By 1934, Schlanger's calls for a better movie theater auditorium repeatedly involved his concerns with visual distortion. Not only were theaters arranging seats improperly for current films, but auditorium structures were of increasingly urgent relevance due to shifts in the industry's preferred cinematographic techniques. As Schlanger explained, movies were beginning to showcase action across the entirety of the frame rather than just the center, both due to the Academy's development of the 3 x 4 projection aperture and in an anticipation of mainstream widescreen. For this reason, distortion at the screen's edge would mean not just loss of peripheral detail but of the focus of the film's shot.[60] Considering these new visual requirements, Schlanger argued that "the *exhibitor* must demand more scientific design of the theatre,

57. Ibid.
58. Ben Schlanger, "Planning so Patrons Can See the Picture Comfortably," *Motion Picture Herald*, November 14, 1942, *Better Theatres* section, 64–65.
59. For more on chair design and seating plans, see Jocelyn Szczepaniak-Gillece, "Revisiting the Apparatus: The Theater Chair and Cinematic Spectatorship," *Screen* 57, no. 3 (Autumn 2016): 253–276.
60. Ben Schlanger, "Production Methods and the Theatre," *Motion Picture Herald*, April 8, 1933, *Better Theatres* section, 8–10; "Use of the Full Screen Area Today," *Motion Picture Herald*, June 3, 1933, *Better Theatres* section, 11–13.

starting right in with the selection of the site, to make sure it is adaptable."[61] Additionally, his architects must understand the requirements for proper seeing in the theater; hiring sightline specialists and conducting two-person and dummy patron vision tests in the auditorium were of the utmost importance.[62] In developing his standards for idealized theaters, Schlanger even suggested that, once perfected, theatrical space could start to dictate the shape of film rather than vice-versa.[63] In fact, in 1970, just one year prior to his death, Schlanger patented a cinematographic system that would "provide a high level of visual impact, simulation of visual experience and the effect of participation to the audience by projecting a series of images each of which comprises a high resolution psycho-physical focus region and diminished discernible detail outwardly thereof." Because "theatrical motion-picture presentations under design-controlled conditions and environment can become a separate experience of a magnitude which cannot be attained by any other entertainment form," the objectives of the invention included creating high visual impact by providing methods for exhibition that dramatically regulated the conditions of movie-viewing for maximum effect.[64]

What Schlanger was seeking to create was, in essence, a fully controlled environment where space, object, and human vision work together to impress integral information upon the spectator. The controlled space of the laboratory shifts to the controlled space of the optically perfected movie theater. Thus the neutralized theater was connected not only to larger aesthetic models in film texts, but to older film spaces, such as Edison's Black Maria from the turn of the century. As Brian Jacobson has demonstrated, the Black Maria not only recalled the laboratory, but demonstrated the power of early filmmaking for wielding environmental control in order to "enframe" cinematic subjects.[65] In this sense, Schlanger's theatrical abyss relied similarly on industrial traditions of organization, management, and discipline—all hallmarks of the apparatus's stealthy indoctrination. Within neutralized theatrical environments, perception becomes instant, inalienable, immediate, while vision was directed through manipulation of the space in which the spectator sat. Although Schlanger was trained as an architect and not as a scientist, concepts from science infiltrated his theatrical designs and proposals. Such science was undeniably tinged with magic and with metaphysics; Schlanger's

61. Ben Schlanger, "Changing Factors in Theatre Vision," *Motion Picture Herald*, December 15, 1934, *Better Theatres* section, 31 (emphasis original).

62. Ibid., 6–36.

63. Ben Schlanger, "Standard Practice in Theatre Design," *Motion Picture Herald*, September 21, 1935, *Better Theatres* section, 8–35.

64. Ben Schlanger, "Methods of Cinematography Patent," US3502400 A, March 24, 1970.

65. Brian Jacobson, "Black Boxes and Open-Air Spaces," in *Studios Before the Systems: Architecture, Technology, and the Emergence of Cinematic Space* (New York: Columbia University Press, 2015), 23–54.

perfected optical conditions were always geared toward immersion, an impossible illusion never fully attainable but always desired. What science could purchase for Schlanger's movie theaters was a new kind of perception, one that both mimicked and heightened human vision. In a reworking of the relationship between science and aesthetics, Schlanger echoed the centrality of scientific seeing to filmic seeing: that both might function best in a space of control, that both might work as tools of measurement, but also that both depend on a specific environment to be read correctly. From the eye through to the mind, modern perceptual immersion required both a place designed for immediacy and a new comprehension of volumetric visual space, full of energies threaded through a relational universe of things, theories, spirits, and harmonies. In order to access these mysterious structures, film must be proximal to its viewer, not just in terms of the close-up's powers, but the screen's relation to the spectator. The screen, then, must not only be integrated into the space of viewing through auditorium neutralization, but also through the elimination of its optically definitive frames: the antiquated proscenium arch, and the black masking that set it distinctly apart from the rest of the theatrical surround. The screen must no longer be a framed and separate image, but a window opening onto a world witnessed by the spectator.

## DEMASKING THE SCREEN, REMOVING THE FRAME

Illustrated by both theories of the close-up and Schlanger's interest in visual acuity, proximity and enormity in the American theater enjoyed much longer periods of experimentation than solely the second widescreen movement in the 1950s. Among the attempts to bring the audience closer to the screen prior to generalized widescreen, screen demasking constituted a major object of scrutiny. Although standard practice for the first half of the twentieth century, screen masking has rarely been the subject of extensive analysis in exhibition history. Yet the gradual removal of screen masking over several decades instigated debates around embodiment and disembodiment in the widescreen boom. Whereas masked screens prior to the 1950s set film apart and visually evoked its relationship to a framed picture, demasked screens welcomed a cinema of presence. Exhibition's removal of masking mirrored changes in high art, where objects and performances expanded from sharply defined borders out into the space of spectatorship, exemplified by spaces such as Frederick Kiesler's 1942 Art of This Century gallery and its unframed paintings, or later "happenings" in public spaces by artist cooperatives such as Fluxus.[66] At the same time, new predominance of picture windows in suburban houses

66. Peggy Guggenheim claimed the lack of frames in Art of This Century was her idea rather than Kiesler's. Regardless of whose concept it originally was, the lack of frames

and more innovative use of glass in modernist domiciles, curtain walls, and windshields suggested both a new mobility and a malleable shape to the traditional window that could shift according to the spectator's perspective, position, and environment.[67] In this sense, the slow discarding of masking over several decades both echoed efforts in the gallery and museum world and reawakened debates regarding the place of the body in looking. Where the definitive borders of masking might keep spectators secure in the separation between picture and body, masking's removal heralded a visual immersion in which eye and object shared the same world. This vision was alternatively bodily and aphysical, the envelopment of the spectatorial body and the denial of its existence; for both ideals, masking ushered in the era of successful widescreen and highlighted its ensuing ambivalence toward bodily status and transportation. Masked, the screen appeared like a play due to the predominance of unnecessary stages and proscenium arches, but also like a flat, framed picture hung on the wall. With the removal of masking, or its relegation to aspect ratio adjustment, the screen recalled not so much a painting as a window

was a subject of much interest for media coverage at the time: "The pictures, which are largely unframed, are exhibited detached from their backgrounds. Some are joined to brackets which project a foot or more off the walls, while others are shown similarly fastened to columns improvised of wood or cord. As Miss Guggenheim explained, the object is to provide a framing of space for the pictures instead of the usual artificial frameworks" ("Peggy Guggenheim's Collection of Modern Art on Exhibit Today," *New York Herald Tribune*, October 21, 1942); "The paintings, which are to be presented in an entirely new way, will be shown without frames and appear to be suspended in mid-air" (*New York Times*, October 16, 1942); "[W]e find all of the art framed not within an individual rectangle or square of its own, but instead by the 'spatial' architecture that forms the whole gallery and of which the painting is definitely a part" ("Gallery Premiere Assists Red Cross," *New York Times*, October 21, 1942); "Miss Guggenheim believes that frames are 'always wrong' and 'kill a picture'" ("Isms Rampant: Peggy Guggenheim's Dream World Goes Abstract, Cubist, and Generally Non-Real," *News Week* [Dayton, OH], November 2, 1942); "A revolution in modern display techniques, depriving paintings of their frames and hanging them anywhere but on walls, has been effected here by art collector Peggy Guggenheim and architect Frederick J. Kiesler" (William Platt, "Neither Frame Nor Wall Used for Paintings," *Dallas TX News*, November 22, 1942). All clippings from "Art of this Century" clippings, Guggenheim Archives, Peggy Guggenheim Foundation Papers, Series 2, Scrapbooks, 1936–1979, Box 000505: Peggy Guggenheim.

67. For discussion of the curtain wall, see Reinhold Martin, "Atrocities, or, Curtain Wall as Mass Medium," *Perspecta* 32 (2001): 66–75; for discussion of the mediated picture window, see Lynn Spigel, "Installing the Television Set: Popular Discourses on Television and Domestic Space, 1948–1955," in *Private Screenings: Television and the Female Consumer*, ed. Lynn Spigel and Denise Mann (Minneapolis: University of Minnesota Press, 1992): 3–40; and "Designing the Smart House: Posthuman Domesticity and Conspicuous Production," *European Journal of Cultural Studies* 8 (November 2005): 403–426. Sandy Isenstadt briefly explores the question of the windshield and cinematic viewing as similar modern conditions, although he remarks that driving is embodied compared to cinema's disembodiment, in "Auto-Specularity: Driving through the American Night," *Modernism/Modernity* 18, no. 2 (April 2011): 213–231.

**Figure 2.4:** Century Theatre, Detroit, MI. From the Manning Brothers Historic Photographs Collection.

onto a changing, moving, proximal world. Thus the shift from masking the filmic image to opening the screen's borders occasioned a metaphorical shift in the status of the screen from the frame to the window.

From early on in film exhibition through the mid-1950s, projectors cast moving imagery onto a screen often with double borders: first a heavy, black frame of fabric masking, then the proscenium arch, an antiquated reminder of film exhibition's architectural legacy deriving from live theater (Figures 2.4 and 2.5).[68] Proscenium arches remained in place for so long primarily due to the movies' association with the stage. Although Schlanger, among others, argued for the removal of the arch and therefore the separation of theater and film into their own specific artistic realms, the continuing popularity of the proscenium through the widescreen revolution illustrated an extended struggle to define film's place in the larger aesthetic sphere as either unique or indebted to the theater.[69] Unlike the proscenium, though, masking represented a piecemeal

68. Despite Thomas Tallmadge's urge in 1928 to "abolish the old-fashioned ever loaded proscenium . . . divorce the motion picture from vaudeville and jazz, from tawdry decoration and vulgar architecture," proscenia remained in mainstream use for decades. Thomas E. Tallmadge, "The Screen, a New Art, Should Pave Road to a New Architecture," *Exhibitors Herald and Moving Picture World*, March 17, 1928, *Better Theatres* section, 9.
69. A lack of proscenia was often a feature of the art house. By the early 1950s, canny exhibitors understood that differentiating movie theaters from television and

**Figure 2.5:** Annex Theatre, Detroit, MI. From the Manning Brothers Historic Photographs Collection.

solution to technological as opposed to metaphorical problems. The rationale for masking rested mostly on shaky projection; like most technologies in their infancies, cinema and its technical accoutrements boasted less-than-perfect capability in the 1900s through the 1920s. Masking absorbed light spill and hid the dancing edges of a jittery frame; by cutting off small portions of the frame, masked screens stabilized the film image. As William Paul summarizes, rationales for masking shifted from exhibitor to exhibitor:

> Over the years, various reasons were offered for the masking: the dark surround made the image appear brighter, which helped with general problems of

thereby increasing profits could be accomplished both by removing the frame—impossible to do with television—and securing film's status as art compared to television's status as simple entertainment. The Beekman Theatre in New York, opened in 1952 by the Rugoff Corporation/Rugoff & Becker chain, had no proscenium and curtains instead of masking, adding to its "atmosphere of relaxing charm, subtly appealing to the aesthetic demands of the discriminating theatre patron. . . . Offering the utmost in comfort and beauty and incorporating the finest modern innovations in design and efficiency, the New York City art house is a constructive answer by astute theatremen to competitive forms of amusement, particularly television. The stimulation of a satisfying motion picture, enjoyed in surroundings such as the Beekman offers, cannot be duplicated from the easy chair." "Ready for That TV Competition," *Boxoffice Magazine*, June 7, 1952, *Modern Theatres* section, 9.

illumination; it squared off the image to make less apparent the keystoning caused by sharp projection angles of high projection booths; it concealed the vibration of projection equipment. Whatever the justifications, masking had the odd effect of making a small image seem even smaller and, by virtue of the double framing, at a fairly great remove from the audience.[70]

Paul explains that masking, originally thought to increase reality effects by brightening and steadying the image as it was projected through undependable projectors, was eventually found to decrease immersion in the picture by blurring the image while at the same time sharply defining—setting apart—the space of cinematic action from the place of viewing. Despite some earlier experimentation, masking remained mainstream practice in most theaters after Academy ratio changes and full integration of sound-on-film technology, in large part due to force of habit.[71] By the mid-1950s, however, advances in optical technology began to make clear that a causal relationship between brightest screen image and sharpest screen image was not necessarily provable; instead, optimum visual acuity was related to low contrast as opposed to the high contrast created between bright image and dark masking.[72] The discarding of skeuomorphic masking not only decreased distracting contrast, but also highlighted a general shift in exhibitors' understanding of what a film could be: from a frozen, immutable, and labeled artwork to an image of worldly, sensory experience. A demasked screen boasted a more "realistic," "participatory," "engaging" film; a demasked screen promised a new life for an old cinema, one where immersion, action, and movement became heftier, more integral categories.[73]

Demasking began to take hold during a moment when frames were concurrently disappearing from gallery display. As frames were no longer necessary for describing contemporary art as art, they were similarly no longer necessary

70. Paul, "Screening Space," 147. Paul also discusses de-masking and the Synchro-Screen in *When Movies Were Theater: Architecture, Exhibition, and the Evolution of American Film.*

71. In 1953, decades after projectors had been effectively stabilized, Lou Gerard, in conversation with Herbert Barnett, president of SMPTE and executive vice-president of Cinerama, Inc., stated that "the trend is slightly away from black masking." Lou Gerard, "Planning to Install a Wide Screen?," *Boxoffice Magazine*, August 4, 1953, *Modern Theatres* section, 15.

72. See, for example, Gio Gagliardi, "Optical Objections to Screen Masking," *Motion Picture Herald*, March 24, 1951, *Better Theatres* section, 44.

73. By the 1950s, the words "realistic," "participatory," and "engaging" were more and more consistently deployed as positive cinematic/theatrical descriptors in exhibition journals. "Participation" in particular became the word of choice for exhibitors explaining the popularity of the widescreen experience. See Ariel Rogers, "Smothered in Baked Alaska: The Anxious Appeal of Widescreen Cinema," *Cinema Journal* 51, no. 3 (Spring 2012): 74–96.

for describing the movies as movies.[74] While met with much fascination in the press, Frederick Kiesler's unframed images in Art of This Century were unusual but far from singular in terms of deframing experimentation. Detlef Mertins explains that Mies van der Rohe's New National Gallery in Berlin's inaugural Piet Mondrian retrospective (1968), containing unframed art suspended in the air, was part of a history of Mies's innovative artistic display of interaction and contact. As early as his Pressa exhibition in Cologne in 1928, he realized the usefulness of unframed images for developing a "unity of the arts within a new open and fluid spatiality."[75] Mies's interest in freestanding or floating objects in the gallery pointed to a larger modernist investment in phenomenology, interaction, immersion, and collusion of art and experience.[76] At mid-century, then, art in a modernist context could be more massive than its container and inseparable from quotidian life; cinema's possibility also became integration with the flows of everyday experience. From frame to window, the movie screen swung open onto a view of the world.

Schlanger quickly developed a reputation for demasking. Known by the late 1930s in exhibition circles as the "architect with a passion for proper theatre sight lines," Schlanger was described as "bent on abolishing masking" in order to let projection light spill onto all sides of the screen.[77] And in July 1939, patrons of New York City's Edison Theatre on Upper Broadway saw the first projection of a motion picture on a demasked screen in the United States. While a model had been presented at a meeting of the Society of Motion Picture Engineers in 1937, the Edison boasted the initial practical American exhibition of demasking paired with surrounding light variance.[78] A border of light spill around the screen varied in intensity according to changes in the projected image's foot-lamberts. In the theater, "no screen supports are visible; the picture appears to be floating in space, in the midst of an area of changing light. Surprisingly, many viewers find screen definition improved."[79]

74. Discussion of the removal of frames in gallery spaces was undeniably one of the radical reinventions of the modern art museum leading to both the rise in public- and education-oriented museums and the American museum's later crisis of identity. For further discussion of this crisis, see Daedalus: Special Issue on America's Museums 128, no. 3 (Summer 1999). For further exploration of the spatial ideologies of the museum and its assertion of a passageway between the "real" and the infinite world of aesthetic experience, see Amir Ameri, "The Spatial Dialectics of Authenticity," SubStance 33, no. 2 (2004): 61–89.

75. Detlef Mertins, "Mies's Event Space," Grey Room no. 20 (Summer 2005): 65.

76. Although "suspended" might suggest a hanging framed painting, Mies's exhibition contained unframed art; suspension in the case of unframed objects signified integrated and organic display as opposed to graph-like separation.

77. "Monthly Chat," International Projectionist 14, no. 7 (August 1939): 5.

78. James J. Finn, "Television, Projection Feature S.M.P.E. Meeting," International Projectionist 12, no. 10 (October 1937): 27–28.

79. At the time, masking's reinforcement of light contrast was sometimes thought to increase visual acuity. This assumption would be disproved by some studies in the 1930s, but most extensively in the 1950s. "New York Theatre Uses Maskless Type Screen," Motion Picture Herald, August 19, 1939, Better Theatres section, 6.

**Figure 2.6:** From *International Projectionist*, January 1952.

Dubbed the Synchro-Vision Screen (later to be modified with the assistance of engineer William Hoffberg to the RCA Synchro-Screen) and constructed by Schlanger and electrical engineer Jacob Gilston, this new technology constituted a radical change (Figure 2.6). Removal of the screen's thick frame resulted in greater optical acuity, arguably due to the elimination of sharp contrast between black masking and bright image as well as a newly allowable reduction in levels of projector light, yet also shifted the manner in which spectators conceived of and thus engaged with the screen. Whereas before the screen was sharply bounded from the rest of the auditorium by its surrounding frame, the demasked Synchro-Vision Screen visually blended into the walls of the theatrical space. Without "screen supports," the picture appeared to be "floating"; without obvious boundaries between screen and auditorium, the picture could more easily inhabit the space of spectatorship. Combined with an efficient and functional auditorium, the demasked screen foreshadowed a mainstream large-screen movement.[80] While the Synchro-Vision Screen kept the standard Academy ratio of 1.33:1 with a basic 4:3 width-to-height aspect, its at-the-time unique usage of light spill and no masking illustrated a new investment in the screen surround's environmental vacuity.[81] Although screen

80. The Edison had recently been renovated, and was left at least through August of 1939 with no painting over its plain white plaster walls. See ibid.
81. Anne Friedberg discusses changes in the Academy ratio during the widescreen revolution as related both to television and the automobile. Anne Friedberg, "Urban

aspect ratios would not change in the mainstream for another decade and a half, the Synchro-Vision screen exemplified ties between neutralized cinemas and enrapturing screen expansion.

The SMPE, Schlanger, and others involved in the neutralized cinema movement and on the forefront of cinematic technology advocated for widespread change in black masking from 1939 onward, recommending its entire elimination, reduction in size, or replacement with a luminous surround material that would reflect light falling on the screen from the projector and increase both visual acuity and the impression of the picture "bleeding" into the theatrical structure.[82] In June of 1939, the SMPE's Projection Practice Committee formed a special group to determine if "many objections to the masking of the screen and complete darkening of the surrounding area" were, in fact, accurate.[83] By 1941, Robert W. Russell of the Training Film Projection Laboratory recommended "removing the area of the picture from its fixed frame," describing the potential effect as one in which "great new frontiers of cinematic effect are opened up by making the screen area the entire proscenium wall."[84] Removing masking both promoted a fuller image by allowing for the entirety of the filmed image to be shown onscreen, and proposed a new form of cinema screen: one with a low contrast, and thus less hard definition against the darkness of auditorium walls, and one with either nondelineated or light-based borders, and thus with more metaphorical spill into spectatorial space. Synchronous screen surrounds, such as the RCA Synchro-Screen, became the gold standard in the early 1950s for film engineers and scientists, if not always for exhibitors.[85] The subsequent creation of an ethereal window "floating in space" recalled Richard Wagner's

Mobility and Cinematic Visuality: The Screens of Los Angeles—Endless Cinema or Private Telematics," *Journal of Visual Culture* 1, no. 2 (2002): 183–205.

82. See, for example, "Screen Masking Is Now under Broadening Attack," *Motion Picture Herald*, November 11, 1939, *Better Theatres* section, 5; Ben Schlanger, "Plans & Materials: Checking the Screen," *Motion Picture Herald*, January 10, 1942, *Better Theatres* section, 24; "Functionally Revised while Being Enlarged," *Motion Picture Herald*, June 10, 1942, *Better Theatres* section, 10–11; "Designs & Devices: Luminous Screen Frame," *Motion Picture Herald*, July 15, 1942, *Better Theatres* section, 10–20.

83. The Committee would, of course, eventually advocate for the removal of masking to promote visual acuity. The group's chairman was Harry Rubin, supervisor of projection at Paramount; in the 1950s, Paramount introduced VistaVision, the studio's successful attempt at an in-house large-screen format and the system of choice for the Williamsburg transcineums. "Auditorium Lighting Needs Being Studied," *Motion Picture Herald*, June 24, 1939, 5.

84. "Pictures on the Wall," *Motion Picture Herald*, October 18, 1941, *Better Theatres* section, 9.

85. "Elimination of Screen Masking," *International Projectionist* 26, no. 3 (March 1951): 29. "With reference to the elimination of black masking, observations by acknowledged authorities since 1920 have indicated the desirability of illumination of screen surroundings."

*mystischer Abgrund* at his Festspielhaus in Bayreuth, both evoking a modern operatic spectatorship of awe, projection, and empathy and suggesting an endless cinematic spectatorship with vision and community at its core.[86] By moving into audience space, the demasked screen also began to make available the phenomenological spectatorship such as that described by Vivian Sobchack, where the screened image is an entity that fills up the room and meets us at our positions in the seats.[87] In removing black masking, experimental theatrical exhibition recalled the work of Epstein and Balázs while anticipating later theoretical relationships to the screen.

While the Edison Theatre was quite striking to the average moviegoer, evidenced by *Motion Picture Herald* coverage, completely demasked screens did not take over mainstream exhibition for over a decade after the Synchro-Vision Screen's debut. Although a demasked screen was widely held as an ideal, engineers and exhibitors recognized its usefulness in allowing some screen flexibility, particularly in theaters without substantial funds for meeting the pace of changing screen ratios. Even once demasking became more commonplace, masked screens still retained some hold on exhibition through the 1960s, partially due to unstable aspect ratios in the widescreen era. In 1946, the Island Theater in Hamilton, Bermuda (Reisner & Urbahn; Schlanger & Hoffberg), designed to reflect the calming and serene effects of tropical color and temporality, boasted a "floating screen" (Figure 2.7), still an object strange enough to warrant the following description: "In the auditorium the effect is perhaps best of all. The screen . . . is unmasked; the patented arrangement of screen and surround gives synchronous lighting of the surround by light spilled from the picture, destroying sharp contrast, fading hard outline, varying with picture intensity. . . . No irrelevant decoration is allowed to interfere with this pleasant dramatic effect."[88] The result according to *Motion Picture Herald* was that the

> elimination of a 'picture-frame' effect—either by masking or proscenium opening—is accomplished in the Island Theatre . . . by placing the screen virtually against the forward wall, which, due to convergence of the forward side walls, is only a little wider than the screen. The image is thus placed in a field of self-created light (which modulates according to variation in film density): with this 'natural' field supplemented by light of low intensity supplied by filament lamp strip sources concealed behind the edge of the screen.[89]

86. For more on the *mystischer Abgrund*, see Juliet Koss, *Modernism after Wagner* (Minneapolis: University of Minnesota Press, 2010).

87. Vivian Sobchack, *The Address of the Eye: A Phenomenology of Film Experience* (Princeton, NJ: Princeton University Press, 1992).

88. "A Bermuda Theater with 'Floating Screen,'" *Architectural Record* 105, no. 4 (April 1949): 87.

89. "Picture Integrated with Auditorium," *Motion Picture Herald*, March 25, 1950, *Better Theatres* section, 21.

**Figure 2.7:** From Jay Emanuel's *Theatre Catalog*, 1953–1954.

Completing the light spill effect, vertical corrugations on the surrounding gray sidewalls, like those later installed in the Tacna, reflected the light emerging from the projected image.

By 1950, the "ideal condition" in the movie theater was that "the viewer should temporarily lose his identity . . . and have no reminder of the fact that he is in a building looking at a screen"; dark masking, however, "has the effect of pushing the action on the screen away from the viewer, of making the picture look remote and unreal" (Figure 2.8). [90] The year 1951 in particular was filled with studies regarding visual acuity and masking, industry calls for removal of masking, and the openings of multiple theaters with demasked screens, while screen technological developments such as curvature required total masking removal.[91] It is no accident that these studies proliferated only a year before Hollywood's eighteen-month-long 3D craze, or two years before

90. Gio Gagliardi, "To Mask or Not to Mask? Isn't It Time to Decide?," *Motion Picture Herald*, September 3, 1950, *Better Theatres* section, 35–36.

91. Cinerama, of course, being one of these; although *This Is Cinerama* did not premiere until September of 1952, the process had already been developed by Fred Waller in 1951.

**Figure 2.8:** Ad for RCA Synchro-Screen, from *Motion Picture Herald*, November 15, 1952.

Cinemascope was patented. Expanded screens were on the rise in American exhibition, and demasking offered a major step forward.

In early 1951, a fully curved Transcolor screen with no masking and a minimized proscenium debuted at the Paris Theatre in New York; produced by the Transcolor Screen Company and designed by Otto Hahn, the screen was mounted on a duraluminum frame created expressly for a doubled convex curvature.[92] The Paris was one of the first successful American art house theaters, and its early adoption of unmasked screens indicated the usefulness of demasking for cinema's relationship to art as well as its separation from the stage.[93] As evidenced by Warner-Leeds's elegant architectural drawings from the design stage of the theater, the Paris was always intended to appeal to an elite class of art house cinemagoers (Insert 2); its use of the Transcolor demasked screen highlights the relationship between modernist immersion,

92. "Curved-Type Screen at New York's Paris Theatre," *Motion Picture Herald*, March 3, 1951, *Better Theatres* section, 24.

93. See chapter 4 for additional discussion of the Paris and its eventual manager, New York art house king Donald Rugoff.

film appreciation, good optics, and cinephilia. Screen masking was deemed unsatisfactory, unscientific, and to blame for the evils of eye strain.[94] A study by the Optical Society undertaken in 1951 found that sharp contrast between bright and dark such as those found in commonplace masked screen auditoriums resulted in eye strain, fatigue, and discomfort. Instead, the society urged exhibitors to provide a small area of transitional illumination— such as that created with the Synchro-Vision Screen—between brightly illuminated screen and dark auditorium walls.[95] Based on findings such as these, the projection practice committee of the now renamed SMPTE (Society of Motion Picture and Television Engineers) developed recommendations for minimum screen sizes and brightness values:

> 1. The *width* of the picture on the screen should be not less than *one sixth* of the distance from the center of the screen to the *most remote seat*. 2. The distance between the screen and the front row of seats should not be less than 0.87 of a foot for each foot of picture width. 3. The brightness at the center of a screen for viewing 35mm motion pictures shall be between 9 and 14 foot-lamberts when the projector is running and no film is in the gate.[96]

Similarly, the SMPTE reiterated that visual acuity increased with brightness only up to the level of ten-foot lamberts. Beyond this, visual acuity does not significantly increase; far below, and eye strain is a consistent problem. To avoid halation—glare resulting from a film with too high a contrast ratio— overall brightness should be increased during such picture conditions. Removing masking and blending screen reflection into the auditorium would immediately reduce contrast without necessitating prohibitively high levels of brightness.

Demasking not only solved these problems of high contrast, but was also of a metaphorical concern. According to George Schutz, the industry's response to whether masking should continue was "long past due" in 1951.[97] In light of the "new thing" no longer being the movies but, rather, television, returning to the theater its former quality of "exciting distinction" was of increasing urgency. The cobwebs must be dusted off the cinema; rather than a staid and antiquated form, it must be remarketed to the public as a living, breathing, revolutionary experience. One of the primary ways of hastening

94. John L. Irwin, "Remodeling with Accent on the Focal Point," *Theatre Catalog* (Philadelphia, PA: Jay Emanuel Publications, 1952), 228.

95. Gagliardi, "Optical Objections to Screen Masking," 44.

96. Gio Gagliardi, "Screen Conditions for Good Vision," *Motion Picture Herald*, March 24, 1951, *Better Theatres* section, 44–45 (emphasis original).

97. George Schutz, "The Search for Ways to Make the Theatre's Picture Newly Unique," *Motion Picture Herald*, May 5, 1951, *Better Theatres* section, 13.

this marketing transition, for Schutz, was both to expand and to demask the screen. In addition to eye strain and contrast problems, masking "reduces the naturalness of color films. Moreover, it rigidly frames the action—makes it so obviously just that, a moving *picture*. This is an inherent condition of television. It need not be one of the theatre screen."[98] Cinema should no longer be a picture, but an experience in motion. Demasking not only promoted an ease of screen enlargement but also served to rarify the cinema-going experience into something colorful, immersive, and expansive—increasingly urgent given television's threat.[99] Thus television's permanent mask—its rigid borders continually demarcating the space of action—should not be repeated in the film theater. Rather, the cinema should define itself *against* the walled off and individualized image on the television and be a communal, public, awe-inspiring object. By late in the year, Walter W. Wehr, owner and manager of the Park Theatre in Pleasantville, New Jersey, declared black masking to be "as dead as silent films," as much a vestige of early exhibition as, by this time, the cavernous palaces and their elaborate decoration.[100] Although George Schutz's reluctance to completely assent indicated a time of transition, he noted audience reactions that included "the picture is clearer" and "the acting seems more real." For Schutz, the "absence of the frame, with the picture suspended, as it were, in its own light, gives the performance a greater grip on the senses. Which means stronger realism of the scenic material, greater impact of dramatic action."[101] With synchronous light surround matching illumination levels of projection, the spectator could better imagine the image not ending at the edges of the screen, but moving forward, bleeding out into the space of the surround and therefore into the space of spectatorship, maintaining an impression of expanse.[102]

The resounding success of the RCA Synchro-Screen, Schlanger and William Hoffberg's newer version of the Synchro-Vision Screen of the 1930s, and consistent recommendations issued by the SMPTE helped pave the way for a new industry standard of demasked screens. By 1952, black masking, in use for decades since early exhibition, was considered by many to be "a relic of the

98. Ibid.
99. Indeed, the "art urgently needs every technical advantage it can acquire," both to set it apart from television and ensure film would continue to be considered a cutting-edge technology. At the same time, in 1951, a major television manufacturer introduced plans to create a "halo" border reminiscent of theatrical light spill around the televised image to increase visibility, reduce eye strain, and make the "picture look larger." See "Looks Like Screen Masking Could Be on the Way Out," *Motion Picture Herald*, August 4, 1951, *Better Theatres* section, 22.
100. George Schutz, "Screen Border Elimination: A Start toward More Realism," *Motion Picture Herald*, November 10, 1951, *Better Theatres* section, 12.
101. Ibid.
102. This, in turn, was thought to increase realism. See Ben Schlanger, "Adapting Existing Auditoriums to 'Full Vision' Movies," *Motion Picture Herald*, December 1, 1951, *Better Theatres* section, 12.

art's early crudities," "always an evil—for years a necessary one. . . . With color pictures, it is twice an evil. Now the evil is no longer necessary."[103] New York exhibitor Leo Brecher, who by mid-1952 had installed three Synchro-Screens throughout the city, explained that the Synchro-Screen "is the result of over 20 years study and experiment in the science of human vision. The improvement in sheer ease of seeing and in bringing vividness to the image on the screen, in both black-and-white and in color, have already struck hundreds of our patrons as breathtaking."[104] An ad for the Synchro-Screen similarly asserted audiences' delight with the new technology, with quotes from patrons hailing its "softer picture," and declaring that the "picture looks bigger," and "old black masking seemed morbid; this new screen seems more cheerful" (Figure 2.9).[105] In tandem with trends toward eliminating stages and proscenium arches, the Synchro-Screen created a continuous space between screen and auditorium—even an endless space—for an intertwinement of observer and filmic object. According to Gio Gagliardi, the spectator could be a "*participator*, the idea being that the patron, while sitting in any part of the auditorium, should not have a feeling of being a remote spectator of scenes inside a picture frame, but rather that he is transported to the world of the story, with the action leaving the reality of life going on around him."[106] For exhibitors incorporating recommendations based on angles of vision, spectators must be encouraged to imagine the screen as excessive for a fullness of participation.[107] The psychological effects of such an undertaking would be complete illusion, total immersion—a Bazinian experience, a gestalt filmic object into which spectators could release their minds. Looming in the context of an erased, almost vanished auditorium structure, the demasked and enormous screen could balance visibility and invisibility into a highly structured architectural empathy where audiences could feel by seeing. The modern demasked screen calculated experience through sensory-psychological manipulation.

Still, screen masking did not entirely disappear in the 1950s.[108] New models for masking such as the Synthetic Vision Corporation's automatic formatting system proposed flexible and variable curtains that could adjust the screen's

103. "Mask Elimination Takes Engineering, Not Gadgeteering," *Motion Picture Herald*, February 9, 1952, *Better Theatres* section, 34.
104. Ibid.
105. Ad for RCA Synchro-Screen, *International Projectionist* 27, no. 6 (June 1952): 7.
106. Gio Gagliardi, "Working toward a Better Story-Telling Screen Image," *Motion Picture Herald*, April 5, 1952, *Better Theatres* section, 32 (emphasis original).
107. "If we are coming to a decision that black masking must go, let's remember the ultimate objective—to get rid of the delimiting frame. That is basic to advances which yet may come." "The Aim Is to Get Rid of the Picture *Frame*—Black or Light," *Motion Picture Herald*, June 7, 1952, *Better Theatres* section, 18.
108. Some examples of masking remained in place to account for varying aspect ratios into the 1960s, particularly as the craze for widescreen continued throughout the 1950s and thereby necessitated flexible screen sizes and lengths.

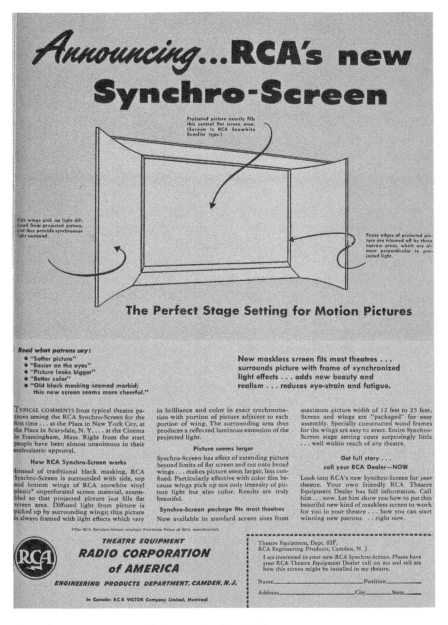

**Figure 2.9:** From *International Projectionist*, June 1952.

frame according to a film's aspect ratio or other projection needs.[109] Through the rest of the decade, changeable masking was included even in new renovations, such as the Waverly Theater in Greenwich Village, New York,

109. "Curtain-Mask System for Varied Picture Size," *Motion Picture Herald*, July 3, 1954, *Better Thatres* section, 44–45.

where a 1958 remodeling featured both the removal of the proscenium arch and the inclusion of masking for three possible image sizes controlled at the projection booth.[110] Up through the early 1960s, then, a modernized theater might hold a synchronous light bath screen with illumination spill falling on all sides of the frame onto light colored surround, or mutable masking, newly automated and somewhat controllable. For both options, flexibility proved to be an essential category; synchronous spill changed according to differentiations in picture hue intensity, while mechanized masking could be adjusted according to image ratio and size. At mid-century, modernization of the screen's surround, then, relied less on form than on flexibility. Yet into the mid-1950s, neutralized theater advocates remained staunchly on the side of demasked screens, insisting on the effect of "presence" they created. The demasked screen became an instrument of proximity, from framed and distanced view to permeable and flexible pathway.

Screen masking flexibility, then, maintained the modernized theater's debt to functional modernism, but also reflected exhibition's ambivalent attitude toward bodily immersion. Flexible screens and screen borders implied the usefulness, for varied exhibition strategies, of a plastic architectural space to respond to a malleable spectatorial position. Flexibility allowed architectural change alongside technological change and helped maintain film's status as *the* modern art: flexibility was inherently modern and inherently filmic.[111] Making the architectural space of the auditorium, already an environment with which the spectator was intended to identify, into a dynamic and flexible entity not only encouraged immersion in a range of pictures, but suggested to the modern spectator her own potential flexibility. If the staid nature of a building could be transformed into an array of uses and statuses, then so too could the spectator, in the process losing her stable sense of physicality and gaining expansive endlessness through visual immersion. To eliminate the rigid enclosure of the masking also implied the elimination of the rigid borders of the body. The "floating" screen framed in light surround evoked a spatial incorporeality paired with a mode of particularly cinematic trans-portation: walls of light, a screen of light, abstracted concepts of light and movement, and a spectator projected forward into the susurrating pulses of cinematic experience.

110. "Revised for Neighborhood Clientele in Manhattan," *Motion Picture Herald*, May 10, 1958, *Better Theatres* section, 31–32.

111. Indeed, screen flexibility was a major cinematic characteristic that separated film from the antiquated stage: if a "simple way of applying [peripheral modulation] could be created, the art would lose none of its unique flexibility, while gaining superior impact." Schutz, "Putting the Big Picture into Theatres," 11. See also Ben Schlanger, "Theatres and the New Techniques," *Motion Picture Herald*, September 5, 1953, *Better Theatres* section, 12–52.

# CHAPTER 3

# A Mobile Gaze through Time and Space

*Neutralization in the Era of Widescreen, 1950–1960*

## SCREENING INTO THE FUTURE

The Cinema, a theater Ben Schlanger described as one of the finest ever built, opened in 1951 in Framingham, Massachusetts at Shoppers World Mall (Figure 3.1), the first shopping mall in the Northeast and only the second in the country.[1] Built for a total cost of $8 million, the mall was anchored by a huge Jordan Marsh, while a 227-foot-wide dome protected both the department store and the smaller restaurants and forty-four shops housed within. Like other malls to come, Shoppers World responded to transformations in the demographics of the American population: in 1940, Americans owned 32 million cars, but by 1950, that number had soared to 50 million.[2] In order to access this rapidly growing market, shopping centers needed to be accessible to roads as well as prepared for the onslaught of automobiles. Nearby, the Massachusetts Turnpike had just been completed, making Framingham an ideal spot for the prototypical mall-ification of the United States; Shoppers World boasted six thousand parking spots for cars zooming in from turnpike traffic. Media hype around Shoppers World worked: twenty-five thousand curious visitors attended the mall's opening, despite the fact that the first game of the World Series was held the exact same day.[3] Greeting consumers at the

1. See Ross Melnick and Andreas Fuchs, *Cinema Treasures: A New Look at Classic Movie Theaters* (St. Paul: MBI Publishing, 2004).

2. Morris Ketchum Jr., "A New Theatre in a Regional Shopping Center," *Theatre Catalog* (Philadelphia: Jay Emanuel Publications, 1952), 24.

3. Granted, the Red Sox were not playing. Nancy Shohet West, "Framingham Exhibit Brings the Original Shoppers World to Life," boston.com, March 20, 2013, http:

**Figure 3.1:** The Cinema at Shoppers World. From Jay Emanuel's *Theatre Catalog*, 1952.

unlocked doors was a new era of bountiful of consumer goods no longer primarily accessible from freestanding downtown stores and public transportation. Instead, a decentralized and wealthier population could buy both everyday objects and luxuries in massive suburban township malls with sprawling parking lots to house the cars necessary for getting there and for bringing purchases home.

In addition to immediate transportation and capital needs, the builders of Shoppers World and other new centers like it sought to respond to the leisure interests of the burgeoning middle class. Theaters, therefore, were a necessity; without a theater, Morris Ketchum, main architect of the structure, observed, "the balanced program of retailing, amusement and service units . . . cannot be achieved. With them, the center can offer a top selection of every type of downtown customer attraction."[4] For Ketchum, theaters were essential for malls—and malls were becoming essential for theaters. If the suburbanization of the population was hitting the film industry in new and unexpected ways, then the great American pastime of conspicuous consumption could be tied more forcefully to filmgoing practice. The mall, then, integrated the theater

//www.bostonglobe.com/metro/regionals/west/2013/03/13/framingham-exhibit-brings-original-shoppers-world-life/ehIlj5dsudZB8jHgUx4rdJ/story.html.
    4. Ketchum, "New Theatre," 24.

into new mainstream ways of moving through time and space, signified by the automobile and its rapid-fire gaze, by the microcosmic globalized tourism contained under a shopping center's dome, and by the expansiveness implied in both the blossoming American highway system and the increasingly large cinema screen. Travel both temporal and spatial meant seeing in sequence, through glass unbounded by frames. If, for Ketchum, "regional centers are rapidly changing the shopping and theatre-going habits of a large segment of our country's population," they were doing so not merely through the reification of capital's intertwinement with cinema, but also through new ways of seeing through time and space exemplified by trends in American postwar culture.

Such a gaze through time and space has its roots in the panorama, the diorama, and eventually the arcade, as well as the figure who moves among them: the flâneur or, per Anne Friedberg, flâneuse. For Friedberg, as well as Giuliana Bruno and Vanessa Schwartz, spectators of the panorama and diorama learned to be traveling eyes prepared physically and mentally for cinematic immersion.[5] Within the arcade, their gaze was mobilized in a marketplace "where consumption itself became the spectacle."[6] The architectonics of protocinematic urban viewing insisted on a mobilized gaze that would soon be virtualized for an immobile spectator. Thus the early movie screen evolves into a "mobile display window"; by extension, the late twentieth-century shopping mall is the "topos" of postmodern urban visuality.[7] Yet Friedberg moves directly from silent cinema to a 1980s United States where malls proliferate, without pausing to consider the early mall and its relationship to cinema. If the 1980s spectator caught in a virtual and mobilized gaze views and is viewed in sequential consumerism, what of spectatorship in the mid-century American moment of widescreen and the early mall? The architectures produced there are additional pieces of a larger filmic structure that reifies transportation's suture with screen. In so doing, they revisit the domination of American perspectives by massive screens that evoke westward expansion, by the ideals of democratic citizenship, and by the pleasures of purchasing while viewing. The birth of Shoppers World and other malls like it can therefore be understood as a juncture in American spectatorship's trajectory that consolidates travel, vision, myth, and industrial capitalism.

Inside Shoppers World, the 1,500-seat Cinema formed the structure's jewel (Figure 3.2). A system of passageways and footpaths led pedestrian

---

5. See Giuliana Bruno, *Streetwalking on a Ruined Map: Cultural Theory and the City Films of Elvira Notari* (Princeton, NJ: Princeton University Press, 1993); and Schwartz, *Spectacular Realities*.

6. Anne Friedberg, *Window Shopping: Cinema and the Postmodern* (Berkeley: University of California Press, 2013), 69.

7. Ibid., 89 and 109.

**Figure 3.2:** The Cinema at Shoppers World. From Jay Emanuel's *Theatre Catalog*, 1953–1954.

traffic from parking lots, mall areas, or the central green in efficient lines toward the theater lobby. Rather than the typical narrow vestibule and hidden lobby found in urban theaters, the Cinema's entrance deliberately echoed the glass window display techniques present in the rest of the mall area. The ticket counter, concession stand, lounge, and balcony stairway were readily accessible to public eyesight in an image of openness, light, and expanse. Once inside the auditorium, wide-eyed audiences encountered an enormous, maskless RCA Synchro-Screen stretching twenty-five by thirty feet across the front of the theater (Figure 3.3). The screen was set in a curved plaster wall with a "special surface" containing a light value precisely matching that of the screen.[8] Wall panels widened near and facing the screen in order to direct reflected light away from spectators' eyes, while screen edge and wall met one another across a thin frame of plastic intended to blend the two together. During projection, the Synchro-Screen, plaster, plastic band, and corrugated wall surfaces harmonized into an "unlimited space" with screen glow serving as the only illumination. According to Ketchum, the resulting effect was one of "intense realism" where the "actors almost seem to be moving in space close to each member of the audience."[9] Schlanger's seating plan divided the total capacity between the main floor and the balcony. Rather than focus on

8. "The Cinema," *Theatre Catalog* (Philadelphia: Jay Emanuel Publications, 1953–1954), XXX.
9. Ketchum, "New Theatre," 30.

**Figure 3.3:** The Cinema at Shoppers World. From Jay Emanuel's *Theatre Catalog*, 1953–1954.

consistent aisle widths, rows of pushback chairs were placed "freely in strict reference to screen sightlines."[10] Because the aisles contained variable widths, patrons entered and exited efficiently and calmly. Like the Shoppers World pathways and corridors that subtly encouraged shoppers' consistent travel from store to store, the Cinema gently reinforced a spectatorship of flexibility, flow, and quiet cohesion for better travel inside the theater, out to cars, and into the film itself.

All of the designers who worked on the project, including Schlanger, William Hoffberg, and the main building architects at Ketchum, Giná & Sharp, sought a "purely functional design" so that a "definite physical scheme is offered for the advancement of motion picture exhibition."[11] This combination of functionalism with attention to transportation exemplified much of 1950s neutralization. From the late 1940s to the early 1950s, theaters lacking in adequate parking experienced a downturn, yet those located within shopping centers remained solvent. Like stores in those centers, such theaters took advantage of the increase in automobile traffic.[12] Typically, analyses of 1950s exhibition in the context of the automotive gaze look to the drive-in as the exemplar of American postwar viewing patterns. And certainly the rise in drive-ins was a defining factor of American exhibition both after the crisis

10. "The Cinema," *Theatre Catalog*, XXX.
11. Ibid.
12. Ketchum, "New Theatre," 31.

and once wealth grew after–World War II. Numbering fewer than one hundred prior to the war, American drive-ins proliferated rapidly in postwar suburbanization years, totaling about two thousand by 1951.[13] Through much of the 1950s, drive-ins dominated theater-building sections of exhibition journals such as *Motion Picture Herald, Boxoffice,* and the annual or biannual *Theatre Catalog* published by Jay Emanuel. Yet few have pointed to the impact of the automobilic gaze on widescreen cinema, particularly in terms of its conceptual attributes.

To be sure, the car had a causal effect on 1950s exhibition: exhibitors understood the necessity of parking lots, of capturing suburban audiences likely to attend theaters by way of highways instead of city streets, and of welcoming those who simply did not wish to leave the comfort of their cars. But in addition to the verbatim echo of increased car ownership, the automobile's specific way of seeing shaped the traditional theater's technology and design. In the 1930s and 1940s, unmasked screens swung the filmic image open from a picture in a frame to a window onto a world. In the 1950s, the enormous, unframed screen continued to expand into a vision of virtual disembodied travel, much like that exemplified by the experience of the car. Certainly, this was an idealized version, given that the American postwar dream of car travel was one of open roads, highways, and individualized conquest and discovery, rather than recognition of other drivers, tolls, and endless lines of honking gridlock. But idealized car travel promised an experience of being "at" the scene—both engaged and passing by, able to stop and see rolling visions of America, in control of what one perceives, but an external observer who peers closely yet remains anonymous by virtue of the machine within which one travels. The car, like the apparatus within the neutralized cinema, or like widescreen in the 1950s, is an object of witness. Widescreen and car add layers of "realism" to visual experience, but both maintain an elusive spectatorial distance from what is seen. Both enable travel through time and space, but both do so by ensuring a balance between visual immersion and physical separation from their windows onto the world. In this way, the car's evocation in 1950s exhibition cements how Schlanger understood widescreen: as a technology of presence.

## PRESENCE AND PARTICIPATION IN WIDESCREEN RHETORIC

Much evidence supports the claim that widescreen should be seen in terms of active spectatorship; in particular, exhibitors' frequent use of the words

13. Rodney Luther, "Drive-In Theaters: Rags to Riches in Five Years," *Hollywood Quarterly* 5, no. 4 (Summer 1951): 401–411. Luther's study surveyed the Minneapolis-St. Paul area where six suburban drive-ins served a population of over a million people.

"participation" and "realism" encourages this reading. As Ariel Rogers explains, "participation" was regularly cited during the 1950s as a spectatorial ideal, while Alison Griffiths describes a similar immersive view in the context of embodied vision in the cathedral, the planetarium, and IMAX.[14] John Belton's extensive history of the movement and its technologies similarly focuses on the physically active and participatory properties of immersion, asserting that at Cinerama's premiere in 1952, "the frame of the theater proscenium seemed to disappear, and the audience had the uncanny sensation of entering into the events depicted on the curved screen. . . . Cinerama launched a widescreen revolution in which passive observation gave way to a dramatic new engagement with the image."[15] Yet Schlanger insisted that the proscenium decidedly did *not* disappear, and therefore should be removed to promote filmic illusion—if it did disappear, then its elimination would hardly be as urgent as Schlanger insisted.[16] Belton ascribes the success of widescreen in the 1950s—compared to the failure of the first serious attempts in the 1930s—to the postwar technology boom and to the reinvigorated economy's allowance for more widely available leisure time; certainly, the decade's increase in domestic spending, suburbanization, freer weekends and evenings, and larger juvenile population, along with transforming filmic technologies, created an environment particularly conducive to a funhouse-esque cinema.[17] In addition to these factors, shifts in screen dynamics related to demasking from the 1930s to the 1950s as well as the stranger arguments on the more radical side of 1950s exhibition further nuance the history of widescreen. For Schlanger, immersion could mean something other than experience of the body, and "participation" and "realism" owed a peculiar debt to highly structured visual experience.

Alongside activity, "participation" could imply a communal yet disembodied sensory projection, while, rather than the sensations of quotidian life,

14. See Ariel Rogers, *Cinematic Appeals: The Experience of New Movie Technologies* (New York: Columbia University Press, 2013); and Alison Griffiths, *Shivers Down Your Spine: Cinema, Museums, and the Immersive View* (New York: Columbia University Press, 2008).

15. John Belton, *Widescreen Cinema* (Cambridge, MA: Harvard University Press, 1992), 1–2. Proscenia were subject to much debate throughout the widescreen revolution, with some clamoring to discard them completely and others claiming they could be adjusted to be compatible with the new formats.

16. Schlanger began calling for proscenium elimination in specific cases in 1931 (Ben Schlanger, "The Economics of Theatre Remodeling," *Motion Picture Herald*, April 11, 1931, *Better Theatres* section, 18). In his Sutton Theatre, completed in 1934 and formerly a stage theater and then a bank building, the "unnecessary" proscenium was removed during remodeling ("Changing a Bank into a Theatre," *Motion Picture Herald*, July 28, 1934, *Better Theatres* section, 6). By 1935, Schlanger urged the elimination of all "traditional architectural ornamentation" such as the "extraneous ornamental proscenium" (Ben Schlanger, "Standard Practice in Theatre Design," *Motion Picture Herald*, September 21, 1935, *Better Theatres* section, 8).

17. Belton, *Widescreen Cinema*, 52.

"realism" could signify the mimicking of perception and the creation of an alternate world. While "participation" as defined by Belton and Rogers may have been the most prominent widescreen goal, others argued for the importance of "presence": being *at* rather than *in* the scene. For Schlanger, whose work in the 1950s focused often on the experimental end of the widescreen boom, visual angles were the only filmic aspect that truly created participation, or, in his preferred terminology, presence: "In designing a theatre for the new [widescreen] techniques we need not provide for deeply curved screen as a means of attaining 'presence,' or as it is sometimes confusingly called, 'participation.' Subtended viewing angles alone control the degree to which the spectator has a feeling of being at the scene."[18] "Presence," therefore, implied a separate world accessible by integrating object and spectator through visual and mental projection—significantly, one in which the spectator was mentally but not bodily submerged. The unmasked window of the screen, then, functioned to enhance the verisimilitude of the image as well as the contemplative aspects of widescreen cinema—immersion in the voyeuristic image rather than a bodily roller coaster. Although mental projection and reinforcement of the eye's centrality were not an endgame for all widescreen proponents, justified interest in the bodily effects of widescreen cinema has obscured such investment in visual immersion in the historical record.

Given the tension between participation and presence, then, the discussion of these categories allows a fuller picture of the widescreen revolution as a product of multiple, sometimes competing discourses. While a majority of exhibitors and promoters engaged primarily with sensation, others understood the gigantic screen as empathically and psychically rather than bodily liberating. Almost unfailingly, these claims came from those invested in modernist architectural aesthetics as the "right" way to view film, due in part to phenomenological structures inherent to architectural modernism that encouraged an abstracted spectatorship, such as Frederick Kiesler's "endlessness." For Kiesler, "the first radical step toward the creation of an ideal cinema is the abolition of the proscenium and all other stage platform resemblance to the theatre which we find in motion picture houses. . . . The interior lines of the theatre must focalize to the screen compelling unbroken attention on the spectator."[19] Functional modernism, efficiency, and mechanization had little place in the cinematic world for the chaos of the total physical sensorium; vision, however, retained a streamlined, smooth, and clean aesthetic association. Where cinema could

18. Ben Schlanger, "Theatre Design *in* the New Techniques," *Motion Picture Herald*, January 7, 1956, *Better Theatres* section, 27.

19. Kiesler, it should be noted, was a surrealist rather than purely functional modernist. Yet his investment in attentive immersion made him a trailblazer for neutralized spectatorship. Frederick Kiesler (credited as Friedrich Kiesler), "Building a Cinema Theatre," *New York Evening Post*, February 2, 1929 (Lillian and Frederick Kiesler Archives, Archives of American Art, Smithsonian, Box 46). Reprinted in

not imitate proprioception or olfaction, it could mimic vision and hearing. For American mid-century widescreen exhibition, the concept of immersion bore some commonalities with what Michael Fried describes as "absorption": total belief in the full reality of the image and its hermetic existence, as well as the ability to enter into it unselfconsciously.[20] For Fried, such objects exist for themselves, on their own, independent of the viewer or their environment. Theatrical art, on the other hand, requires the spectator's presence.[21] Exhibitors' ideals of immersion, however, alternately included spectatorial presence, spectatorial participation, and spectatorial witnessing, suggesting the efficacy of immersion over absorption: immersion hints at the unfeasibility of total bodily relinquishment along with the ambivalent desire for it.

Screen size was the subject of decades of debate for its impact on visual acuity, but also dictated the spectator's affective relationship to the moving image. Belton explains that the palaces' lack of enormous screens to compensate for the auditoriums' cavernous size created a strange spectatorship where, as theaters grew larger, the projected image appeared smaller.[22] Use of the image as a portion of the entertainment program in the late 1920s resulted in a continuation of "multi-event" presentations, "and 'distraction' remained the dominant form of spectatorial engagement."[23] Although experimented with throughout the 1920s and 1930s, widescreen projection remained an exhibition novelty until the mid-1950s.[24] In light of this, the response to the "distractions" of the multievent palace included reducing the number of events in the entertainment program to one film, decorating functionally for attentive spectatorship, and seeking out large-screen formats as powerful display techniques to work in tandem with, rather than against, a unified cinematic presentation.[25] To this end, neutralization's rallying cry of "unification" continued in the widescreen era, with an enlarged screen ideally "blended" into the rest of the theatrical space, whether through light bleed, the elimination of black borders, or excessive curvature. By unifying an enormous screen

Kiesler, *Frederick J. Kiesler: Selected Writings*, ed. Siegfried Gohr and Gunda Luyken (Stuttgart: Verlag Gerd Hatje, 1996), 16–18.

20. See Michael Fried, *Absorption and Theatricality: Painting and Beholder in the Age of Diderot* (Chicago: The University of Chicago Press, 1980).

21. Michael Fried, "Art and Objecthood," in *Art and Objecthood: Essays and Reviews* (Chicago: The University of Chicago Press, 1998), 164.

22. Belton, *Widescreen Cinema*, 36.

23. Ibid., 51.

24. In 1930, between three hundred and one thousand widescreen systems were installed in theaters across the United States, with MGM's system as the frontrunner. Still, few of the theaters had capability for projecting properly onto the screens. "More Than 300 Wide Screens Installed in Theatres of U.S.," *Motion Picture Herald*, October 18, 1930, *Better Theatres* section, 23.

25. For an account of the rise and fall of the multi-event cinema, see William Paul, *When Movies Were Theater: Architecture, Exhibition, and the Evolution of American Film* (New York: Columbia University Press, 2016).

and a neutralized auditorium, the theater could further unify the spectator with the film and with her surroundings, minimizing bodily experience for the sake of a community of vision. In this sense, the demasked, expanded screen aligned with an austere theatrical space to prompt the decisive shift in 1950s exhibition discourses toward a form of mainstreamed neutralization. Although not all exhibitors shared the goal of disembodied vision through widescreen, unification of theatrical space and concentration on the screen found enhanced relevance in 1950s exhibition.

Thomas Elsaesser describes classical Hollywood (and, to a certain extent, international) film style as contingent upon two diegetic forms: closed and open. These forms imply two modes of cinema as frame and as window:

> The difference between closed and open film form can thus also be seen as a reformulation of the difference between window and frame: the window offers a detail of a larger whole in which the elements appear as if distributed in no particular way, so that the impression of realism for the spectator is above all a function of transparency. By contrast, foregrounding the frame shifts the attention to the organization of the material. The window implies a diegetic world that extends beyond the limit of the image while the frame delineates a filmic composition that exists solely for the eyes of the beholder.[26]

For Elsaesser, windows and frames manage relationships among distance, proximity, object, and spectatorship. Both metaphorical statuses imply an erasure of the illusion's parameters and a vanishing apparatus. Like many historians of film theory, Elsaesser focuses on film form as an indication of ontological shifts; similarly, most film histories pinpoint formal elements of cinematographic, sound, and editing structure as the most salient sources of spectatorship's changing paradigms.

Yet it is not solely in the film itself but in the entirety of filmic encounter where such new theories are fully put to the test. The space of seeing affects the spectator's view of a perfect and enclosed diegetic sphere or a window onto a world just like, alongside, or within our own. While an open cinematic formal structure might suggest a window onto a world, the window can be closed off by a screen bordered with a black frame. The space of exhibition cannot help but have an impact on cinema's larger form. William Paul has noted the effects of architectural space, screen ratio, and screen size in transforming shot patterns and film form in classical Hollywood; thus, while deframing the screen might not entirely have had an impact on all filmic form, it did, in fact, influence larger American cultural assumptions about how a film screen—and thus

---

26. Thomas Elsaesser, *Film Theory: An Introduction through the Senses* (New York: Routledge, 2010), 17–18.

spectatorial encounter with cinema—is experienced.[27] For a wider set of cinematic forms, one that includes architectural space within the filmic apparatus, a range of factors have an impact on film's diegesis, but, more importantly, the entirety of filmic experience. A filmic text is more open or more closed off, more accessible to immersive entry or more rigidly structured, more akin to human perception or more stylized to account for different modes of sensory address according to the conditions in which it is shown—something that exhibitors were theorizing virtually from the time of film's mainstream success. In this sense, widescreen as an open cinematic form was generally inaccessible until film could be shown in a spatial environment particularly conducive to expansiveness, no longer hindered by strict visual boundaries.

By 1952, the average screen size in American movie theaters had risen from approximately sixteen feet in the 1930s and eighteen feet in 1942 to around twenty feet, with some outliers already reaching twenty-six to thirty feet. This new era of cinematic exhibition welcomed color, 3D, and large formats— a level of invention that, according to exhibitors, had not been experienced since the dawn of sound in the late 1920s.[28] After declining attendance numbers post–Depression and World War II and a two-year ban on theater construction from 1951 to 1953, widescreen heralded a moment of economic optimism.[29] The wealth and expansion promised by new film technologies led Berk and Krumgold, an amusement property firm in New York, to publicly declare, "Two years ago you couldn't give theatres away, but now the situation has changed to such an extent that it is becoming difficult to supply the demand."[30] Unlike sound, however, the hopeful outlook for the 1950s proved to be a product of multiple innovations: larger screens, stereophonic surround sound, and stereoscopy together offered a wider range of potential filmic product. Demasking resulted in a

> liberat[ion of] the image from a picture frame surrounded by architecture. The available area of the performance is flexibly expanded, allowing tremendous effects of scale, giving director and cinematographer more creative tricks as well

27. William Paul, "Screening Space: Architecture, Technology, and the Motion Picture Screen," *Michigan Quarterly Review* 35, no. 1 (Winter 1996): 143–173; and *When Movies Were Theater.*

28. "Pictures Are Getting Bigger Than Ever, Too—On the Screen," *Motion Picture Herald*, March 1, 1952, *Better Theatres* section, 14; and "Trends," *Motion Picture Herald*, March 22, 1952, *Better Theatres* section, 8. These are approximate numbers, as there is typically discrepancy in exhibitors' journals.

29. Lester Rees described "skyrocketing grosses" in 1953 as indicative of a moment of renovation and optimism for theater owners, predicated on the new widescreen advances ("Theatre Modernization Hits Rapid Pace," *Boxoffice Magazine*, January 9, 1954, *Modern Theatres* section, 8–10); for information on the end of the ban, see "Introduction," *Boxoffice Magazine*, January 3, 1953, *Modern Theatres* section, 7.

30. "A Greater Theatrical Medium in the Making," *Motion Picture Herald*, January 10, 1953, *Better Theatres* section, 10.

as better control of them, and at last letting the show to occupy a dominant instead of a minor part of the field of vision. Such a screen world, we believe, should be as little invaded as possible by definable structure. Its edges should seem to peter out, you might say, into infinity. That would relate the screen with auditorium design most intimately. . . . Unmasking the screen should not mean substitution of just another, less objectionable, kind of *border*. And that is why we have created the maskless screen *with a synchronous surround*—that is, a surround created by the projected image—as being specifically one of the "new devices" of motion picture technique, part and parcel of the development of the motion picture into a greater theatrical medium.[31]

Here, the unmasked screen was explicitly tied to widescreen. Both substituted rigid, "definable" structure for cosmic languages of infinity, scale, and expanse; in addition, both illustrated exhibition's general belief that directing and cinematography were intimately connected to screen environment. These advances of demasking, 3D, and widescreen technologies were thought to make the cinema into a more realistic machine, but also a "greater" one, what Leonard Satz called "the first really dramatic improvement in picture presentation in over twenty years."[32]

While the unbordered film world inspired lofty rhetoric, part of the rationale for the lauding of these immersive techniques was their utter separation from television. For Schlanger,

television images at home, and even in large screen theatre TV, are at their best with close-up shots; both fail in showing detail when middle and long shots are used. Present television scanning methods impose these limitations. The predominant use of the large close-up in the motion picture during the last 30 years had its advantages, but it also restricted the art of cinematography, making it stilted and artificial; and it discouraged the development of large-screen and wide-angle cinematographic techniques.[33]

Along with more mainstream use of color film, widescreen projection and wide-angle cinematography resulted in an arguably more realistic filmic experience. Discarding the close-up due to its lack of fundamental filmic-ness and its link to the televisual, however, was somewhat of a turnabout. Whereas

31. Generally, standard aspect ratios were preserved at this time. Aperture plate filing, for example, could help retain the lateral arc of vision at three times vertical vision. "A Greater Theatrical Medium in the Making," 11 (emphasis original).

32. Leonard Satz, "Panoramic Vision Gives Dramatic Improvement in Screen Presentation," *Boxoffice Magazine*, September 1, 1951, *Modern Theatres* section, 12.

33. Ben Schlanger, "The Rising Revolution in Motion Picture Technique," *Motion Picture Herald*, January 10, 1953, *Better Theatres* section, 14.

close-ups had, in the 1920s through the 1940s, seemed the most filmic of all shot forms, in the wake of television, their status was more ambivalent. Television's intimacy and domesticity supplanted cinema's reach toward the minute and the magnified; massive scale was a more economically viable tactic to dissociate film from television. According to Schlanger, factors such as seating patterns had previously helped retain the close-up as a formal cinematographic element. Given that antiquated seating arrangements often resulted in less-than-optimal visual acuity in most parts of the auditorium, close-ups were required in order to allow all spectators to see in detail:

> There have been proponents of larger pictures for many years. . . . But the conditions of cinematography which were themselves encouraged by the typical seating pattern of theatres had a reciprocal effect of keeping picture sizes as they were. Predominant among the cinematographic factors of such effect was the *close-up*. This device allowed the smallest detail to be seen clearly from remote points of the auditorium. It also supplied a sense of "intimacy," by seeming to bring the viewer closer to the screen through sheer magnification.[34]

For Schlanger, the era of widescreen made the close-up superfluous; whereas smaller screens might require close-ups as techniques of immersion, larger screen production appeared instead to be characterized by long and medium shots of a more "spectacular" variety. As a longtime designer of theatrical architecture, Schlanger could acknowledge the direct impact of exhibition patterns on films themselves—a unified spectatorship formulated not only in the moment of watching, but also in the moment of production.

An illustration accompanying Schlanger and Schutz's 1955 article "Visualizing the Theatre for a New Era" demonstrates exhibitors' investment in reinforcing the communal effects of widescreen technology compared to the distancing effects of television. On the left side of the page in a small pencil-sketched illustration, a family of three sits in a living room in separate easy chairs, watching a tiny television screen from at least one body length away (Figure 3.4a). Each family member is separated from the others by sharply delimited chairs. Their faces are turned toward the screen; the picture's beholder can view only the backs of their heads. In contrast, to the right, a large charcoal illustration of an audience watching a movie in a darkened auditorium takes up the entire page (Figure 3.4b). No chair is fully separated from the other by strong and bold lines; similarly, there is no hard line of separation between screen and auditorium. Instead, the film image gradually bleeds and dissolves into the space of the auditorium, much as spectators' seats and

---

34. Ben Schlanger, "Sizing the Picture for 'Wide-Screen,'" *Motion Picture Herald*, October 10, 1953, *Better Theatres* section, 16–18 (emphasis original).

(a)

(b)

**Figure 3.4a and 3.4b:** From "Visualizing the Theatre for a New Era," *Motion Picture Herald, Better Theatres* section, March 26, 1955.

bodies melt impressionistically into each other. Even in the material selection of charcoal rather than pencil, the artist depicts the fluidity of large-format cinema compared to the strict delineations of boundaries in television's home viewing. Where television implies domesticity, bounded personal space, and separation between image and audience, projected widescreen cinema suggests community, a shared familial and national experience, and a sense of being "at" the profilmic moment. Cinema allows for the melting away of the body into a mass of attentive community, and the dissolution of one spectator into another as visual contemplation becomes the central focus.

In addition, the choice of subject that spectators are viewing speaks to exhibitors' forceful opposition of film to television in an even more curious way. The family at home, watching television, sees little more than a vague line onscreen that could be a mountain but remains unclear. By contrast, the audience at the depicted theater views a scene of cacti, a cowboy on a horse, a fence, mountains in the distance—in short, a widescreen western, the most spatially, temporally, and politically American of genres. Television not only reduces one's space and vision to that of the home, but is the less *American* spectatorial experience. Film in the theater, however, provides images of manifest destiny and of western expansion from sea to shining sea. The presence promised by widescreen and by the neutralized theatrical experience is one of travel through a national spatial consciousness, conquest, and culture by way of the horse or its contemporary analogue, the car.

Although television's "liveness" tends to be considered its most powerful attribute, the illustration suggests another layer of nuance between television and film.[35] While television might be shown live, its patterns of exhibition elide the spontaneity possible in cinematic space. Film may be shot and edited months prior to its exhibition, but bears immediacy through public exhibition and, at this moment in particular, enormity of scale. Seeing something live and the illusion of being "at" the scene depicted are two separate phenomena; one can only be fulfilled by television, but the other can only be fulfilled at the movie house. Schlanger described the experience in another article from the same year:

> The viewer should not be "picture"-conscious. Instead, he should essentially feel as though he were at the scene. When the screen has physical relationships to the auditorium like those of a good-sized painting to a living room, it is just that—a picture on a wall. This artificial, unconvincing quality of a motion picture performance is the more damaging to the illusion as smallness in actual

35. Liveness as television trope is most famously described in Mary Ann Doane's "Information, Crisis, Catastrophe," reprinted in *The Historical Film: History and Memory in Media*, ed. Marcia Landy (London: The Athlone Press, 2001): 269–285.

dimensions is supplemented by a bold, rigid frame and, further, by points of light that intrude into perception of the picture from beyond the screen.[36]

Here, Schlanger describes the "artificial" and "unconvincing" aspects of the smaller, bounded screen not only as similar to those of a picture in a frame, but as a framed picture hung in a living room. Not only is this image reminiscent of artificiality, smallness, and stillness, not only is it similar to a motionless and antiquated art object, but it is domestic and everyday, located within the home interior rather than the art museum. Grandiosity is achievable through massive scale, but massive scale is only achievable in public. To visually dominate, a screen must be public, outside the boundaries of comfortable home life, and able to transport its spectators to the moment and place of the profilmic scene.

For these reasons, exhibitors looking to reinstate film's status as a medium of magnitude, novelty, and spectacle welcomed widescreen technologies as well as the drive-in and its return to the fairground cinema.[37] For Belton, widescreen experiments such as Cinerama reinvigorated cinema's emotional urgency and reinstated the centrality of attraction and immediacy.[38] Hollywood higher-ups such as Al Lichtman, former director of sales at Twentieth Century-Fox, explained that part of the problem was, as Herbert E. Bragg, Fox's assistant director of research, described in 1953, "the ever-increasing resistance of the public to the ordinary motion picture."[39] The public wanted more: larger screens, bigger events, sensational experiences. Yet an additional major difference separated the enlarged cinema screen of the 1950s from the power of earlier film experience. Cinematic architecture had also undergone radical debates and consequent transformations, including lessened ornamentation and fewer vestigial stage attributes. Widescreen demanded American exhibition's acquiescence to aspects of the neutralized cinema, such as the removal of the proscenium arch to accommodate larger screens or the demasking of the larger screen.

In 1953, exhibitors debated whether widescreen systems and proscenia could coexist, with some arguing that larger screens could be installed behind the arch so that proscenia need not be "ruthlessly torn out . . . just for

36. Ben Schlanger, "Adapting Theatres to the Big Picture," *Motion Picture Herald, Better Theatres* section, July 2, 1955, 20.

37. Waller's *This Is Cinerama* famously showcased the Atom Smasher roller coaster, thereby cementing the roller coaster's status as a touchstone for the widescreen movement. For image, see still from Cinerama brochure in Rogers, "Smothered in Baked Alaska," 77.

38. Belton, *Widescreen Cinema*, 93.

39. Herbert E. Bragg, "The Development of CinemaScope," reprinted in *Film History* 2 (1988): 360.

the sake of having the house appear functional."[40] By 1956, however, the theater auditorium's cutting-edge "new look" was usually that of an archless space: "While the widescreens have created new patterns in seating and some other changes in auditorium styling, the most pronounced change is, of course, in the proscenium area. The projection of pictures in the new screen ratios has required that almost the entire front width of the building be opened up for the installation of the widescreens."[41] In 1957, Kenneth MacGowan, producer of *La Cucaracha* (Lloyd Corrigan, 1934), the first live-action three-strip Technicolor process film, and chair of the Department of Theater Arts at UCLA, described the architectural conditions for widescreen as follows:

> One very serious problem about the wide screen is how to fit it into the average proscenium. (Cinerama gets around this by thrusting the curving sides of its screen out into the auditorium.) The majority of America's 17,000 theaters can use screens not much more than 25 feet wide. The situation is worse in Great Britain and on the Continent. In houses with narrow prosceniums, the height of the picture in CinemaScope or SuperScope has to be less than the height of a picture on normal film; or else the sides of the shots have to be cut off with masks, and then the wide screen isn't really wide. Even VistaVision has its architectural troubles. In large theaters, overhanging balconies may cut down the height of its ideal 1.85:2 screen, or force the tearing out of seats at the back of the lower floor. In the late 1920s, when Hollywood began to develop the wide screen, the Wall Street boom was at its height, and the big theater chains, controlled by the producers, were ready to build larger houses designed to handle the new shape. We may shortly see a trend toward fewer and larger theaters—if the wide screen holds off the TV menace.[42]

As MacGowan's observations demonstrate, widescreen required the acceptance of neutralization: the removal of stage theater characteristics such as proscenia and ill-designed balconies; reduced masking; and an auditorium

---

40. Haviland S. Reves, "Essentials of Wide-Screen Installation," *Boxoffice Magazine*, October 3, 1953, *Modern Theatres* section, 15. Twentieth Century-Fox's CinemaScope manual released in 1953 similarly spoke to the anxieties of exhibitors, addressing in its installation section the following question: "Can a picture of twice the width of the present picture be secured within the proscenium, or must it be brought forward of the proscenium, thereby shortening the throw, or must structural alterations be arranged which might either shorten or lengthen the throw?" The manual also notes that Fox's CinemaScope package did not come with masking included. "What Every Exhibitor Needs to Know about a Cinemascope Installation," *Boxoffice Magazine*, August 4, 1953, *Modern Theatres* section, 12.

41. "In New or Remodeled Theatres, the Proscenium Arch Bows Out to Widescreen," *Boxoffice Magazine*, July 7, 1956, *Modern Theatres* section, 12.

42. Kenneth MacGowan, "The Wide Screen of Yesterday and Tomorrow," *The Quarterly of Film Radio and Television* 11, no. 3 (Spring 1957): 239.

constructed for screen needs.[43] MacGowan points to an often overlooked feature of widescreen technology: a need for changed theatrical space in the wake of changed cinema screens and filmic technologies. To encourage a widescreen immersion focused on the film itself and its apparatus of screen, projector, and camera—all of which had to be altered for the widescreen experience—the theater first had to become a mechanism of motion picture immersion. Alongside the changing screen, the mid-century theater constituted a complementary visual technology. For some exhibitors eager to test the limits of the new cinema screen's possibilities, the symbiotic harmony of large and/or curved screen and architecture as filmic technology not only expanded profits and combatted the threat of television, but also cemented film's status as an immersive phenomenon.

The meaning of "immersion," however, was hardly standardized. Despite the frequency with which they are assumed to be universal in meaning, "immersion," "participation," and "realism" were increasingly loaded and multivalent terms in the 1950s. For a theatrical designer and theorist like Schlanger, "realism" did not refer to the extant world outside of the cinema, but instead to an alternative reality made from the sutured elements of movie and theater that, once activated by the spectator's vision, could fully substitute for exterior experience. Schlanger preferred the term "presence" to "participation" for reasons of spectatorial calibration; in his view, spectators should witness but not act. The participation lauded by so many widescreen exhibitors placed spectators at the center of aesthetic activation. By contrast, presence implied the spectator's existence at the profilmic scene paired with his incorporation as an equal—not an authority—to camera, screen, and projector in a vision machine. In order to realize the potential of the traditional theater, the auditorium must be made, "in effect, part of the projected picture, giving the audience a sense of realistic presence at the scene."[44] In this model, the spectator was observer rather than active force: "The effect may be called 'participation,' but in our use of that term here is not meant a feeling of being *in* the scene, but rather *at* it."[45] Less participant than witness, the spectator in this version of large format cinema was more contemplative, more critically distanced, and, by virtue of being visually immersed, afforded a level of unbiased pseudoexpertise. To be present is to see; to participate is to affect the outcome. Widescreen here thus took on the status of both an American expansive automobilic view and a perfected scientific experiment, where the observer sees but does not influence.

43. Theatrical size was, however, a palpable difference: while many neutralized cinemas were smaller than palaces, larger screens could potentially mean a return to the larger theaters of pre-Depression America.

44. Schlanger and Schutz, "Visualizing the Theatre for a New Era," 38.

45. Schlanger and Schutz, "A Greater Theatrical Medium in the Making," 38 (emphasis original).

Vision was the ideal sense for performing this operation not only because of cinema's reliance upon it, but because it could occur with very little physical movement, and therefore trick the spectator into forgetting her physical body. In a 1953 article highlighting detailed diagrams of visual ranges, Schlanger argued that visual perception is divisible into three groups:

> (1) With no, or very little, movement of the eyes or head; (2) with movement of the eyes and/or the head [in which the subject does not feel conscious of the movement]; (3) with eye, head and sometimes body movement, consciously, to cover a wide range, which may even be as much as full circle coverage [a turn-around]. The greatest part of visual experience falls within the second group, with the next largest falling in the third.[46]

Cinematography and projection should therefore focus on the second visual range to enact full presence, which hinges on unconscious movement. Widescreen at its best, then, tiptoed between mobility and immobility in a further evocation of film's virtual travel.

Cinerama's exhibition advocates who conceived of the format as an "audience-participation" device were targeted by Schlanger as "tak[ing] audiences for rides—no pun intended." The model's inability to effectively "engulf" its audience with a picture of 120 feet in width diminished its intended illusion and rendered it unsatisfactory—not the experience possible with a neutralized auditorium and a screen enormous in both width and height.[47] Along with other widescreen formats—as opposed to Schlanger's preferred large-screen formats—Cinerama's width was developed based on understandings of visual scanning as typically more horizontal than vertical in movement—yet how much more horizontal than vertical motion the human eye engaged in was not established. A stretch of only the horizontal cinematic plane relied on shaky data and reasserted film's association with theater: "Actually, a screen that is wide to an exaggerated degree comes close to imitating the stifling pattern of the proscenium opening of a stage theatre."[48] Only widening the screen was a regressive movement for cinema, which had always been able to show "foreground, middleground and overhead areas at once, which has been one of the factors making it a story telling device infinitely superior to the stage with its exclusively horizontal aperture. It certainly cannot be advisable to discontinue this flexibility, one of the most potent forces of cinematographic art."[49] For Schlanger, large format cinema's spatial endlessness, flexibility, and multidimensional presentation, as opposed to its sense of bodily thrill, constituted its greatest powers.

46. Ben Schlanger, "Theatres and the New Techniques," *Motion Picture Herald*, September 5, 1953, *Better Theatres* section, 12.
47. Ibid.
48. Ibid., 13.
49. Ibid., 52.

Finally, large-screen formats should not be separate from the rest of the theater; rather, they should be the focal points of an integrated visual machine. Although widescreen afforded further opportunity to privilege the screen, Schlanger insisted that exhibitors should consider it, along with the spectator, a part of the cinematic-architectural apparatus:

> The movie theatre deserves the chance to fulfill its potentialities. . . . The improvement has been great and is the more remarkable for the ingeniousness with which it has been made widely available. But the machinery of it is still, from the broadest point-of-view, an attachment. It has had to be. It is yet in development, however, and from this research and usage must eventually come some unity of experience as to what is best for the purpose. Theatre design free of past practice should now begin to figure in this experience in order to bring forth a system that co-ordinates and integrates all functions from camera to audience.[50]

Via large-screen formats and modernized interiors, cinema's unified machine could become the dynamic, communal, transportive, unified, and revelatory public form espoused by revelatory film theorists and anticipated by earlier urban visual modes. Rather than functioning as a horizontal "attachment," widescreen should take its place within a larger system traversing temporal and spatial lines: from camera recording profilmic scene, to projector showcasing film at any number of times in any number of places, to neutralized auditorium space, to stilled witness.

While Schlanger's integrated cinema operated somewhat at the outskirts of mainstream discourse, his urging of a unified filmic and architectural experience was influential overall. Comparatively, Haviland F. Reves described theatrical conditions for 1953 in *Boxoffice Magazine* as follows:

> Historically, the theatre has been viewed as a place for the presentation of live entertainment, and the traditional proscenium symbolized that condition. Today it is very subordinate to the screen itself in fact. Basic aspects of the modern approach are:
> 1. The stage as an entity in itself should tend to vanish from the theatre.
> 2. The audience should participate in the theatre.
> 3. The screen should be the dominating factor in the theatre.
> 4. The desirable physical objective is to achieve full peripheral vision from the maximum number of seats.[51]

---

50. Schlanger, "Theatre Design *in* the New Techniques," 29.
51. Reves, "Essentials of Wide-Screen Projection," 15.

While audiences are called upon to participate rather than witness, certain tenets of the neutralized ideal remain central: the screen as dominating force, a vanishing stage, fullness of vision. And overall, the palpable excitement in exhibitors' publications in the 1950s ranged from the bodily enticing spectacle of the new American standard of amusement-centric entertainment to a futuristic, liberated American sensorium. For these and other avenues for widescreen, large-screen formats promised the grandeur of expansive American visual conquest and a sweeping view on a new world. Even in the loudest insistences on widescreen's amusement park desires, exhibition in the era of widescreen maintained material traces of disembodied space, of film theory, and of long-standing traditions of aesthetic contemplation that denied the body for the sake of the mind. Such negotiations of seemingly opposed impulses reflected the modern spectator's continuing contested status.

## "DISEMBODIED INTELLECTUAL ABSTRACTION": THE COLONIAL WILLIAMSBURG TRANSCINEUMS

According to exhibition discourse, the spectator of 1950s widescreen was at once enticed by entertainment, transported to times and places outside of her body, struck dumb, and participating in or present at the filmic scene. While exhibitors imagined contradictory versions of the perfect widescreen spectator, some characteristics remained consistent: the spectator of widescreen was modern, flexible, and American. In this sense, the shifting ideologies of widescreen spectatorship implied an American viewer at mid-century for whom art traversed new ground between high and low; moving imagery was both intimately domestic on television and enormously public on film; fast communication across vast distances was widely available, yet homes were more and more suburban; and domestic travel was increasingly accessible in personal vehicles on interstate highways, while journeys into space were a more concrete possibility. Close attention to widescreen rhetoric untangles multiple iterations of exhibition's presumed spectator, but also sheds light on the larger shape of American viewing ideals at mid-century.

Within this set of conditions, Schlanger built one of the few theaters of his that still stands untouched: the transcineums at Colonial Williamsburg, Virginia. Not only were these theaters some of the most experimental widescreen theaters of the 1950s, but they appeared at a venue treading the line between education and entertainment; they were sponsored by the Rockefellers, one of the most influential American funding families of the twentieth century; they were constructed with special attention paid to advances in optical technology; they explicitly linked the origins of the nation with the movies; and they expressed a mode of virtual travel tied to burgeoning American highway tourism. Film at Colonial Williamsburg was a tool of revolution and

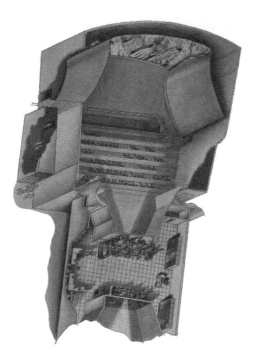

**Figure 3.5:** Overhead drawing of transcineum structure. The Colonial Williamsburg Foundation.

of patriotism, a shining example of American ingenuity, a national investment in the power of vision, and an appeal to the mobile yet individualized spectator traversing the far-flung borders of the United States. Schlanger's American approach to spectatorship found its beginnings in the neutralized cinema's emergence in the late 1920s–1930s, but reached its height in the transcineums, where a combination of visionary theatrical architecture and quintessentially American funding together wove a narrative of a machine-made aesthetic experience where spectators bore witness both to the remade past and a futuristic technological utopia.

Now mostly forgotten, the transcineums opened to the public in 1957 to great domestic and international acclaim. The twin theater setup boasted two identical auditoriums, a shared projection room, and double s-curve lenticular screens over 50 feet in projection length and 120 feet in actual length that extended from the front stage area out into the audience seating space Figure 3.5.[52] Originally designed to project for Todd-AO, the theaters

52. Curvature was another screen fad in the 1950s, thought to increase "realistic" participation along with widescreen, but relatively swiftly became relegated to novelty, museum, and attraction sites due to the impracticality of standardized curvature. See John Selby, "Variable Curvature Proving Answer to Screen Headaches," *Boxoffice Magazine*, May 4, 1957, *Modern Theatres* section, 40; and John Belton, "The Curved Screen," *Film History* 16, no. 3 (2004): 277–285.

**Figure 3.6:** Interior transcineum with film. The Colonial Williamsburg Foundation.

eventually showcased a combination of VistaVision single-strip projection and Todd-AO sound with 65 mm and 70 mm film.[53] Like many other curved screen examples, the transcineums were always intended to be unique, mostly showing a film shot and conceived of specifically for this single place (Figure 3.6). The Rockefeller Foundation's considerable wealth allowed the transcineums and the center in which they were built to be relatively large in scope. More importantly, the project's end goal never had to be profiteering, but could focus on more amorphous sights: increased presence, spectatorial awe, educational enrichment, and integration into a positive vision of a shared American national past. For this reason, designers envisioned the transcineums as "conditioning chamber[s] or time lock[s] in order to create the proper mood for [the audience's] journey into another century" and to introduce spectators to the Williamsburg experience of historical tourism— essentially a time machine whose advisors would include luminaries from the worlds of architecture, literature, theater design, and Hollywood.[54] This "time

53. Todd-AO's system aimed to recreate Cinerama but with a single projector and film strip, and culminated in a special lenticular aluminum-coated screen with a multitude of tiny embossed "lenses" covering the fabric's entirety. Williamsburg's screen would eventually also be lenticular, although not made by Todd-AO.

54. Max Abramovitz from Kenneth Chorley, November 6, 1953, Colonial Williamsburg Foundation, Archives & Records, Block 33, #6, Hotel and Reception Center,

lock" or "conditioning chamber" centered on two paired strategies of sensory immersion: functional architecture and cinematic widescreen.

Despite Colonial Williamsburg's mission of historical preservation and re-enactment, the Information Center was a modernist structure nearly from the beginning. The main rationale for this was that the Center would be a gateway or transitional area between the modern world and the colonial space of Williamsburg's area of re-enactment. In addition, the Center's designers valued an architectural style that could be more or less invisible. Compared to a colonial building, a modernist Center would be less intrusive on the public's vision, and, like a neutralized theater, could obscure itself in order to privilege the visual experience within.

By the 1950s, functional modernist architecture could represent multiple consummately American (and Puritan) values: rationality, simplicity, humility, fastidiousness, thrift, community, and efficiency. Now less a high-brow European import and more a visualization of American democracy in action, functional modernism was an appealing style for a live historical attraction depicting the United States' national emergence.[55] In a document from 1952 detailing current Center plans, the layout and design would meet

> functional requirements, yet [being] simple and modest in appearance so as not to become architectural features themselves and thereby distract the visitors' attention from the restored area. . . . Also, since the interiors of the buildings were required to be largely functional and modern in both furnishings and equipment, it did not seem necessary nor desirable to attempt to capture the colonial style on their exteriors. . . . It also became obvious to all from further studies and sketches that extremely progressive modern designs would tend to be a shock and distraction to the visitors interested in the pure colonial architecture in the nearby restored area.[56]

"Simple," "modest," "functional," and "modern" here might be substituted with "neutral." Yet to create a "neutralized" visual environment at the very center of the most American of American attractions bore considerable implications

September–November 11, 1953. Hollywood's involvement was multifaceted; among the project's advisory board was Louis Novins, President of Paramount Pictures, who undoubtedly influenced the eventual choice of the VistaVision system. Louis A. Novins to Kenneth Chorley, September 28, 1953, Colonial Williamsburg Foundation, Archives & Records, Block 33, #6, Hotel and Reception Center, September–November 11, 1953.

55. Beatriz Colomina has argued that mid-century modernism's rhetoric of happiness and prosperity was part of a propaganda campaign tied to the American military. Beatriz Colomina, *Domesticity at War* (Cambridge, MA: MIT Press, 2007).

56. "The New Visitor Reception Facilities Architectural Design," Colonial Williamsburg Foundation, Archives & Records, Block 33, #6, Hotel and Reception Center, January–July 1952.

for Williamsburg's democratic ideology. The emergence of American history becomes unadulterated, unquestioned, and teleological—a foregone conclusion without doubt, tangent, or question. To be visually neutral not only allows a space to privilege its contents—it also makes invisible the process through which it was constructed.

Although "modernist" here meant a style easily digested and functional rather than the potential "shock" and "distraction" present in its more extreme versions, some experimentation still permeated design concepts. Wallace Harrison and Max Abramovitz—high-profile modernist architects in the 1950s—and their shared firm took on the main architectural duties. But in March of 1954, Williamsburg's Mitchell Wilder and John Goodbody also met with counterculture architectural phenomenon Buckminster Fuller, whose work on geodesic domes and utopian industrial and building design were iconic images of the space race and, later, psychedelic mind expansion movements.[57] This version of modernism could therefore consist of something both public and visionary, both grounded in tradition and evocative of the spirit of American ingenuity. Similarly, expansive cinematic and architectural techniques could be harnessed both for the wild possibilities of the avant-garde or Hollywood's standardized suturing vision, the frivolity of three-dimensionality in *Kiss Me, Kate* or William Castle's bodily shock horror cinema, the broad thrills of roller coasters in *This Is Cinerama* or the rationality of American democracy. Immersion through burgeoning architectures and technologies could allow mid-century cinematic spectators to enter any number of brave new worlds.

Alongside architectural experimentation, preliminary designs for the media auditoriums in the Information Center involved substantial discussions of innovative filmic formats. In a 1952 meeting, representatives from Williamsburg argued that

> the projection equipment for the auditoriums should be as spectacular as we can obtain and still be practical. Our investigations should cover multiple screens, three-dimensional projection, facilities for projecting television, and consideration for using both 16mm and 35mm equipment. . . . We should consult Eastman Kodak and Mr. Waller [Fred Waller, inventor of Cinerama] to see how far they have progressed with plans for multiple screens and three-dimensional equipment.[58]

57. Fuller was not able to assist in the eventual shape of the project, but Mitchell Wilder, director of presentation at Williamsburg, expressed interest in working with him on preliminary designs of the building. Mitchell A. Wilder to Buckminster Fuller, March 11, 1954, Colonial Williamsburg Foundation, Archives & Records, Block 33, #6, Hotel and Reception Center, January–March 1954.

58. Permanent Reception Center Planning Session Memo, July 30, 1952, Colonial Williamsburg Foundation, Archives & Records, Block 33, #6, Hotel and Reception Center January–July 1952.

In keeping with interest in Waller's achievements, in March of 1953 Harrison proposed using Cinerama, while by December of 1953 additional possibilities included 3D, remote control light panels, television projection, backlit slide projection, moving shadow boxes, or even films with live narrators as guides through the "decompression chamber" who would "step with you through the 'picture window' until you were on your way along the pathway to the restored area."[59] In some unexpected way, the experience should be "spectacular."

Based on Max Abramovitz's recommendation, Schlanger was brought onboard the Center project as theatrical architect and consultant in June of 1954. Abramovitz knew Schlanger from New York; several years prior, Abramovitz & Harrison worked alongside Schlanger, Le Corbusier, and Oscar Niemeyer in designing the United Nations headquarters, which opened in 1952. A few years later, the firm would again work with Schlanger on the redesign of Lincoln Center, where Schlanger installed a continental seating plan. Nearly immediately after Schlanger joined the project, discussions of the theaters shifted significantly from using an array of technological gimmicks to perfecting visual experience. Particularly because the project was envisioned as "an orientation theatre [with] the ideal conditions for presentation of a wide screen production" and "a small house with every seat located as near as possible to the ideal position," Schlanger, with his nearly quarter century's worth of experience, seemed the perfect choice for auditorium design.[60] Schlanger immediately emphasized "minimizing the impact of the building upon the visitor, i.e., playing down the interior architecture in order that the dominant note is the action on the screen," maintaining a focus on consistently effective pictorial illusion, developing a system of an enormous screen paired with a film with no close-ups, and the use of either Todd-AO or VistaVision projection. In the first meeting with Schlanger, the committee decided that "it would be fruitless for us to proceed with our sketch plans of various ideas for the building and not to relate such plans to the optical factors involved."[61] Just a few months prior, ideas for the theaters leaned more toward slide

59. Confidential Memo to Kenneth Chorley from E. P. Alexander, March 13, 1953, Colonial Williamsburg Foundation, Archives & Records, Block 33, #6, Hotel and Reception Center, January–April 1953; Memo to Mr. E. M. Frank from M. E. Campoli re: New Reception Center, July 14, 1953, Block 33, #6, Hotel and Reception Center, May–August 1953; Discussion Minutes to Max Abramovitz from Carlisle Humelsine, December 16, 1953, Block 33, #6, Hotel and Reception Center, November 12–December 1953.

60. Carlisle Humelsine to George Wells, Chairman, American Optical Company (Buffalo, NY), June 21, 1954, Colonial Williamsburg Foundation, Archives & Records, Block 33, #6, Hotel and Reception Center, January–March 1954.

61. To the Files from M. A. Wilder re: New Information Center, Mr. Schlanger, Consultant, June 15, 1954, Colonial Williamsburg Foundation, Archives & Records, Block 33, #6, Hotel and Reception Center, January–March 1954.

shows, immobile displays, and live narration—evidently, Schlanger was very persuasive.[62]

Consequently, once Schlanger appeared, filmic and theatrical conditions that mimicked the eye's behavior supplanted multiple media formats similar to Kracauer's "panoply of effects"—a microcosmic narrative of film exhibition's move from vaudeville to singular film object. Inside the auditoriums, functionality would be taken to the extreme. In a September 1954 board meeting, the proposed transcineums were described as having "no decoration in the interior inasmuch as all walls and ceiling are thought of as a part of the optical illusion which, under the conditions when there is no picture being projected on the screen, show no break between the ceiling, walls, and screen and there are no fixtures, etc., which permit the viewer to acquire a sense of scale in the room. The phrase used 'an optical vacuum' in which one is unable to gage distance or size is to be desired."[63] Such an "optical vacuum" avoided any "sharp rectangular border for our screen image. Instead, [Schlanger] has been exploring various alternatives which permit the image to be blended into the shell of the theater by a gradual diminution of light and color."[64] To maintain the illusion of an entirely disappeared place floating unmoored in space and time, no clocks would be allowed in the auditoriums. By eliminating "all such points of reference which could be seen by the spectator while viewing the projected picture," the optical vacuum made a seamless transition between eye information and screen information, with no distinction between visual perception and the experience of projected film.[65] It is hardly an exaggeration to call this Schlanger's ideal theater.

As discussion concerning the transcineums' shape, size, and function evolved, the film to be projected within them similarly underwent radical conceptual transformation. Given the anticipated use of either Todd-AO or VistaVision large-screen formats, exhibition requirements dictated the film's form from the outset.[66] To complement the theaters' interior design, Schlanger recommended a modified use of natural lighting that would keep in place the "realistic quality" of the film. Schlanger explained that, while Hollywood usually uses "flat lighting," the film made for the Information Center could be

62. New Information Center, April 27, 1954, Colonial Williamsburg Foundation, Archives & Records, Block 33, #6, Hotel and Reception Center, January–March 1954.

63. Memo to Kendrew from Wilder re: New Information Center, September 8, 1954, Colonial Williamsburg Foundation, Archives & Records, Block 33, #6, Hotel and Reception Center, July–September 1954.

64. Memo to Files from Goodbody re: New Information Center Film, December 29, 1955, Colonial Williamsburg Foundation, Archives & Records, Block 33, #6, Hotel and Reception Center-Program, September–December 1955.

65. Ben Schlanger to T. W. Drewery, July 16, 1956, Colonial Williamsburg Foundation, Archives & Records, Block 33, #6, Information Center, July 1956.

66. Todd-AO screen and/or sound formats would require special projection requirements, while VistaVision would not.

shot entirely in wide angle with "attention calling devices" deployed in certain areas of the screen. Wide angle had, at this point, become Schlanger's preferred cinematographic technique: it was distinctly not televisual while closely mimicking natural visual perception. Thus, rather than rely on close-ups, which are filmic and not perceptual, the film could enlist light contrast to either enhance or downplay areas of the screen.[67] Beyond lighting and contrast issues, the film also began to take shape less as a narrative and more as an instrument of audience immersion. Although film critic, journalist, and screenwriter James Agee was first attached to the project, his interest and investment in character and story proved to be a sticking point for Williamsburg staff who, following Schlanger's lead, sought control over the film from an exhibition standpoint.[68] Agee insisted that slavery should be at the forefront of the film as a "constant irony, considering 'Liberty' and 'Independence' and something like 'Equality' as underlying themes; but this irony must be as constantly sharpened by new insights for our audience about the relationships between black and white, between slave, master, and freeman."[69] Yet Arthur Tourtellot from the Rockefeller Foundation voiced concerns about Agee's script, arguing that its depiction was inappropriate and embarrassing.[70] Eliding bodies in the theaters therefore reflected an elision of historical shame. A focus on slavery might disrupt the seamlessness of film, technology, and theater by forcing audiences to acknowledge uncomfortable moral dilemmas uncovered by movement into the past. Neutralizing the exhibition space served to neutralize—and naturalize—an idealized birth of American democracy.

In this sense, Agee was too fixated on the historically authentic dimensions of narrative rather than a tool for time travel. Similar issues emerged in the directorial selection process, which eventually culminated in the choice of George Seaton, Paramount director of *Miracle on 34th Street*; like Agee, "many directors, however, are more concerned with cast performance than camera technique and if we were to select this kind of director for our final production it might not help us very much to have him involved in the experimental filming. We are not so much concerned at the present with character performance as we are with psycho-physical reactions to the process itself."[71] The

67. A. L. Smith to Alexander, August 26, 1954, Colonial Williamsburg Foundation, Archives & Records, Block 33, #6, Hotel and Reception Center, July–September 1954.

68. Agee's death on May 16, 1955 occurred during his contract period with Williamsburg, although both he and Williamsburg staff were certain by that time that his script would never satisfy both parties.

69. Agee Script, 15–17, Colonial Williamsburg Foundation, Production Archives, June 13, 1955.

70. Arthur Tourtellot to Carlisle Humelsine, June 29, 1955, Colonial Williamsburg Foundation, Production Archives.

71. Seaton's reputation as a highly professional, if not innovative, Academy award-winning director of inoffensive material surely contributed to his being the "safe" choice for the project. Other directors suggested for the project included John Huston, Fred Zinneman, Larry Watkin, Frank Capra, and Elia Kazan. Memo to files from Art Smith

Williamsburg film was therefore aligned with screen gimmicks of the 1950s via technology as well as bodily reaction, stimulation, and visual manipulation rather than story and character.[72] As with earlier iterations of neutralization, spatial constraints and their impact on the spectator bore greater import than the film's narrative effect.

Agee's interests also included "traditional" storytelling techniques related to painting and the stage. In his treatment for the Williamsburg film project, Agee noted that

> with the use of Todd-AO many of the most powerful devices of traditional filmmaking—notably the close-up; cutting, panning, dollying and pull shots— must be dramatically curtailed. We forget most that is traditionally meant by a movie—though some of these traditional devices, used sparingly, can have powerful effect—and realize from the start we draw less on these traditional devices of that art than on painting, particularly on heroic-scale painting, and on the stage. What we will work toward, in that case, will be a kind of Mural in Motion (and Sound), static and permanent and unique to Williamsburg. For it is from painting and the stage (for instance) that we will learn more how to direct the eye and the ear of the audience toward a sometimes relatively minute part of the screen than we can learn through traditional movies or through our own experiment.[73]

Static. Traditional. Permanent. Agee's film contrasted sharply with the flexible, modern, and mutable energies upon which neutralization depended. Alongside Schlanger, Agee sought to eliminate close-ups, as well as other camera "tricks" unsuited to mimicking human vision. Yet whereas Schlanger and many other widescreen proponents of the 1950s proposed a new cinema of participation or presence, of unframed windows onto cinematic worlds, Agee saw film as painterly and stage-oriented. His "mural in motion" was stilled rather than transportive. For Schlanger, who had worked for decades to eliminate the "picture on the wall" effect of screen masking, film as a painting or a play was a hopelessly antiquated vision. Instead, eyes and ears should be directed through calibrated environment, acuity, seating charts, and

re: New Info Center-Experimental Shooting, December 9, 1954, Colonial Williamsburg Foundation, Archives & Records, Block 33, #6, Hotel and Reception Center, Audio Visual Equipment, 1954; Memo re: Production of Film for New Reception Center, from Wilder, November 8, 1954, Colonial Williamsburg Production Archives.

72. Eventually, however, the transcineums would be described as visually rather than bodily immersive—not so much relatives of Cinerama as of a more conceptual approach to large-screen formats.

73. James Agee, "Some Notes on the Williamsburg Film," Colonial Williamsburg Foundation, Production Archives.

viewing conditions—a mechanized, modern, attention-oriented approach to spectatorship decisively different from the museum or the stage.

With Schlanger's input, the transcineums and *Williamsburg: The Story of a Patriot*, their eventual film, came to be conceived of as transportive, transitory, and transitional in purpose, transparent in design. Imagined to be an intermediary space between the modern present and the colonial past, theaters, maximally curved screen, and specifically shot film would screen out the everyday in pursuit of historicity and pastness. For Schlanger, this meant "providing a proper transition between the projected image and the remaining side walls of the auditorium," and making the "screen surround material and the picture screen itself . . . the same."[74] Schlanger had expressed a desire to cover all the completed theater surfaces except for the rear wall with the same fabric out of which the screen was made.[75] Although the theaters eventually were covered in perforated stainless steel rather than screen material, Schlanger's vast space signified a belief in screen environment as a mode of imaginative—yet civic—transportation. For this reason, he urged the elimination of any semblance of masking from the theater, as it "makes the viewer acutely aware that he is seeing a screen image as if framed by a window." Instead, Schlanger recommended "a surround treatment in which there is a more gradual diminution of color. He believes that this can be achieved without any awareness of the technique as such on the part of the audience. He holds that such a surround effect will create for the viewer a greater feeling of awareness of the image and a greater sense of participating in the film action." In regard to lighting during projection, "Mr. Schlanger plans to have no lighting—except low-level seat lighting for safety purposes—other than that which is reflected from the projected image on the screen. The shape of the theater is that of a neutral shell, with the use of additional screen material to blend the screen image into the shell in such a way that the theater environment itself becomes part of the total film experience."[76] As for the screen itself, it grew throughout the planning process, from 46'3" in 1955 to 48' in early 1956 to its final size of 52' by 26' in projection space. Two

74. Schlanger to Smith, March 13, 1956, Colonial Williamsburg Foundation, Archives & Records, Block 33, #6, Information Center-Model 1956.

75. Memo from Ben Schlanger re: Colonial Williamsburg New Information Center Theatre and One-Half Full Size Model, April 22, 1956, Colonial Williamsburg Foundation, Archives & Records, Block 33, #6, Hotel and Reception Center, April 1955.

76. Schlanger's reference to the screen image being framed as if through a window is a curious one, given his reliance on the window metaphor for the screen in much of his writing throughout the 1950s. I interpret his use of the word "window" here to refer to a heavy wooden frame that separates inside from outside. The screen here would be more akin to, for example, the floor-to-ceiling windows at Mies van der Rohe's Farnsworth House that deliberately suggest an integration of interior and exterior worlds. Memo to Files from Goodbody re: NICA Film, January 16, 1956, Colonial Williamsburg Foundation, Production Archives.

surround s-curves where the projected image "blended" into gradual obscurity veered out toward the sides of the stage and into the audience, making the entirety of the screen 120' in length—at the time of construction, the longest indoor screen in the world.[77]

Enormous screen, neutral theater covered in perforated steel from walls to ceiling, and film without close-ups developed specifically for its space—shot after design and most construction was completed on the transcineums—comprised a sophisticated apparatus to mimic human vision. In 1954, approximately halfway through theatrical design, Arthur L. Smith described the goal of developing

> a near perfect audience involvement film—this has never been attempted in the full sense of present implication. . . . What is meant by "improved viewing"? In a project such as Colonial Williamsburg currently contemplates, we propose to seat a select audience in front of a large screen and provide a visual experience that seems real and believable. . . . It must so closely approximate normal vision that the audience, in effect, is the camera and everything that is seen has the same effect on the screen as it would have to the eye—if the camera had been a human eye. Human vision, from the present viewpoint, is a process in which the eye finds only one small area sharp at a time. . . . Since the eye does not possess a telescope device, the typical movie close-up with the long focal length lens is not normal. . . . As action moves from one side of the screen to the other the eye characteristic lens system should similarly move with it. This may be termed the "moving pupil" system. There is considerable evidence that the moving pupil system with its peripheral modulation factor is practicable. Dr. O'Brien has calculated that peripheral modulation could be used for the Todd-A-O system.[78]

The "moving pupil" system encapsulates the transportive yet immobilized qualities of the transcineum: an eye that moves, a body that remains still, the environment changing in sequence around the spectator like the experience of a passenger in a car. In January of 1955, Schlanger and other representatives from Williamsburg traveled to Buffalo and Cambridge, where they met with Dr. Ernst Wolf from the Department of Physiology at Wellesley and with Dr. W. J. Crozier from the Laboratory of Physiology at Harvard. Crozier was known for his attempts to eliminate the flicker effect—one solution he proposed involved running film at 30 fps—while Wolf had previously consulted with television manufacturers regarding eye fatigue and strain from

77. Goodbody to Ben Schlanger, January 20, 1956, Colonial Williamsburg Foundation, Production Archives; Memo to Files from Arthur L. Smith re: New Information Center Film, November 14, 1956, Colonial Williamsburg Foundation, Production Archives.

78. Memo to Files from Arthur L. Smith re: New Information Center Program, November 8, 1954, Colonial Williamsburg Foundation, Production Archives.

television's contrast of dark space with cathode tube illumination.[79] At these meetings, the visitors discussed screen masking elimination and flexibility, further demonstrating the project's connections between optical science, aesthetics, technology, and neutralization.

Once open, the transcineums found extensive coverage in American media outlets.[80] In "Design for Illusion," his article for *Motion Picture Herald*, Schlanger described the paired film and theater as a "conditioning" experience that filled the entire range of vision for all spectators (Insert 3).[81] Reverberation within the "dead" auditoriums was calibrated to outdoor conditions and achieved through maximized absorption from sound buffering material that blanketed the space behind the metal walls. In typical fashion, Schlanger explained that total immersion could not happen without such a carefully designed environment: "Development of and experience with this project proves that, while the requirements for achieving a convincing degree of presence-at-the-scene depend to a great extent upon the production and the projection system, complete illusion is not fully attained unless the viewing space and seating scheme are designed to give that system certain conditions of perception."[82] Metal partitions between rows were particularly essential; their abnormally high scale prevented spectators from seeing those in front of them and therefore reduced peripheral stimulation (Figures 3.7 and 3.8). Ideally, the transcineums seamlessly integrated human and camera perception and fully substituted one for the other:

> A major objective is liberation of perception to every possible degree from effective invasion of material extraneous to the picture. . . . Since long before the motion picture, this department of a theatre building has been called an *auditorium*. Conceived for the motion picture as at Williamsburg, we call it a *transcineum*. . . . We apply *transcineum* in space for viewing a motion picture in

---

79. New Information Center Planning Committee—Buffalo-Cambridge Trip, January 20, 1955, Colonial Williamsburg Foundation, Archives & Records, Block 33, #6 Hotel and Reception Center-Audio Visual Equipment, 1954.

80. Mentions of the theaters include "Colonial Williamsburg to Film in Todd-AO Process," *Business Screen Magazine* 16, no. 7, 1955, 10; "Todd-AO Subject Is Set for Williamsburg Center," *Film Daily*, November 1, 1955; "Seaton to Do Documentary," *Hollywood Reporter*, November 25, 1955; "Dedicate Williamsburg Foundation Theatres," *Motion Picture Daily*, April 2, 1957; "A New Screen Presentation System to Make Its Bow at Colonial Williamsburg," Boxoffice, February 2, 1957; Bosley Crowther, "Showmen's Challenge: Time Now for Dynamic New Film Theatres," *New York Times*, December 1, 1957; Arthur L. Smith and Benjamin Schlanger, "The Colonial Williamsburg Theaters for a Wide-Screen Participation Film," *SMPTE* 70, no. 9 (September 1961): 677–679; Ben Schlanger, "The Evolution of the Williamsburg System: Motion Picture System from Camera to Viewer," *International Projectionist* 37, no. 1 (January 1962): 8–16.

81. Ben Schlanger, "Design for Illusion," *Motion Picture Herald*, June 8, 1957, *Better Theatres* section, 7.

82. Ibid., 14.

**Figure 3.7:** Transcineum seats. The Colonial Williamsburg Foundation.

which conditions are so contrived as to allow the spectator to be aware only of the projected image and immediately surrounding area with the latter so integrated into the performance area itself as to be subservient to the picture. . . . The total screen area as seen from the last (8th) [row] fills the comfortable range of a spectator's vision, which means that *everyone* seated in the transcineum is not normally aware of the side walls and ceiling beyond the performance area. This elimination of personal spatial and environmental references allows the picture to dominate.[83]

Schlanger refers here to a "liberation of perception" in his masterpiece widescreen space—a bodiless projection into imaginative time and space. Paired with barrier walls between rows, the removal of spatial, temporal, and perceptual reference points both masked other audience members and retained a sense of communal viewing, resulting in the spectator "being immediately at the scene, *mentally in it*, as a kind of disembodied intellectual abstraction"—a presence bearing forceless witness to the filmic vision.[84] As in typical continental seating plans, a lack of aisles except on the far left and far right

83. Ibid., 15 (emphasis original).
84. Ibid., 16 (emphasis original).

Figure 3.8: Williamsburg audience, 1957. The Colonial Williamsburg Foundation.

discouraged audience members from standing or mingling during the performance. By strictly regulating perception, bodily comfort, screen size, and viewing distance in the transcineums, Schlanger looked toward total disembodied immersion—an abstracted, perfected spectatorship, both communal and perceptual, and purely attentive. Schlanger's use of the term "abstraction" can be understood as a reference to abstract art for consumers of 1950s American culture, particularly American Abstract Expressionism's recent exportation to the rest of the globe. Via "disembodied intellectual abstraction," Schlanger cast cinematic experience in response to a larger critical discourse that still frequently refused to acknowledge film as art. If the viewing of a film can result in a "disembodied intellectual abstraction" rather than merely a muted escapist pleasure, film and its house formulate a unique discipline to be canonized alongside opera, fine art, and symphonies.[85]

85. Indeed, certain physical attributes of the transcineums proved to be useful for some of these very same art forms. The seating layout for Wallace K. Harrison's redesign of the Metropolitan Opera House building in 1966, "devised by Ben Schlanger, one of Harrison's many consultant specialists, had to be figured out in such a way that no person in the auditorium saw the stage past more than two heads. Hence the staggered seating and uneven spaces between some of the seats." Lincoln Center's

Calling his theaters "transcineums" rather than "auditoriums" served three strategies: first, it qualified film's relationship to live theater; second, it affirmed that the theaters' perceptual structure was directed at vision at the expense of the other senses; and third, it reinforced the structure's transportational qualities. For Schlanger, because cinema's formal elements and environment were radicalized both in terms of screen size and ideal spatial arrangements, film in concert with architecture had become something distinct from the Greco-Roman tradition of live theater. A play is heard and watched; a film transports. A play's spectatorship is flat and staid; a film's bears witness, reaching toward bodily experience in order to transcend it. In removing the root "audito," Schlanger insisted that the transcineums were less places of listening, more where something moves or is moved across. Paired with the "moving pupil system" of projection, Schlanger meant the transcineums to be understood as a place, first and foremost, of stilled bodies and moving eyes. Silent, in their seats, spectators would be kept motionless by the grandiosity of the image while their eyes traveled across the screen. The Williamsburg transcineums were of such massive import for Schlanger because, as he explained, they "established that there is a critical link between the art of film *production* and film exhibition, and that to ignore it would be to miss an opportunity for great stimulus in the industry."[86] For Schlanger, the transcineums could irrevocably demonstrate the implicit link between production and exhibition, one that had been ignored by film producers, by most contemporaneous writing on film, and later by significant swathes of film theory. The transcineums' environment insisted on structures of reception for viewing practice—an insistence that, at least in this particular instance and for this particular designer, mattered more than the elements of the film itself.[87]

At Williamsburg, then, the transcineums were not only a Rockefeller pet project of visual education and historical reenactment.[88] While perhaps not

general redesign was, like Williamsburg, funded by John D. Rockefeller III. Wallace K. Harrison Architectural Drawings and Papers, Collection 1: Box 6, WKH "Lincoln Center & Metropolitan Opera/Miscellaneous 1967 to Date," "Bridge to the Future," *Opera News*, September 17, 1966, Avery Architectural and Fine Arts Library, Columbia University.

86. Schlanger, "Design for Illusion," 22 (emphasis original).

87. The film made for the transcineums, *Williamsburg: The Story of a Patriot*, is a costume drama depicting a British supporter in pre-revolutionary America who learns that he is a true American and therefore a supporter of the rebellion against England. Most notable about the film's formal structure is its lack of close-ups.

88. In addition to considerable interest in scientific research and public health, the Rockefeller family was deeply invested in the arts in general and film in particular as an educational phenomenon, and John D. Rockefeller III's long-standing interest in the impact of film on spectators provided a rationale for the project. Just a decade prior to the Williamsburg project in the 1940s, the Rockefeller Foundation was heavily involved in preserving films with MoMA and Archibald MacLeish and the Library of Congress (Janna Jones, "The Library of Congress Film Project: Film Collecting and a United

everyone involved realized it, the transcineums were an experiment concerning viewing patterns in the American mid-century that highlighted the importance of enlarged screens and minimized environmental cues for spectatorship. Williamsburg may have seemed a counterintuitive location for speculative research involving functional architectural form, fringe approaches to new technologies, advances in optical science, and the interplay of production and exhibition. Yet its link to the birth of the United States draws a line stretching from American neutralized architectural space to film viewing to discourses of twentieth-century spectatorship in general. What the neutralized cinemas sought to induce was a highly efficient and disembodied aesthetic experience—a mechanized revelation suitable for the homeland of Taylorism, the factory assembly line, and a streamlined consumer culture invested at once in individualism and a shared sense of community. This consumer culture culminated in the late 1950s in the figure of the automobile, which brought visitors to Colonial Williamsburg and transported stilled but watching Americans across a country built on western expansion. The transcineums were definitively opposed to drive-in culture, but leaned nonetheless on the icon of the car and its individualized yet community-oriented attributes, at once separating one person from the next and connecting them by way of mass-produced highway networks. Furthermore, the transcineums represented a transformation of modernism at mid-century; what was once the domain of high-brow European elites was now a marker of American consumerism, efficiency, and better living through technology. Whereas 1930s modernist theaters might uneasily recall tensions between a democratic, everyman United States and an intellectual, elitist Europe embroiled in constant war, modernism in mid-century America was transformed, in the movie theater and in the general cultural sphere, into a marketable egalitarian phenomenon—at its root, into something that could be bought. Functional modernist architecture was no longer just for the avant-garde, but folded into an American ethos of hard work, democracy, and the labor of patriotism. Placing some of the work done on the surface—in the transcineums, privileging the labor of viewing and projecting, eliminating stylistic cues that distract not only from a film but also from the effort required for seeing and showing, and embracing a machine-like aesthetic of gleaming metal and smooth screen—functional modernism highlighted national values of ingenuity, efficiency, progress, and invention. In the transcineums, modernism,

State(s) of Mind," *The Moving Image* 6, no. 2 [2006]: 30–51), related to efforts begun in 1935 focused on motion pictures including grants for the establishment of the Film Library at MoMA. The Rockefeller Foundation, "Our History," Rockefellerfoundation. org, https://www.rockefellerfoundation.org/about-us/our-history/.

movie, and mobility labored together in a united task of creating a distinctly American spectatorship.

Because this space's impossible goal was to mimic the eye—to replace physical perception with a mechanized yet transcendent vision—the transcineums both lifted the neutralized movement to its pinnacle and doomed its overreaching hubris to failure. As Arthur Smith explained, the transcineums were meant to "closely approximate normal vision" so all that is seen "has the same effect on the screen as it would have to the eye—if the camera had been a human eye."[89] Partially, this can be explained in terms of location specificity; the transcineums were not nor ever intended to be typical theaters, and instead were designed as models for similar educational attractions.[90] Still, film provided the ideal medium for this work, implying the necessity of some essential element of cinema. The transcineums proposed that one purpose of mechanized vision is the disintegration of boundaries between machine and eye, both in terms of perceptual experience and environmental image of screen blending into theater blending into audience space. Yet as Schlanger explained, the transcineums enacted a "disembodied intellectual abstraction," which resulted in an additional step in the process. First, vision must be studiously mimicked; then, lines between human and camera perception erased; finally, vision is freed into intellectual abstraction, where bodies are no longer required in order to sense, to see. The futile dream of the transcineums, in tune with the strange awestruck avenue of monumental large-screen formats, was to erase the spectatorial body, releasing its roving eye into an ether of expansive movement and ultimate perceptual transportation: from the car to the time machine and back again.

Like the transcineums, neutralized auditoriums in general leaned toward concepts of "floating voids" or "optical vacuums," impossible metaphors that illuminated neutralization's dichotomies: to properly view a film, one must see nothing else at all. In calling the transcineums "floating voids," Schlanger reflected upon neutralization's overarching contradictory impulses: to escape into transcendence via ideologies of nation and profit, to erase space through the careful regimentation of space, to evoke a projected state of bodilessness through measured physical environment, and to separate spectators from grounded lived experience by drawing them closer to an elusive filmic encounter. Developing the illusion of nothingness—the void at the center of the neutral theater—required an obsessively detailed mechanism to float in a mysterious, invisible space. Within an optical vacuum, nothing rises between eye and film, nothing distracts viewer from viewed, and nothing appears to

89. Colonial Williamsburg Foundation, Production Archives, Memo to Files from Arthur L. Smith re: New Information Center Program, November 8, 1954.
90. While he hoped to replicate the system, Schlanger used the term to refer only to the mechanism of paired theater and film structure at Colonial Williamsburg.

exist except vision and screen. Inside the dematerialized auditorium, emptiness makes space for visions, images, and a spectatorship of purified presence. The theatrical void unmoors and disorients, but also transforms sensory experience and allows different spaces and times to converge in the place of visual contemplation. In Schlanger's movie theaters, film and empty space met directed perception to cease bodily movement for the sake of visual movement, creating a system of travel based in abstracted community, immersion, and cinema's strange automotive effects. For this reason, and neither for their location in Williamsburg nor their specific film shown, the transcineums constitute the most salient example of Schlanger's aesthetic goals. In transforming the house of cinema into a minimized space with a maximized screen, Schlanger framed film as art, by defining it as an experience in which we lose ourselves to a higher power, and argued that its viewing was utterly distinct from other available forms.

The transcineums eventually used Paramount's VistaVision process, given that Todd-AO had yet to be proved as a fully operational, long-term widescreen solution; VistaVision, which could be projected in 65 mm or 70 mm, was both more compatible and more flexible than many of its widescreen competitors. Knowing VistaVision could never be quite as wide as CinemaScope, Paramount marketed it as a "big-screen" process that proved the importance of height in a moment fixated on width.[91] While it may have made financial sense compared to Todd-AO or the comparative expense of CinemaScope, VistaVision also bore a metaphorical benefit for a project dedicated to memorializing—and resurrecting—the past. Large as opposed to long, tall in addition to wide, VistaVision's verticality in addition to horizontality aligned with both the kinds of buildings constructed to memorialize and contemporaneous skyscrapers designed for marvelous impact in urban centers.[92] As Sigfried Giedion explained in "The Need for a New Monumentality" in 1958, modern monuments should be constructed not as "haphazard world's fairs, which in their present form have lost their old significance, but newly created urban centers should be the site for collective emotional events, where the people play as important a role as the spectacle itself, and where a unity of the architectural background, the people, and the symbols conveyed by the spectacles, will be achieved."[93] With their recreation of the past, their physical sense of screen enormity and height, their fixation on collective experience, their investment in unified perception, and their insistence on spectatorship as the key to activating aesthetic events, the transcineums fulfilled some of the

91. See Belton, *Widescreen Cinema*, 125–126.

92. In the transcineums, VistaVision was projected horizontally, allegedly to promote "realism."

93. Sigfried Giedion, "The Need for a New Monumentality," in *Architecture, You and Me: The Diary of a Development* (Cambridge, MA: Harvard University Press, 1958), 39.

promise of Giedion's speculative modern monument. In another evocation of a modernist mode at work in the United States, their height echoed the soaring scale of the corporate skyscraper. By seeking an experiential window onto the past, the transcineums celebrated the stunning visual conditions of large-screen technology and offered an alternative architectural model for modern monumentality that embraced magnitude, perception, unity, community, and projection both internal and westward.

Concurrently, Schlanger's involvement gave the project an investment in purified vision. "Disembodiment" and "abstraction" were not likely categories for a Rockefeller project, compared to "education," "film," and "history." Schlanger's striking terminology speaks not to Williamsburg's interests but to a mid-century experimentation present both in high art and in American cinema presentation. In this sense, although the transcineums were designed to showcase only one movie, they formulate both an outlier *and* a node of American exhibition in the 1950s. Although their importance as evidence of cinematic experimentation at mid-century has been mostly forgotten, they are still in operation today. The film's congenial approach to the United States' revolutionary heritage ignores the horrors of slavery or the nuances of political interests in favor of a utopian depiction of the country's birth.[94] Yet when one walks into the transcineums—both of which are early examples of anechoic chambers with no aural reverberation—sounds become hushed. Inside the theaters, muted lights, blue in one theater and red in the other, bathe the auditoriums in soft monochrome (Inserts 4 and 5). Gleaming perforated metal covers most visual surfaces, liquefying the reflected colored light and evoking the interior of a sleek, streamlined ship from a science fiction film. Seated in a cold row with minimized dividers between seats, one finds the bottom edge of one's view frustratingly but intentionally cut off by the

94. Particularly for Williamsburg, which during the colonial era was composed of a 50 percent African American population not shown at all in 1957's re-enactment area, this history was pained and shameful. Yet with segregated movie theaters into the 1950s and even 1960s and a divided populace linked by a shared investment in tourism, the surrounding town dealt with ongoing debates and tensions for decades. Arthur Knight describes the racial implications of segregated movie theaters in the town of Williamsburg (not Colonial Williamsburg) in "Searching for the Apollo: Black Moviegoing and Its Contexts in the Small-Town US South," in *Explorations in New Cinema History: Approaches and Case Studies*, ed. Richard Maltby et al. (West Sussex: Wiley-Blackwell, 2011), 226–242. A photo from 1957 shows three African American men working in the film projector booth of the transcineums, while another shows an African American tour guide outside the theaters (NICA and Projection Booth, Special Collections, Block 33, 57-CL-935 and BL33–26, Colonial Williamsburg Foundation), but Colonial Williamsburg allowed African American visitors only one day per week through the 1950s. In the 1970s, CW began to hire black interpreters and change its position on depicting slavery. Today, dealing with that legacy is at the forefront of CW's educational interests (Rachel Manteuffel, "Colonial in: The Complicated History of Colonial Williamsburg," *Washington Post*, June 9, 2011).

top of the tall bench in front; there is no option but to accept the blockage. No one else appears to be in the theater except those by one's side. In such a relatively small space of 250 seats, the screen still appears far too large, completely impractical, snaking from one end of the stage to the other in curved symmetry. Its giant sides fan out into over 120 feet of total screen length, their wide swaths to both left and right recalling the curvature of the eye or the movement of throwing open a window. Nothing, one might realize, would ever look quite right when shown here. Like all ideal projects, it is a failed experiment of an ideal theater and ideal cinematic perception with no ideal movie ever available to show. One might sit, then, in a silent metal room culminating in an absurd expanse of screen, willing the film not to start, imagining in those last few minutes what perfect movies could spill out of the projector, inhabiting and filling the entirety of the theater's endless space.

## PERFECT VISION, SENSORY DEPRIVATION

In 1970, artist Peter Kubelka's Invisible Cinema opened to the public at Anthology Film Archives (AFA) in New York.[95] As an experiment in sensory deprivation, Kubelka's construction relied on three sides of blinders surrounding audience members' heads on the tops of their theater seats, hopefully resulting in the spectator's full attention focused on the screen. Art world avant-garde glitterati including Andy Warhol, John Lennon, and Yoko Ono were photographed attending the Invisible Cinema; until it closed in 1974, four years after its opening, it was another bright spot on New York's ownership of the map of the cultural elite. Kubelka's experiment was hailed as a radical reinterpretation of spatial and perceptual relationships in the movie theater, an example of the exciting art scene on the American East Coast, and a part of the emergence of an art-focused cinema overseen by Jonas Mekas. In the auditorium replete with hooded seats and coverings of black velvet on all surfaces but the screen, there were, as Kubelka said, "no curtains in front of the screen as, unlike most film spaces, it was not conceived as an imitation of a theater. In order to completely eliminate everything but the screen from the visual field special seats were designed which shielded sight to both sides and made it impossible to see one's neighbors."[96] Viewers sat upright in rigid seats, because, Kubelka noted, "the position of the body is very important for the mind." In regard to the theater's communal aspects, Kubelka argued that while one's eyes were shaded from views of neighboring audience members, "you always felt there was someone on your side. You knew that there were

95. Peter Kubelka, "The Invisible Cinema," *Design Quarterly* 93 (1974): 32–36.
96. Ibid., 32.

many people in the room. . . . Architecture has to provide a structure in which one is in a community that is not disturbing to others."[97]

What Kubelka, as well as many art world—both gallery and film—critics failed to mention, however, was a similar experiment at the Williamsburg transcineums over a decade earlier. Given Williamsburg's lack of artistic cache compared to AFA, the elision was hardly surprising. Yet the presence of an immersive, attention-focused cinema in two such dissimilar places showed the neutralized cinema's continued investment in bridging the gap between elite and mass art as well as its ongoing interrogation of cinephilia's spatial meaning. Simply being associated with movies meant that, for the first part of the century, the neutralized cinema was tied to popular as opposed to rarified discourses. In using architectural techniques to reframe cinema as a potentially radical art form rather than merely a popular entertainment, however, the neutralized theater also argued for the importance of space in calibrating spectatorship. The space of seeing blueprinted the reception of the object it housed.

In this sense, the neutralized cinema broke new ground for the second wave of cinephilia in the 1950s and 1960s and its attendant fixations on proper viewing and spatial experience. In terms of their relationships to art movements and to architectural modernism, as well as their odd location in a place poised between education and entertainment, the transcineums slipped through multiple cultural spheres. Regarded at once as a novelty, a folly, a beautiful example of modernist architecture, a state-of-the-art theater, and a confounding space in both purpose and design, the transcineums could never find a secure and stable audience. They remain under near-constant threat of removal, their technological marvels outdated, their film slow-paced and overly sincere for jaded audiences, their mystifying design evoking more curiosity than wonder. In addition to their relationship to the high art world, the transcineums also implied a spectatorial interest in the networks stretching among transcendence, motionlessness, and sensory deprivation. Like many other enormous screens of their day, the massive screen they enclose strikes its spectators into a state of both confusion and awe. Blocking the heads of other spectators, preventing movement by refusing to allow aisles between rows, deadening all sound except from the film, and thereby attempting to transport viewers to the profilmic scene, the transcineums proposed a spectatorship of total intellectual projection, total bodily disavowal. Alongside perfected sightlines requiring neither head nor upper body movement, predominant characteristics of earlier neutralized cinemas implied that the transcineums were spaces designed for oblivion. The transcineums vaunted perfected, attentive vision by attempting to block out both other spectators and other senses.

97. Ibid., 34.

The film projected might therefore achieve a sense of harmony with the viewer's perception, resulting in an "optical vacuum" wherein spectator and artwork intertwine in a solitary, disembodied state of communion. Present to the viewer, the film would appear as a total entity, promising revelation and transcendent understanding. Like a monument, the enormous screen suggested the overcoming of temporal and spatial gulfs through awe and solemnity, the halting of time's progression into an accessible fixture in space.

Yet such an undertaking was, at its heart, destined for failure. To make film into a complete entity, Schlanger and the other designers—and, later, Kubelka, as well as creators of IMAX films and other manipulators of what Alison Griffiths has called "the immersive view"—needed to develop a complex perceptual apparatus that could perform the task of effacing itself. In the end, the transcineums were indeed "designed for illusion," although perhaps not quite the illusion Schlanger intended: the illusion of completion, of presence, of aesthetic communion, possible only through a series of tricks and calibrations whose seams and stitches were concealed, a kind of "invisible cinema" in that the cinema, and its audience members, disappeared into the gulf of reverie. Schlanger's dream of "disembodied intellectual abstraction" could be conceived of only through a representative and symbolic embodiment. In citing the work of the body—keeping viewers frozen in place, dulling the other senses, fixing vision on the screen—the transcineums' designers attempted to deny the very physicality to which they appealed. Like many forms of orchestrated presence, the transcineums were most successful in drawing back the veil of purified vision. Behind the perforated metal walls and seamless screen were technology, machinery, and ideology: the cogs, wheels, and work that make up cinematic revelation.

The transcineums and, by extension, aphysical widescreen can therefore be understood as attempts to soothe and to suture, but also to awe, to strike dumb, and to still in order to secure a place for cinema as a category of human experience. Their reach toward perfected vision reveals an alternative history of enlarging screens: visceral immersion not for its own sake, but to deny the body and privilege the eye. By inhabiting the spectator's space, the enormous screen proposed that it was no longer a separate entity, but could fill the entirety of the viewer's visual world. As an opening window, or as a mode of automobilic vision, the wide and high screen of the 1950s served to shift cinema's status from entertainment to art to definition and replication of the world itself. The transcineums' planners dreamt of spectators enraptured and motionless except for their roving eyes, an erasure of the boundary between machine and eye, an eventual replacement of eye with machine, and a liberation of vision from body through a targeted set of objects and experiences. This new cinema was a multifaceted apparatus of built environment, technology, screen, and spectator designed for both illusion and transcendence.

**Insert 1:** Eleazer and Ben Schlanger, 1913. Courtesy Sue Isman.

**Insert 2:** The Paris Theatre, Manhattan, NY, architectural rendering. Charles H. Warner Jr. architectural records, 1940s–1990s, Avery Architectural and Fine Arts Library, Columbia University.

**Insert 3:** Interior transcineum composite image. The Colonial Williamsburg Foundation.

**Insert 4:** "Blue" transcineum. The Colonial Williamsburg Foundation.

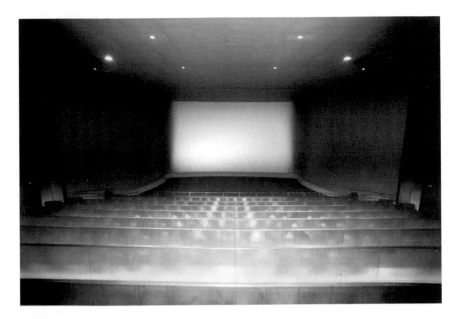

**Insert 5:** "Red" transcineum. The Colonial Williamsburg Foundation.

**Insert 6:** Cinema I & II exterior. Abraham W. Geller architectural records and papers, Avery Architectural and Fine Arts Library, Columbia University.

**Insert 7:** Cinema I & II interior. Abraham W. Geller architectural records and papers, Avery Architectural and Fine Arts Library, Columbia University.

**Insert 8:** *Proliferation of the Sun* and *Blackout*, Black Gate Theater, 1967. Aldo Tambellini Art Foundation.

**Insert 9:** The Paris Theatre, Manhattan, NY, architectural rendering. Charles H. Warner Jr. architectural records, 1940s–1990s, Avery Architectural and Fine Arts Library, Columbia University.

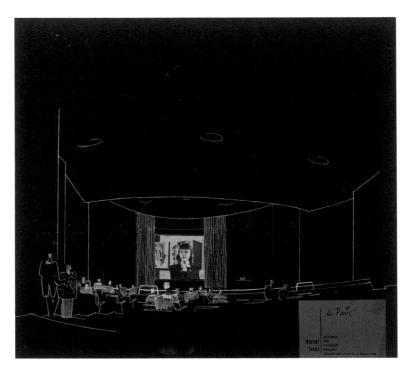

**Insert 10:** The Paris Theatre, Manhattan, NY, architectural rendering. Charles H. Warner Jr. architectural records, 1940s–1990s, Avery Architectural and Fine Arts Library, Columbia University.

**Insert 11:** The Elinor Bunin Munroe Film Center. Film Society of Lincoln Center, Albert Vecerka/Esto.

**Insert 12:** The Elinor Bunin Munroe Film Center. Film Society of Lincoln Center, Albert Vecerka/Esto.

# CHAPTER 4

# Cinephilia in Ruins

*An Audience of the Elite, 1960–1970*

## CINEMA I & II

By the early 1960s, neutralization had been subsumed into general American theatrical style. The neutralized theater's visual traces—directional lighting, lack of ornament, comfortable yet structured seats, perfected sightlines—made for good companions with its conceptual lineage of film as art and theater as temple to attention. Yet along with neutralization's acceptance in the larger exhibition sphere came its uneasy pairing with what would at first glance seem to be outmoded gestures toward opera and the stage. While American art house exhibition at mid-century owed much to neutralization's efforts, the prospect of art and foreign film's profitability as well as a wealthier postwar American populace translated to a reintegration of glamor and luxury into cinematic experience. Art houses of the 1950s and 1960s often included excesses formerly linked to the palace or the stage, such as chandeliers, curtains, and floor-to-ceiling lobby windows; in this sense, the architecture of cinephilia's second wave reinscribed neutralization's debt to capital and represented an uncomfortable denouement. This moment cemented neutralization's artistic and capitalist status, and highlighted the ruins of certain forms of modernization in popular discourse. Meanwhile, underground exhibition, the profitable art house's negative space, sought instead to make something new out of modernization's failures. In the degradation of ruined underground space could be found the potential for a new expression founded on the calculated intertwining of vision, communal experience, and space: the goals of neutralization reworked in an apocalyptic postwar environment. Film exhibition was both high art and ruinous failure, located in the spaces of the cinephilic

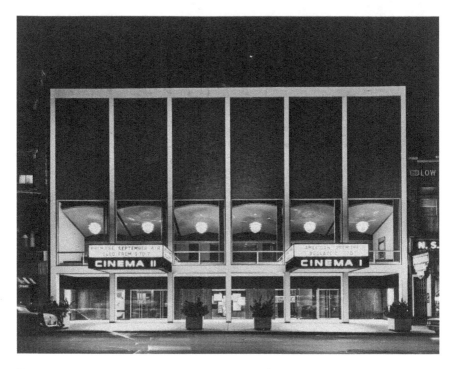

**Figure 4.1:** Cinema I & II exterior. Abraham W. Geller architectural records and papers, Avery Architectural and Fine Arts Library, Columbia University.

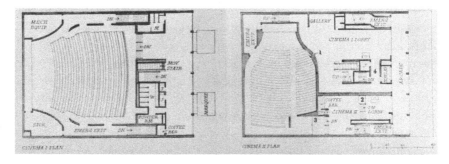

**Figure 4.2:** Cinema I & II plans. Abraham W. Geller architectural records and papers, Avery Architectural and Fine Arts Library, Columbia University.

art house and the enigmatic underground. Together, these two seemingly opposed places trace the legacy of neutralization, ideal spectatorship, and contemplation in the era of moving imagery through the 1960s and point toward exhibition's twenty-first-century avenues.

In June of 1962, Abraham Geller and Ben Schlanger's award-winning Cinema I & II opened on Third Avenue at Sixtieth Street in New York City (Figures 4.1, 4.2, and 4.3). The first official twin cinema in the country as well as the first completely new movie house built in Manhattan in three decades,

**Figure 4.3:** Cinema I & II artichoke chandelier. Abraham W. Geller architectural records and papers, Avery Architectural and Fine Arts Library, Columbia University.

Cinema I & II represented two linked phenomena: the emergence of the multiplex and the second wave of cinephilia in the late 1950s and 1960s in the United States.[1] In an example of the burgeoning profitability of art film, the country's first multiscreen theater was built expressly for the purpose of showing foreign imports and other "intellectual" fare. Considerable funding was sunk into the project, which implied the level of probable audience sophistication and expectation and therefore owner Donald Rugoff's anticipated financial returns.[2] Cinema I's auditorium sat 750, while Cinema II sat 300; the cost per seat was over $1,000, twice the average for new theater construction at the time.[3] As the first open-façade theater space in New York City, Cinema I & II's entire second floor was open to view from Third Avenue, "resulting in a foyer reminiscent in character and proportions of that of the Opera in

1. 5-D Master, 1962–1964, Abraham Geller Collection, Box 2:51, Photographs, Cinema I & II, Manhattan, NY, Avery Architectural and Fine Arts Library, Columbia University.
2. Twin theaters would begin dotting the nation, particularly in suburban locales, during the early 1960s alongside drive-ins. See Christofer Meissner, "A Revolutionary Concept in Screen Entertainment: The Emergence of the Twin Movie Theatre, 1962–1964," *Post Script* 30, no. 3 (Summer 2011): 64–65.
3. "Twin Cinemas: Flexible Showcase for Films," *Architectural Forum*, September 1962, 120–124.

Paris."[4] A covered arcade ran the length of the theater's front, where vitrines showed not "the customary posters . . . [but] three-dimensional constructs similar to those used in department-store display windows (Insert 6)."[5] Stairs flanked either side of the larger upper auditorium, with a sloped platform at the front leading to the screen.

Perforated aluminum coated the walls inside both auditoriums, while the front slope and walls were covered in vinyl (Insert 7). As in the Williamsburg transcineums, the metal draping the auditorium walls reflected light from the screen and illumination between show times, creating an atmosphere of elegant otherworldliness.[6] Vinyl coverings visually suggested a screen extending past its own boundaries, "wall-to-wall," moving into the space of the audience, while a lack of additional lighting meant patrons' eyes would "automatically focus on the screen."[7] Acoustical tile ceiling suspensions hung down from the ceiling for nonreverberative sound. Cinema I & II's combination of luxurious surroundings and piety toward cinema encouraged the association of film with fine art, nights out, bright city life, and quotidian escapism that cemented domestic entertainment's incommensurability with the theater; according to press at the time, Cinema I & II's approach possessed an "interior glamorous enough to woo the public away from the home television."[8] In addition to its elegant decor, the structure offered free coffee in lounges that doubled as art galleries. Described in the pages of *Architectural Forum*, Cinema I & II was at once operatic and modern, chic and neutralized:

> Except for the copper chandeliers, all lighting is recessed and surrounded with a gold metallic lining which gives the light a warm, pleasant quality. Once inside the theaters themselves, the simplicity of the gray perforated metal walls and acoustical tile ceiling focuses attention on the wall-to-wall screen. The neutral, curving side walls eliminate harsh contrasts and form a subtle relationship with the movie by reflecting the light intensities as they change on the screen. Curtains and old-fashioned black frames have been eliminated and the picture actually blends into the walls, although black ribbons can be lowered from the

4. Press Release, Joe Wolhandler, Public Relations, 15 April 1962, Box 3:1, Folder Public Relations, 1961–1989, Abraham Geller Collection, Avery Architectural and Fine Arts Library, Columbia University.

5. Ibid.

6. Schlanger would decorate many of his late 1950s and 1960s cinemas with metal walls, including the Shoppers' Haven, which opened in Pompano Beach in 1960. Robert A. Mitchell, "Glamourizing the Screen Part 2: Masking the Modern Screen," *International Projectionist* 38, no. 10 (October 1963): 4–6.

7. "New York Theatres Offer Novel Solution for Continuous Seating," *International Projectionist* 37, no. 7 (July 1962): 10.

8. "Two-in-One Art Movie," *Interiors Magazine*, November 1962, Abraham Geller Collection, Box 1:33, Files Large Projects, 1962, Avery Architectural and Fine Arts Library, Columbia University.

ceiling to frame narrow-screen films. Colored lights take the place of curtains during intermissions. Architect Schlanger has placed his screens only 54 inches from the floor, which was carefully inclined so that sight lines are direct, and the audience does not have to watch at an uncomfortable upward angle.[9]

In Cinema I, a continental seating plan allowed for aisles only on the left and right side of the theater with nothing cutting cut through the rows in the middle. Artist Ilya Bolotowsky painted a 45' x 2' mural along the rear wall of Cinema I's ground-floor lobby, while additional sculptures by Stephanie Scuris, artworks by Sewell Stillman, marquee lettering by Norman Ives, and black marble slab coffee tables designed by Geller contributed to an atmosphere of enlightened high art. In his *New York Times* review of *Boccaccio '70*, the first film shown at the theater, Bosley Crowther described the movie's qualities of "glamour, sophistication, color, wit and sensuality (not necessarily in that order), all of which blend very well in the enveloping air of a facility that is to be devoted to the showing of sophisticated films."[10] Here, not just any film blended into a neutralized theatrical space. In keeping with the lessons learned at Williamsburg, Cinema I & II's architecture melded with high-caliber, prestige, and international film product. The movies that blended into the screen surround required similar gestures toward sophistication and refinement in order to equal the effects of the auditorium space.

All in all, Cinema I & II promised a theater for serious moviegoers intent on sophisticated filmic fare *and* on the accoutrements assumed to go along with it: a complete cultural experience encompassing theater, lobby for socializing, art gallery, and café. Despite the luxurious lounge and lobby space, however, Cinema I & II's auditorium interiors were decidedly neutralized, decorated with nothing but the aforementioned perforated aluminum on the walls and vinyl around the screen. Once the lights went down, the film was the centerpiece of the theater. At this particular moment in exhibition, sumptuous houses for cinema were far from the norm; as Mary Morley Cohen notes in her history of drive-ins, "[T]owards the end of the 1950s and early 1960s, it became increasingly clear that the film industry as a whole was moving away from deluxe theatres—both picture palaces and drive-ins—and towards the smaller and cheaper theatre in the mall."[11] Yet since the mid-1950s, art film had secured a substantial foothold in the United States, particularly as an alternative to home television entertainment, and exhibitors sensed its potential for increasing profits through aspirational markets. Art film encapsulated

9. "Twin Cinemas," 122.

10. Bosley Crowther, "Screen: Three Samplings from Italy," *New York Times*, June 27, 1962, Abraham Geller Collection, Box 1:39, Files Large Projects 1962, Avery Architectural and Fine Arts Library, Columbia University.

11. Mary Morley Cohen, "Forgotten Audiences in the Passion Pits: Drive-In Theatres and Changing Spectator Practices in Post-War America," *Film History* 6 (1994): 483.

the tensions always present in cinema; for John Twomey in 1956, "the film is an economic unit governed by the practices of our capitalistic economy. On the other hand, and seemingly in conflict with its economic nature, a motion picture is the creation of artists. A third element, public taste, must also be considered in any analysis of a film or film type."[12] As a result, the art house presented a particular puzzle for exhibition: should its theater be sumptuous as an opera house, intimate as a little cinema, or something else entirely?

With the construction of Cinema I & II in New York, the Rugoff chain hedged its bets on an audience invested in a spectatorship of elite experience and a lush environment of cultivated connoisseurship. Such an approach to cinematic artistry was tied tightly to conspicuous consumption. The larger appeal of a theater like Cinema I & II was located both in functionality and accessories such as luxurious copper chandeliers surrounded in gold metallic lining and floor-to-ceiling windows in the second-floor lobby that promised the kind of audience visibility associated with opera and the ballet. In this way, Cinema I & II proposed not only a purified visibility of the film in the auditorium, but also a visibility of the *audience*. Suspended above the street level, ticket purchasers mingled on a glass-enclosed and dramatically lit stage floating over Third Avenue. Described above in Joe Wolhandler's press release, the effect was intended to suggest a modern opera house, where audiences would similarly go to see and to be seen: visible both to itself and to others, the audience was identified and marked by its excellent taste.[13] Cinema I & II may have been a neutralized house, but it also exemplified a more significant partnership between neutralization and glamor. While the second wave of cinephilia ensured film's status as art, the greatest example of its widespread success was its intertwining of art with capital. And exhibitors such as Donald Rugoff stood to profit handsomely from the combination.

With Rugoff-esque managers and multiple new import/art film theaters dotting the scene, the 1960s saw the relative completion of the neutralized cinema's work: film was an essential part of an artistic network of rarefication, aesthetics, contemplation, and money. Past the widescreen revolution of the 1950s and its need for close attention to optics, proper sightlines and func-tional design had infiltrated the exhibition scene en masse. Partially, the ur-gency with which neutralization was invested in the 1930s through the 1950s

12. Twomey also explained that the rise of film libraries, documentary film techniques, elimination of trade monopolies, and new postwar import availability were all indicators of a mid-century exhibition need for art house theaters. John E. Twomey, "Some Considerations on the Rise of the Art-Film Theater," *The Quarterly of Film Radio and Television* 10, no. 3 (Spring 1956): 241.

13. Exhibitors courted this image of the art house patron as well-to-do, educated, en-lightened, and intellectual, partially also to avoid censorship of "adult" films. See Barbara Wilinsky, "A Thinly Disguised Art Veneer Covering a Filthy Sex Picture: Discourses on Art Houses in the 1950s," *Film History* 8, no. 2 (1996): 143–158.

had simply fallen away; while the 1920s saw a major boom in theatrical construction, extensive building stalled from the Depression until well into the 1950s.[14] Theaters were, of course, designed and built during those decades, but not nearly as prolifically as during the palace era or the economic boom time of the later mid-century. By 1966, there were increasing "signs of renewed vigor. The popularity of 'the movies' has been rekindled with the construction of comfortable new theatres in suburban locations."[15] George A. Brehm, theater operator in Baltimore, observed that "'the lean days have passed, and amusement seekers are finding fresh entertainment in the wide screen and methods of modern projection.' New residential communities around shopping centers and elimination of parking problems also contribute to the patronage of the modern theatre."[16] In Brehm's Westview Cinema (Fenton & Lichtig, 1966), markers of suburban American wealth festooned the foyer with luxury: a pool, a statue, and ceiling-high windows greeted audiences with reference to boom times, while a VIP party room included stereo sound and Heywood-Wakefield rocking chairs. Suburbanization in the 1960s, and consequent movement of theaters to malls and other areas outside urban locales, meant that exhibition embraced a role as both the new luxury provider and as less a community center than an area of relaxation.

Coinciding with cinematic suburbanization, exhibitors saw postwar audiences as both sources of increasing profits and individuals ready to be seduced by lovely theatrical spaces. Robert K. Tankersley, president of the Theatre Equipment Dealers Association, urged exhibitors to greet the "new movie world" in the following way:

> Today, with all of the new recreations that have come to fill the extra hours of our shortened workday week, movies not only have to be *special* to lure our patrons away from boats, cameras, trips, painting, hunting, fishing, skiing, etc., but the films that are exhibited also must be *special*. We must lure the tired businessman from the television set. We must entice the youngsters from the discotheque. We must take away the housewife from her brood—with cunning, ingenuity,

14. The year 1953 saw the end of a two-year ban on new theater construction, including exhibitors' new ability to use five tons of steel and five hundred pounds of copper per quarter and the removal of limitations on foreign and used steel in general (*Boxoffice*, January 3, 1953, *Modern Theatres* section, 7). Enhanced grosses throughout 1953 led to dramatically increased modernization efforts in 1954 (Lester Rees, "Theatre Modernization Hits Rapid Pace," *Boxoffice*, January 9, 1954, *Modern Theatres* section, 8), while by 1956 theater modernization was up by 104 percent ("104% Increase in Updating of Theatres in Late 1956," *Boxoffice*, January 5, 1957, *Modern Theatres* section, 11).
15. "Kodak Has Best Year in '65; 'Renewed Vigor' in Theatre Attendance, Building Noted," *Boxoffice*, March 21, 1966, *Modern Theatres* section, 18.
16. George B. Browning, "New De Luxe Westview Cinema for Baltimore," *Boxoffice*, January 17, 1966, *Modern Theatres* section, 12.

and forethought. We must offer these segments of our society a kind of comfort and beauty they can get nowhere else. . . . The patron . . . must be treated with the same grace and hospitality as though you were entertaining him in your own home. If he were your guest, you would naturally give him a drink of his choice or food that you know he likes. You would offer him the most comfortable seat in your livingroom. You would cater to his wants and his needs. . . . Let us advertise our films in a way that will woo the patron. Let us look long and hard at the new generation and try to fathom its likes and dislikes.[17]

Compared to earlier efforts at making all audiences into interchangeable beings, exhibition in the 1960s saw value in responding to the individualized needs of each type of viewer. Rather than unification into an assembly line of spectatorial machinery, the theater of the 1960s sought to provide for the individual's desires in order to bring him back to the movies. Neutralization's insistence on a spectatorship of surrender with the viewer rendered motionless by the power of the film held less appeal when so many other forms of recreation were available.

In terms of theater design, "modern" and "functional" were far more mainstream in the postwar era, resulting in a larger incorporation of neutralization techniques in the American movie theater. Still, "functionalism" implied only the architectural style of neutralization—neutralization's investment in community, bodily disavowal, and presence as concepts were not included in functionalism's implications. Although the austerity and simplicity embraced by the neutralized auditorium essentially became the norm throughout mainstream exhibition by the 1960s, partially as a result of economic changes, neutralization as a spectatorial ideal began to dissipate. Comfort, glamor, and individual attention trumped immersion, contemplation, and community in popular 1960s spectatorship. Changes in the structure of Hollywood's production had similarly begun to affect exhibition's footprint. In 1960, Schlanger identified three types of films indicative of current climates: the "block buster," which "can be financially successful in individual instances, but do not necessarily build a firm foundation for a broadly successful art and industry"; the "Art Film," which can provide profits only for a limited number of theaters; and "one that provides quality production for exhibition in a great number of theatres with high exhibition standards."[18] Of these categories, the somewhat disingenuously described third was clearly that which interested Schlanger: nonspecific but wide-ranging in appeal, able to bring in multiple audiences and adhere to the needs of the exhibition footprint. Still, the art film

17. Robert K. Tankersley, "'Get With It . . . !' It's A New Movie World!" *Boxoffice*, April 22, 1968, *Modern Theatres* section, 35–36 (emphasis original).
18. Ben Schlanger, "Theatres for a Popular Art," *Motion Picture Herald*, July 12, 1960, *Better Theatres* section, 128.

became the most appealing for an architect of neutralization. Although the art house theater of the 1960s was hardly an austere space, filled instead like a salon with chandeliers, sculpture, and murals, art cinema encouraged a contemplative and attentive cinephilia that held significant sway with Schlanger.

Cinema I & II delivered on the 1960s art house promise: an entire experience of tastefulness and elegance, where audience members could be seen entering a space that denoted taste, luxury, and sophistication. Vision and being visible found partnership in the high-class mid-century art house cinema. Such a balance between the visible and visibility resonated deeply with Debordian theories of the spectacle where the unification of subject and object through visible social relationships was precisely the goal of capitalism: "The spectacle presents itself simultaneously as all of society, as part of society, and as *instrument of unification. . . .* The spectacle is not a collection of images, but a social relation among people, mediated by images."[19] The society of the spectacle results in the illusion of unity as a system of production, commodification, and capital; the viewer becomes the consumer who consumes illusions. In this sense, the art house was both product of Debord's society of the spectacle and representative of what Tony Bennett has described as the "exhibitionary complex."[20] For Bennett, an alignment of order with culture resulted in a populace that saw themselves as the delivery mechanisms of regulation. Architectural imbrications of power and knowledge, particularly in museum display, encouraged the public to voluntarily submit to versions of what Foucault recognized in the prison system. Yet Bennett identifies a farther-reaching phenomenon—one where a mass audience, not just the incarcerated, entwine themselves into power's networks of knowledge. Art house exhibition therefore maintained and extended a complex of vision, authority, and visibility from earlier forms of neutralization as part of a culture of self-surveillance.

Foucault, Debord, and Bennett consider architectures and optical technologies that reiterate vision's place as the most privileged and abstracted sense, reflecting in turn the abstraction that capitalism performs upon society at large. Much like the neutralized cinema, power's structures insist upon vision as the primary sense for calibrating cultural experience, and on the usefulness of mediations—film, camera, screen, even seating patterns—for calculating the status of vision. Whereas purification of vision in the Williamsburg transcineums encouraged patriotism, here it functioned to indoctrinate the subject into modern capitalism—which are, of course, complementary categories. In the art house cinema of the 1960s, ritzy decoration and attention to markers of wealth in addition to a focus on film as high art

19. Guy Debord, *Society of the Spectacle* (Detroit: Black & Red, 2000), 3–4 (emphasis original).
20. Tony Bennett, "The Exhibitionary Complex," *New Formations* no. 4 (Spring 1988): 73–102.

resulted in what Barbara Wilinsky describes as "the conflicting view on art houses as sites of prestigious culture and as camouflages for purely economic interests."[21] The art house therefore promised fantasies of upward mobility for middle-brow taste cultures and the middle class, and promoted both the democratization of high art for anyone who could pay admission as well as an illusion of differentiation for its patrons from the less enlightened masses.

For Antoine Compagnon, ambivalence toward the public defines the border between modernity and modernism.[22] Art cinema exhibition in the 1960s depended upon similar tensions between mass and elite culture, as had film in general since its inception.[23] In elegant import houses like Cinema I & II, the elitism of the opera house held sway; one could feel like a theatergoer, richer, perhaps, at least in cultural capital, than one necessarily was. Comparatively, the 1960s and 1970s underground cinema was a darker and more enigmatic place, but one still invested in spatial divisions between elite and mass culture. Both kinds of theaters sought to differentiate themselves from the typical Hollywood product: one with sophisticated French and Italian fare, and one with experimental films or happenings. In turn, both differentiated themselves from the hoi polloi. Yet in the art house, the masses were welcomed under the auspices of becoming part of an exclusive audience, while in the underground cinema, scarcity, spontaneity, and singular happenings meant that the general public was necessarily excluded from most of the events. Rarefication was, ironically, in some ways more at work in the makeshift underground world than the high art import cinema, where the difficulty of finding the space and of knowing when and where to attend an event resulted in an elitism of cultural rather than economic capital. In neither space, however, could the neutralized aesthetic properly find a home: not in its last gasps in the art house, with excellent sight lines and projection and a democratic approach to exhibition, but also nods toward the rich decoration formerly associated with the palace, nor in the underground, with its spaces lacking in comfort, perfected optics, and the clean clinical lines of well-funded functional minimalism, but with confounding avant-garde productions and subcultural attitudes not easily digested by the majority of film audiences.

Beyond economic dictates, however, the art house and the underground shed light on the decline of certain aspects of the neutralized cinema as well as its ongoing legacy. First, they proposed two linked pathways for cinephilic film culture in the wake of one of cinema's many deaths. After the breakup of the studio system following the 1948 Paramount Decision and the failure

---

21. Wilinsky, "A Thinly Disguised Art Veneer," 144.
22. Antoine Compagnon, *The Five Paradoxes of Modernity*, trans. Franklin Philip (New York: Columbia University Press, 1994), 29.
23. See Lee Grieveson, *Policing Cinema: Movies and Censorship in Early-Twentieth-Century America* (Berkeley: University of California Press, 2004).

of widescreen to fulfill its promise of total immersive cinema, these two theatrical forms rose from what could be considered cinema's ruins into new possibilities for seeing. Both the art house and the underground also promoted space's primacy for shaping spectatorial seeing. Both structures sought out metaphors that would shape cinematic views—even outside of cinema—for the later decades of the twentieth century and into the twenty-first. The art house, with its pristine lighting, a position often above ground, and sleek modern lines, reflected a mid-century image of space-age utopia, a stylish rocket ship promising the hopes of a new future, a progressive global cinema, and an upward trajectory in terms of both spatial structure and its audience members' hopes for jetting through social, cultural, and economic classes. The underground, with its often-temporary facilities, its termite-like burrowing into the earth, and its fixation on scavenging rarity, evoked a culture saturated with images of the atom bomb and the need to shelter from it. Yet its elusive locations, its make-do approach, and its reverence for filmic, televisual, and video media also unveiled the beginnings of gallery film culture and moving imagery's place in the pantheon of high art. Both art house and underground signified a ruin of film and American popular culture to ferment new approaches to what repeatedly seemed (and still seems) a dying form. And both sustained the central tension of neutralization: how ideology undergirds the ideal optical conditions of the seamless viewing apparatus.

## THE ART HOUSE, NEW YORK, AND URBAN RENEWAL

In the late 1940s, American exhibition fostered a resurgence of interest in international film. The beginning of this second wave of cinephilia crested in the wake of global distribution made possible by the end of the war and booming film cultures abroad. In addition, new difficulties faced by smaller theaters in obtaining Hollywood product, including major antitrust activities in the wake of the Paramount Decision and decreased export business, meant that management was forced to look elsewhere for films to fill their calendars.[24] Alongside changing attitudes toward taste in mid-century America, where entertainment choice and sophistication substituted for economic differentiations, art house and European cinema provided both members of the middle class and nonmainstream theaters with a method for distinguishing themselves from their peers and/or competitors.[25] Given the appeal of taste for making audiences feel part of a highly refined clique, exhibitors latched onto global product as a way to attract the post-1946 "lost audience" back into theaters.

24. Barbara Wilinsky, *Sure Seaters: The Emergence of Art House Cinema* (Minneapolis: University of Minnesota Press, 2001), 67–70.
25. Ibid., 82.

By the end of the 1940s and beginning of the 1950s, the art house phenomenon was well established in urban areas and college towns across the country. But at the end of the 1950s, from about 1957 to 1958, attendance slumped, causing some to wonder if the art house craze had effectively run its course. Some distributors speculated that first-run theaters were dipping too eagerly into the market by showing "quality" and foreign films, thereby preventing the art house from distinguishing itself from the pack.[26] Concurrently, the erosion of the Production Code's stranglehold on American film production and the loosening of censorship's grips meant that Hollywood's output could compete with European cinema's famously sexy sensationalism. Yet into the 1960s, art house theaters continued to expand across the United States; while only five were in operation in Los Angeles in 1957, that number increased to twenty-six by 1962.[27]

The mid-1950s and then the 1960s proved to be a boom time for art house exhibition in many parts of the United States. New York City, however, saw the largest escalation; before 1950, 40 percent of the country's art houses were located within its boroughs.[28] In January of 1962, *International Projectionist* declared the early 1960s a "new art house boom in New York City," noting that four out of six new theaters in development were art houses, with six new screens ranging from three hundred to nine hundred seats set to open that year alone. Among these, two theaters, Cinema I & II and the Walter Reade Coronet atop the Baronet, had two screens each.[29] Others in the building process included the New Town Theatre at Fifty-Fifth and Ninth, the Lincoln Art Theatre at Fifty-Seventh and Seventh, and a Loews at Seventy-Second and Third. In addition to their location in New York, the addresses of these theaters demonstrated the art house's connection to bourgeois mystique. Each one was in Upper Manhattan on both the East and West sides. And each one was planned during the Rockefeller-funded construction of cultural mecca Lincoln Center at 10 Lincoln Plaza on the Upper West Side.

Lincoln Center, for which ground was broken in 1955, was not only an icon of New York's cultural dominance; it was a major achievement of city planner and political stalwart Robert Moses and his program of city renewal from the late 1940s through the 1960s. Moses, a controversial figure with considerable power to reshape the city during his tenure in multiple municipal positions, oversaw a staggering array of projects, from playgrounds and parklands to tunnels, civic centers, and zoos. But Moses's most notorious effort was to transform the city into one of transit—transit particularly

---

26. "Art Circuit Disappearing?," *International Projectionist* 32, no. 3 (March 1957): 37.
27. Wilinsky, *Sure Seaters*, 132.
28. Ibid., 106.
29. "New Art House Boom in New York City," *International Projectionist* 37, no. 1 (January 1962): 17.

marked by its suitability for automobile and truck traffic. Under Moses's influence, New York saw the construction of such massive, defining projects as the Triborough Bridge, the Brooklyn Battery Tunnel, the Verrazano Narrows Bridge, and the West Side Highway, all of which contributed to the nearly seven hundred miles of road added under Moses's watch.[30] In the late 1940s, Moses also oversaw construction of the Headquarters of the United Nations, a project that, according to mayor William O'Dwyer, "was the one great thing that would make New York the center of the world."[31] When the Headquarters opened in 1952, Ben Schlanger's seating design graced the General Assembly Hall.[32]

Robert Caro's biography *The Power Broker: Robert Moses and the Fall of New York*, first published in 1974, shaped contemporary understanding of Moses's impact on New York and, by extension, large swathes of the American urban landscape. In it, Caro describes Moses's obsession with a car-centric culture. While expressways were planned throughout the country in the mid-1940s, they remained unrealized—except in New York. There, Moses began work on six expressways directly after World War II. By 1956, the federal Interstate Highway Act placed the rest of the country in lockstep with New York, due in no small part to Moses's involvement.[33] Alongside his dogged insistence on the need to remake the country into a pathway for the automobile, Moses stridently refused significant investment in public transportation, even as New York became increasingly ensnarled in gridlock and pollution. Such harsh pragmatism underscored many of the cruelties of his work: between 1946 and 1953, hundreds of thousands of New York residents were evicted to clear land for Moses's projects.[34]

While Lewis Mumford declared Moses's influence on the twentieth-century American city "greater than that of any other person," Moses was far from alone in his pursuit of urban transformation.[35] The federal government decided in 1949 to focus on urban renewal as a solution to housing difficulties. Under Moses, New York functioned in large part as a laboratory for the implementation of this approach.[36] And it was in this context of city investment in building and public transformation centered on profitability and motor

30. "Robert Moses," The New York Preservation Archive Project, accessed May 5, 2017, http://www.nypap.org/preservation-history/robert-moses/.
31. Robert Caro, *The Power Broker: Robert Moses and the Fall of New York* (New York: Vintage, 1975), 771.
32. "Editorial Feature: The Accomplishments of Ben Schlanger, Architect," *Theatre Catalog* (Philadelphia, PA: Jay Emanuel Publications, 1953–1954), xxxii.
33. Caro, *The Power Broker*, 11.
34. Ibid., 7.
35. Ibid., 12.
36. Ibid.

transportation that the second wave of cinephilia underwent its most evident physical manifestation.

One of Moses's legacies was the group of so-called Moses's Men, a vast array of administrators, architects, designers, and engineers, many of whom Moses patronized prior to the full establishment of their careers. Moses turned frequently to the same contingent of workers to help redesign his better New York. Among Moses's advisors and builders was famed modernist architect Wallace K. Harrison, at whose estate in Long Island Moses was a frequent guest.[37] Harrison's firm with Max Abramovitz (Harrison & Abramovitz) was active in New York from 1941 to 1976; among their massive projects were Avery Fisher Hall and the Metropolitan Opera House at Lincoln Center, the United Nations Dag Hammerskjöld Library Building, multiple functional modernist corporate office buildings on the East Coast and in the Midwest, and, in the mid-1950s, the new Information Center at Colonial Williamsburg. Harrison and Abramovitz frequently worked with Schlanger. Under Abramovitz's aegis, Schlanger was brought on board to design the transcineums at Colonial Williamsburg, as well as seating plans for the UN and the Met. Through their patronage and collaboration, Schlanger's neutralized approach melded with corporate modernism, the country's urban building boom, and cinema's enmeshment with motor transport to generate a higher brow cinephilic project of capitalist renewal and automobilic viewing.

New York during the art house building boom in the late 1950s and early 1960s was a city in transition: a microcosm of the postwar American architectural experiment, a site of furious debate regarding proper usage of public space, and an example of widespread investment in the age of the automobile and its required connective tissues of bridges, highways, and expressways. It is hardly surprising that new art houses sprang up so rapidly, particularly close to sophisticated addresses on Manhattan's Upper West and East Sides near one of Moses's brightest urban gems: Lincoln Center, with its modernist paeans to the most exalted of performing arts such as symphonies and operas. Such geographical proximity made sense for the development of taste cultures; the refined and sophisticated image of the European picture and American art film certainly appealed to audiences also likely to attend the ballet. City space was constantly at a premium, with few new central locations available for development. Yet many art house cinemas shared another interest of New York urban development: the new vision of public spaces as open, multileveled, grand, and accessible via car.

Cinema I & II was planned specifically to cater to a wealthy audience as evidenced by its position among a group of newer, expensive apartment buildings. Thousands of high-income families who "read books, see plays,

37. "Wallace K. Harrison Estate/SchappacherWhite," *Arch Daily*, December 15, 2010, http://www.archdaily.com/95780/wk-harrison-estate-schappacherwhite.

and can afford to—and do—pay a premium to see foreign and domestic films of high quality in a comfortable, well-appointed theatre" lived in the area.[38] The location of this "jewel" of the Rugoff empire was 1001 Third Avenue between Fifty-Ninth and Sixtieth Streets, just three blocks from the Queensboro Bridge and from the East River Drive/Franklin Delano Roosevelt Drive—one of Moses's early projects. At Fifty-First Street, FDR Drive enters the Sutton Place Tunnel where it winds under apartment buildings until Sixtieth Street; multiple older apartment buildings and homes were razed to accommodate the design. Cinema I & II sat quite close to the Fifty-Ninth Street/Lexington Avenue subway station and alongside the aforementioned preponderance of luxurious buildings, but also in a convenient location for drivers coming west from Queens or even Long Island for a sophisticated evening at the cinema. In 1962, the year the theater opened, Moses was planning to construct a two-thousand-car parking garage at the Manhattan end of the Queensboro Bridge. On top of this garage would be a seven-story department store leased to Macy's.[39] While this plan, which would have required the demolition of a full square block of existing buildings, never came to fruition, it would have funneled audiences of drivers directly into the city for shopping, eating, drinking, mingling, and film viewing, followed by an unceremonious exit via the very bridge by which they entered. In effect, Cinema I & II stood poised in a perfect location to profit from Robert Moses's transformation of New York City into a playground for corporations and the wealthy automobile owner. The democratization of the neutralized cinema would be complete: immersion into the great American dream of individuated transportation, highway travel, expansion, and consumption.

"New theatres are open houses," declared a *Boxoffice* survey of recently constructed buildings in 1962.[40] Among the theaters featured was the Cinema in Menlo Park, New Jersey, where Schlanger consulted, as well as the Cheltenham. A photo of the Cheltenham, which was located in a shopping center near Philadelphia, showed a marquee announcing Sophia Loren in *Two Women*, demonstrating its allegiance to the art house's erudite sheen; the theater's advertised features included parking for five thousand cars and a pearl-coated screen.[41] Both the Cheltenham and the Cinema included multiple-story glass façades, while the Cinema, one of ten shopping center theaters planned by General Drive-In Corp, displayed changing art exhibits with specially constructed room dividers. Each of the Cinema's buildings was

38. "Two Theatres in Two-Level Building Set for New York," *Harrison's Reports*, March 25, 1961, 48.

39. Caro, *The Power Broker*, 742.

40. "New Theatres Are 'Open' Houses," *Boxoffice*, October 22, 1962, 20–21.

41. Ad for the Cheltenham, *Philadelphia Inquirer*, August 31, 1961, http://fultonhistory. com/Newspapers%2023/Philadelphia%20PA%20Inquirer/Philadelphia%20PA%20 Inquirer%201961/Philadelphia%20PA%20Inquirer%201961%20a%20-%205886.pdf.

designed to showcase modern architecture, pristine projection and presentation, and luxe furnishings in an automobile-accessible setting.[42] On-site parking was augmented by facilities at the Menlo Park Regional Shopping Center next door, while the location on Route 1 and proximity to the Garden State Parkway and New Jersey Turnpike meant a steady stream of drivers hastened to the theater.

Like Cinema I & II and the raft of art house and other cinemas opening in the 1960s, the Cinema and the Cheltenham celebrated taste in all its mid-century American implications: chicness, education, art and design, and financial means. As in other buildings inspirational for the times, like Mies van der Rohe's Farnsworth House, the theaters engaged an inside-outside aesthetic exemplified by significant use of glass. As Anne Friedberg explains, glass in modernist architecture developed alongside changes in screen shape and philosophical deployment, which indicated a tension between transparency and opacity, between faithful and virtual view.[43] In keeping with her findings, glass here served a dual purpose: first, an obvious aesthetic reiteration of other modernist architecture, but second, a way to enable wealthy patrons to be recognized as wealthy by virtue of their attendance at sophisticated cinemas. If the auditoriums inside were as darkened as possible to promote immersion, the lobbies and façades were as transparent as possible to allow visitors to be admired from the streets outside. Such admiration cannily made the theaters into a circuit of desire: to view jealously from outside, to pay one's admission to gain entrance, to walk up to a second-floor lobby, to be viewed from outside by the jealous passersby on the street. Yet all that separated patron from outside observer was merely the price of a ticket. The glamorous neutralized art house of the 1960s, then, was a signal of transportation: from highway to theater and from parking lot to lobby, and through the illusion of upward class mobility achieved via the relatively low price of an evening at the movies.

## RUINS, ABOVE AND BELOW

The art house hardly represented the first link between the movies and economics. But its luxurious physical attributes—rich fabrics, tasteful modernist design, painting and sculpture exhibitions, artichoke chandeliers, and sparkling glass façades—put these associations on heightened display. Most of these cinemas, particularly those designed by Schlanger, included precise

42. "A Beautiful Showcase for Menlo Park," *Boxoffice*, January 8, 1962, 4–6.
43. See Anne Friedberg, *The Virtual Window: From Alberti to Microsoft* (Cambridge, MA: MIT Press, 2006).

focus on good viewing, projection, and sound, but most also tended toward pairing these operations with additional attractions: eating, drinking, driving, and shopping. In this sense, they expanded the project of neutralization past the boundaries of film and into the shaping of a larger American consciousness that bound vision, automobile travel, and art into a spiraling force of consumer desire. Mid-century American democratic spectatorship meant entry into a democratic vision of utopia for purchase.

This is not to say that Schlanger's project was something pure prior to this moment, but rather that it aided in marking cinephilia as another facet of conspicuous consumption alongside art-collecting or wine-drinking. The art house and its use of neutralization's dominant attributes—sightlines, streamlining, excellent aural and sonic experience—therefore represented a kind of cinephilic ruin, in that it evacuated certain aspects of its meaning and suspended it between emergence and decay. The luxury of the early 1960s art house diminished one kind of cinephilic ideal (all chairs with good sightlines; technologies of immersion) and inflated another (movie admission as a ticket to upward mobility; the immediate uplift of being seen on a second-floor story through glass). Paired with the visualized ruins of the underground art cinema, the above-ground neutralized art house can be understood as a moment of cinephilia in ruins: the decay of one mode of being, and the birth of another.

Julia Hell and Andreas Schönle explain that while our current conception of ruins as aesthetic objects valuable for contemplation has been available since the secularization of Western society, material traces of the past resonate especially in modernity. Such residues add to an "ambivalent sense of time," where the ruin embodies both unapproachable lost meaning and that meaning's vacuum.[44] The ruin's manifold structure, its confusion between past and present, its depth of and evacuation of meaning, and its layers of temporality, space, and aesthetic purpose make it a powerful totem of twentieth-century temporality. For Georg Simmel, the ruin offered a sense of equilibrium and stability compared to the typical constant movement of aesthetic perception. The ruin's "profound peace" proposed a balance between the progression and fulfillment, or construction and decay, that permeates all artistic work: "The aesthetic value of the ruin combines the disharmony, the eternal becoming of the soul struggling against itself, with the satisfaction of form, the firm limitedness, of the work of art . . . the present form of a past life, not according to the contents or remnants of that life, but according to its past as such."[45] Ruins are a path between past and present and offer visual

44. Julia Hell and Andreas Schönle, introduction to *Ruins of Modernity*, ed. Julia Hell and Andreas Schönle (Durham, NC: Duke University Press, 2010), 5–6.
45. Georg Simmel, "The Ruin," reprinted in *Ruins*, ed. Brian Dillon (London: Whitechapel Gallery; Cambridge, MA: MIT Press, 2011), 24.

comfort to the viewer unmoored by the opposition between the movement of progress and the stasis of form. For Simmel, the value of ruins for the modern spectator was to soothe sensory spatiotemporal experience into something unified, or at least still.

Beyond a fixation with "authentic" ruins, modernism and postmodernism alike have consistently returned to ruins as a philosophical concept useful for articulating their missions and desires. Upon encountering the ruins of the Parthenon, Le Corbusier found himself overwhelmed, returning every day for three weeks to sketch rather than photograph. The crumbling pieces of classical beauty proved both daunting and inspiring, eventually clarifying his desire to create buildings in the perfectionist and mechanistic model of his Greco-Roman ancestors.[46] Andreas Huyssen, referencing Lyotard, argues that the modernist obsession with ruins has resulted in a projection of modernity's fixation on asynchronous time; the building in decay stands in for the horror of passing time.[47] Refiguring the ruin into a trace of the body, Anthony Vidler describes how the transformation of the bodily metaphor for architecture shifted from the early nineteenth through the late twentieth centuries into a kind of "loss" of physical unity made into mere parts by the fracturing of sensory experience in modernity and modernism. In the architecture of Himmelblau or Tschumi, the decaying body is a metonym for "humanist progress in disarray."[48] Despite modernism's goals of progress, humanism, and democratization, by the 1960s it had become more widely understood as an exercise in futility, or, worse, veiled authoritarianism. After what many saw as the failures of utopian modernism, powerfully captured in the destruction of the Pruitt-Igoe housing project in St. Louis or contemporary photographs of the crumbling movie palaces and mansions of Detroit, ruins have come to represent the inability of any movement to improve quality of life or sustain progress, as well as the cynicism with which new generations understand the goals of their ancestors. The intentionality of Pruitt-Igoe's explosion signaled, as Charles Jencks explains, modernism's "mythical 'death,'" where the deliberate transformation of public modernist buildings into ruins became a way of dealing with the failures of modernism's "ideology of progress."[49]

46. William JR Curtis, "The Classical Ideals of Le Corbusier," *The Architectural Review*, September 21, 2011, https://www.architectural-review.com/buildings/le-corbusier/the-classical-ideals-of-le-corbusier/8619974.article.

47. Andreas Huyssen, "Nostalgia for Ruins," *Grey Room* 23 (Spring 2006): 11.

48. Anthony Vidler, "Architecture Dismembered," in *The Architectural Uncanny* (Cambridge, MA: MIT Press, 1992), 80.

49. Charles Jencks, "Postmodern and Late Modern: The Essential Definitions," *Chicago Review* 3, no. 4 (1987): 34. For an interpretation of the Pruitt-Igoe housing project that questions its status as the "death of modernism," see Katharine G. Bristol, "The Pruitt-Igoe Myth," *Journal of Architectural Education* 44, no. 3 (May 1991): 163–171.

For Walter Benjamin, ruins held particular weight for the historian as well as for the modern theorist of aesthetics. In the ruin, Benjamin explained, history is reconfigured from infinite progress to "unstoppable decline."[50] The ruin not only offers evidence of the inescapability of decay, but also provides a model for criticism that resists judgments of value in unified beauty. Instead, the ruin suggests the productivity of fracturing and disintegration for critical discourse:

> Without at least an intuitive grasp of the life of the detail, as embedded in a structure, all devotion to the beautiful is nothing more than empty dreaming. In the last analysis, structure and detail are always historically charged. The object of philosophical criticism is to show that the function of artistic form is precisely this: to make historical material content [*Sachgehalte*], the basis of every significant work of art, into philosophical truth content [*Wahrheitgehalten*]. This restructuring of material content into truth content makes the weakening of effect, whereby the attractiveness of earlier charms diminishes decade by decade, into the basis for a rebirth in which all ephemeral beauty completely falls away and the work asserts itself as a ruin.[51]

In this sense, the detail, paired with the material structure in which it is embedded, is the key for a more productive mode of aesthetic analysis. To ignore the interplay between the minutia of the detail and the larger structure is to fall into what Benjamin sees as the standard trap of banal appreciation of the beautiful. The detail also suggests materiality's integral role for the philosopher of history: ungrounded concepts of the beautiful cannot offer the possibility of truth content that the detail can provide, for the detail is necessarily a material trace.

Indeed, the detail might be compared to revelatory film theorists' interest in the close-up—both promote a spiritual connection to the material world through microscopy and scrutiny. Like the close-up, the detail must be understood in conjunction with or as a part of the larger material structure in which it exists—for the close-up, the entirety of the film—while simultaneously acting as a key to its meaning. It is both unlocked solution and mystic source, both totally material and resplendent with the expansiveness of consciousness and perception. Furthermore, the ruin's promise of historical memory encompasses the elusiveness of momentary fixation, remaking the beauty of the material into enduring truth. Ruins aid in making history authentic by materializing time and maintaining consistency across multiple

---

50. Walter Benjamin, "The Ruin," in *The Work of Art in the Age of Its Technological Reproducibility and Other Writings on Media*, ed. and trans. Michael W. Jennings, Brigid Doherty, and Thomas Y. Levin (Cambridge: Belknap, 2008), 180.
51. Ibid., 184.

temporalities. If ruins are invested with historical memory and the sense of passing time, then they are also objects of thoughtfulness and intimacy. For this reason, humanity's relationship to ruins illustrates our ability to project our own memory, interiority, and sense of consciousness into the material world. Especially relevant, therefore, to modernity, ruins represented a vision of unfolding history not necessarily fixated on progress but located partially in decay. Benjamin understood the ruin as an allegory for modern aesthetic experience that accorded value to disintegration and disarray. In modernity's fragmentation and shock, previous models of aesthetic idealism fixated on the beauty of unity were no longer entirely relevant. Instead, the palimpsest of the ruin provided a template for criticism located in layers of temporality, materiality, and history's forgotten and lost objects.

Benjamin found ruins essential for their mark of pastness and for their status as detritus overlooked by canons. Paul Klee's *Angelus Novelus* depicted, for Benjamin, the angel of history, a figure who is continually blown forward by the storm of progress but whose face turns toward the past. There, he sees a pile of catastrophes consisting of "wreckage upon wreckage," the trash heap of history, where all the terrible events of the past form one enormous monument to regret.[52] Trash, for Benjamin, was both where history inevitably led—the tragedy of collected experience, the decay of death—and also where its redemption might be found. In the discarded pieces left to rot, the leftover, the ignored, and the downtrodden, history's secrets might come shining to life in a fulfillment of the dialectical imagination. Integral to trash's value for the philosopher of history, particularly the Marxist, is precisely its lack of value for contemporary culture, and therefore its elision of commodity fetishism. Once objects created in the context of mass-produced industrial capitalism lose their immediacy and desirability, they also lose their ability to enchant. In the transition to waste, objects obtain a new kind of magic: clarity of vision and expression, the ability to reveal themselves as themselves without the glamor of commodity fetishism. Susan Buck-Morss explains Benjamin's point regarding decay in *The Arcades Project* as asserting that

> the other side of mass culture's hellish repetition of "the new" is the mortification of matter which is fashionable no longer. The gods grow out of date, their idols disintegrate, their cult places—the arcades themselves—decay. . . . Because these decaying structures no longer hold sway over the collective imagination, it is possible to recognize them as the illusory dream images they always

52. Walter Benjamin, "Theses on the Philosophy of History," in *Illuminations*, ed. Hannah Arendt, trans. Harry Zohn (New York: Harcourt, Brace & World, 1968), 255–256.

were. Precisely the fact that their original aura has disintegrated makes them invaluable didactically.[53]

The process of decay lifts the veil of capital to show the truth of what an object, place, or structure really is. For Buck-Morss, the fragment aligns with the detail, as well as with the close-up: a miniscule material trace theorized in conjunction with its larger structure, a too-frequently forgotten object that, despite its tiny size, offers bountiful interpretive rewards. The fragment is the mass ornament stripped, distraction brought to its most radical potential. Like Kracauer's call for film to use its particular distractions for the purpose of revelation rather than suturing spectator to commodity, the ruin might play the role of idealized mass media in awakening the populace. By virtue of their foreign obsolescence and their necessary juxtaposition, ruins and decayed objects from the trash heap of history become strangely, thoroughly, and totally modern. Ruins are quintessential aspects of modernity because they are both of the past and not of it, because they are dialectical and encourage a doubled approach to analysis, and because it is precisely the modern viewer held enraptured by the illusion of capitalist mass production who benefits most from the particular kind of revelation the ruin can provide.

Two aspects of Benjamin's explanation of the ruin bear particular relevance for the art house and the underground. First, for Benjamin, the ruin allows a built object to evade commodity fetishism by sinking into unglamorous decline. Celebrating the potential productiveness—the disassociation of art with capital—inherent to the ruin, the underground experimental cinema of the 1960s looked to a similar model of decrepitude in an attempt to separate art from money. Second, Benjamin describes the power of the object in ruin to become invested with authenticity through its visible relationship with duration. By virtue of being intertwined with passing time, the ruin allows us to project the possibility of memory as well as a kind of historical interiority. Here, the spectator contemplating the ruin understands the poignancy and vibrancy of its markers of duration, and therefore relates to it. While the ruin does not possess a psychical interiority, its degradation through duration suffuses it with a melancholic aura and an implied aesthetic consciousness. Duration abets the ruin's affect.

In the modern imagination, ruins make use of the embattled monuments of the past by creating a new narrative around them, one of collapse, futility, and decay as well as knowledge, revelation, and alternative pathways toward progress, perhaps even questioning the notion of progress itself. A ruin's aesthetic

53. Susan Buck-Morss, *The Dialectics of Seeing: Walter Benjamin and the Arcades Project* (Cambridge, MA: MIT Press, 1989), 159.

for the modern eye relies on its Benjaminian dialectic: at once the productivity and beauty of decline, and the dawning expanded awareness available as a result of learning from destruction. The 1950s large-screen boom resonated with modern transportation, American exceptionalism, and westward expansion; the consequent decline of certain ideals of neutralization, the rapid rise and fall of moneyed art house cinema, and the burgeoning underground exhibition movement of the 1960s and 1970s corresponded subsequently to a modern approach to ruins. With the immensity of large-screen formats, exhibitors sought to recreate an entire world, a world of either participation or witnessing. The hubris and failure of that project, particularly evidenced in the transcineums' attempt to rocket spectators into a reimagined past, were akin to so many modern and modernist collapses, littered with a utopianism that inspires both refusal and nostalgia. For Svetlana Boym, twentieth-century ruins are enigmatic and elusive objects highlighting the multifaceted nature of changing forms of nostalgia:

> The ruins of twentieth-century modernity, as seen through the contemporary prism, both undercut and stimulate the utopian imagination, constantly shifting and deterritorializing our dreamscape. . . . Rather than recycling romantic notions of the picturesque framed in glass and concrete, the ruins of modernity question the making of such a world picture, offering us a new kind of radical perspectivism. From a twenty-first-century perspective, the ruins of modernity point to possible futures that never came to be. But those futures do not necessarily inspire restorative nostalgia. Instead they make us aware of the vagaries of progressive vision as such.[54]

In constructing a new world through the opening window of the movie screen, exhibitors of the large-screen boom sought also to make a new world picture. Divisions between participation and witnessing reflected the variance in immersion's values among different architectural and exhibition schools of thought, and illustrated the tensions between utopianism and ruins. Witnessing, however, brought to mind the observer, both next to and separated in time and space from the aesthetic object, unable to physically affect it but affected by it as the modern onlooker is external to the unreachable pastness of the ruin—except in its interpretation. From the ruins of the cinematic world picture—enormous screen, the impossibility of developing a visual machine for traveling through time, the futility of total disembodiment and visual revelation through mainstream cinematic presentation—came two

---

54. Svetlana Boym, "Ruins of the Avant-Garde: From Tatlin's Tower to Paper Architecture," in Hell and Schönle, *Ruins of Modernity*, 59.

separate impulses, linked in their reliance still on the importance of space in determining the culture of reception. For one, the underground cinema, the filth and decay of cinema's ruins were immediately realized in the chaos of the exhibition space. Envisioned through an apocalyptic collapse of belief in mainstream film and even mainstream culture, experimental films and media events could rise from the detritus of Hollywood's shortcomings and construct a new spectator of the dystopian space age. For the other, the art house cinema of the second wave of cinephilia in the 1950s and 1960s, some theaters began to move above the "ruin" of mainstream cinema in terms of class, cultural, and artistic sophistication, and in terms of literal distance from the ground. The result was a space-age spectator and a cinema of class utopia where sophistication, artistry, and elegance were widely available with the price of admission.

## CINEPHILIA ABOVE AND UNDERGROUND

Benjamin's ruin suggests two models: the unification of beauty and com- modity, and the possible productivity of decrepitude. The spatial ruin of the underground cinema—its lack of finesse and sophistication, its decrepitude— and the operatic splendor of the wealthy art house cinema similarly invite both a literal and an allegorical comparison. Like the unified art work and the ruin's layered temporality, the art house and the underground are am- bivalent spaces that illustrate the ongoing dispersal and increasing anxiety around contemplation in postmodernity. Where the art house signaled a me- tallic and glistening future jetting upward, the underground tunneled deep into a kind of filmic ruin—the disappointments of a visual utopia unrealized by neutralized screens that ultimately reiterated the American industry's ties to class.

In a 1962 article on new theaters going up in New York, including Cinema I & II as well as other art-centered houses, Joseph Morgenstern of the *New York Herald Tribune* noted that

Dr. Edward Teller, the hydrogen bomb expert, suggested a couple of years ago that all new movie houses be built underground to provide ready-made shelters in case of air attack. Messers. Donald Rugoff and Walter Reade please note. The double-decker theaters you are building in Manhattan, far from being snugly subterranean, are so boldly exposed above ground as to be worthless for any- thing but the viewing of movies in comfort. It may be symptomatic of confi- dence in prolonged peace, of a resurgence in the movie business, of the East Side real estate boom, or simply of the tendency of small empires to grow into larger ones, but the Rugoff Theaters, Walter Reade, Inc., Trans-Lux, and RKO are all in the process of putting up spanking new movie houses in New York City, five of the theaters within one block's distance of each other on Third Avenue.[55]

Although Morgenstern's tone was ironic, his linkage of hydrogen bombs and movie theaters illustrated a two-sided tenor in American postwar rhetoric: dystopia, particularly in regard to atomic discourse, and the utopian space-age thrill of exploration, expansion, and travel up and out into the stars. Where some theaters moved underground, others shot above. During the 1950s and 1960s, exhibition in the urban United States branched out into the potentially profitable realm of the foreign import and art venue. Like the little cinemas of the 1920s but with far more financial backing, the art house promised an experience of artistry and sophistication in an appropriate setting. At the same time, experimental filmmakers, tired of Hollywood's stagnancy and excited by 16 mm and, soon, video art, opened their own theaters underneath the mainstream scene. Yet significant overlap between these two divisions appeared in curious places, both in terms of their respective crossings between high and low art, and in what sometimes became their shared place of exhibition.

By the mid-1960s, international art and fringe cult/exploitation cinema exhibition had begun to intersect. Frequently, the same theater showing Fellini or Louis Malle imports would also host late-night horror or sex fare. During and just after World War II, movie theaters became locations of cross-taste and cross-political cultures where audiences ranging from straight unescorted women to gay men to middle-class to working-class patrons could attend the same theater showcasing both grindhouse and art house cinema.[56] Representatives from high- and low-taste cultures shared space in a Bourdieuian sense, attracted to the taste culture not adjacent to but directly opposite their own.[57] Given the still operative power of the Production Code, such theaters were often the only places to see nudity, sex, and violence—Jack Stephenson notes that these areas were, in fact, the "only growth segments of the movie business during the 1950s."[58] Films such as Bergman's *Summer with Monika* were shown in both contexts—original

---

55. Joseph Morgenstern, "At 59th and Third, Art Movies, 5 in a Row," *New York Herald Tribune*, March 25, 1962. Dr. Edward Teller was famously the inspiration for Dr. Strangelove in Kubrick's 1964 film.

56. Mark Jancovich and Tim Snelson, "Horror at the Crossroads: Class, Gender, and Taste at the Rialto," in *From the Art House to the Grindhouse: Highbrow and Lowbrow Transgression in Cinema's First Century*, ed. John Cline and Robert G. Weiner (New York: Scarecrow Press, 2010), 109–125.

57. See Pierre Bourdieu, *Distinction: A Social Critique of the Judgement of Taste*, trans. Richard Nice (Cambridge, MA: Harvard University Press, 1984).

58. Jack Stephenson, "Grindhouse and Beyond," in Cline and Weiner, *From the Art House to the Grindhouse*, 130.

versions for art house crowds, and radically dubbed, rescored, and condensed ones for the grindhouse.[59] As Mark Betz argues, discourses of high and low cinemas during the 1960s were not merely parallel, but shared, engaging in similar marketing strategies and soliciting similar audience interests. Often the central appeal was sex: newspaper ads for French and Italian films like *Bocaccio '70* promised buxom, comely ladies beckoning male spectators in risqué modes of visual address that could just as easily promote a Doris Wishman film. In response, the *Los Angeles Times* began screening its film ads in 1962 for suggestive images—which, as the MPAA noted, most frequently came from art house or import pictures.[60] Yet it was not only in advertising where such crossover could be found; Betz concludes that, in major cities such as New York and Los Angeles, art house and grindhouse cinema shared censorship, prohibition, exhibition environments, and, ultimately, audiences.[61]

Commonalities of certain aspects of ideal space strengthened the bridge between art and sex in exhibition. For both film types, already slipping into and influencing one another in terms of form, the place of viewing proved to be particularly conducive to a symbiotic relationship. Even in Peter Kubelka's Invisible Cinema at Anthology Film Archives, Annette Michelson notes, the very isolation that enhanced spectatorial visual attention on the screen as a mode of nearly religious experience concurrently implied an exemplary setting for watching pornographic media.[62] At a moment when Jack Smith's *Flaming Creatures* could qualify, in the law's eye, as pornography, it could also function as product for an audience seeking stimulation both intellectual and sexual, perhaps even at the same time, most certainly in the same space.

Discourses of art and exploitation in the 1960s invariably found a central location in New York's Times Square, a hotbed of sexploitation and peep show theaters, prostitution, gambling, and even art house cinemas.[63] Among critical voices of the decade, Manny Farber in particular fetishized the practice of "slumming" to catch rare screenings at theaters in Times Square, illustrating the centrality of the space of watching movies and the context of

---

59. Ibid.

60. "L.A. Times Will Screen Its Motion Picture Ads," *Motion Picture Herald*, January 16, 1962, 11.

61. Mark Betz, "Art, Exploitation, Underground," in *Defining Cult Movies: The Cultural Politics of Oppositional Taste*, ed. Mark Jancovich, Antonio Lazaro Reboll, Julian Stringer, and Andy Willis (Manchester: Manchester University Press, 2003), 220.

62. Annette Michelson, "Gnosis and Iconoclasm: A Case Study of Cinephilia," *October* 83 (Winter 1998): 5.

63. Amy Herzog details the rise and decline of peep show loops and exhibition in New York in "In the Flesh: Space and Embodiment in the Pornographic Peep Show Arcade," *The Velvet Light Trap* 62 (Fall 2008): 29–43, while Eric Schaefer explores the advertising and distribution of exploitation film in *Bold! Daring! Shocking! True!: A History of Exploitation Films, 1919–1959* (Durham, NC: Duke University Press, 1999).

viewing experience even for those hungry for the fringes of cinematic taste.[64] In addition to Farber, James Agee and Bosley Crowther promoted the critic-collector's practice of uncovering treasure in unlikely surroundings, where the allure of filmic gems was heightened by their degraded surroundings. For all of these critics, cinematic art could be found in gritty Times Square grindhouse theaters as well as the clinical modern space of the contemporary art museum, and all manner of locations in between. Peter Stanfield describes postwar American film culture as "invented in that 'rocketing' between the 42nd Street theatres, Greenwich Village picture houses, Lower East Side cinemas and MOMA."[65] While this cinephilia reveled in the lurid—and therefore the valuable product that could be uncovered behind metaphorical dumpsters—rather than the pristine spaces of high art and modernism, it also, like earlier neutralized theater moments, found meaning in space itself and in the inter-action between art object and spectator in a specific place of viewing. Certain theaters in New York, including the Charles Theater, Bleecker Street Cinema, Gramercy Arts, Schlanger's Thalia, and Jonas Mekas's Anthology Film Archives, were of particular artistic cachet. Their locations on dirty streets in Times Square, the Village, or the Lower East Side contributed to a film's wor-thiness of being seen; the very process of subjecting oneself to filth implied both the film's importance *and* the impeccable nature of the critic's taste. Both could be mapped topographically.

It was, therefore, no accident that this movement fixated on a spatial met-aphor: the underground. Manny Farber famously explained how "termite cinema" was the opposite of the elephantine: an art that, as Stanfield describes, signified "both a burrowing into and a withdrawal from mass culture."[66] A motley group of outsiders, freaks, and hipsters sought out a descriptor that implied something outside of the norm. By choosing "underground," they revealed the influence, however unconscious, of earlier modernist modes of spectatorship that insisted on the importance of space to determine object-viewer interaction.[67] Farber extolled a delight specific to the repulsiveness of

64. Manny Farber, "Times Square Moviegoers," *The Nation*, July 4, 1953, reprinted in *Cinema Nation: The Best Writing on Film from The Nation, 1913–2000*, ed. Carl Bromley (New York: Thunder's Mouth Press/Nation Books, 2000), 405–406.

65. Peter Stanfield, "Manny Farber & Jonas Mekas," in *Explorations in New Cinema History: Approaches and Case Studies*, ed. Richard Maltby, Daniel Biltereyst, and Philippe Meers (London: Wiley-Blackwell, 2011), 223.

66. Ibid., 218.

67. In using the term "underground" cinemas, I rely on Tess Takahashi's assertion that site must be analyzed in addition to experimental film form, and mostly refer to her second category of screening sites: relatively traditional theatrical spaces typi-cally replete with seats and white screen that tended to show experimental film, video, and even narrative feature-length movies. Tess Takahashi, "Experimental Screens in the 1960s and 1970s: The Site of Community," *Cinema Journal* 51, no. 2 (Winter 2012): 162–167.

the underground's crumbling locations: "the theaters of the Underground—often five or six docile customers in an improbable place that looks like a bombed-out air shelter or the downstairs ladies room at the old Paramount—offer a weirdly satisfying experience. For two dollars, the spectator gets five bedraggled two-reelers, and, after a sojourn with incompetence, chaos, nouveau-culture taste, he leaves this land's-end theater feeling unaccountably spry."[68] The underground space maintains its connections with Hollywood's elegant theaters owned by Paramount, yet gleefully leads spectators not to a sumptuous bedecked auditorium but downstairs to the women's restroom. The space of the underground is "pock-marked terrain," with a "placid spectator suggest[ing] a new concept of honesty and beauty based on beggarly conditions." An underground theater such as Aldo Tambellini and Otto Piene's Black Gate might boast an "ancient unreliable floor," "patches of masking tape," or a tattered carpet that feels "as spongy and sandy as the beach at Waikiki," and appear like a "blitzed miniature cathedral" despite being "an old room of murky origins, painted flat black . . . [with] a bombed-out area in the front half, which houses the screen, and a number of wooden constructions that have been started by a nonunion carpenter and then thrown up as a bad job."[69] As witty as these descriptions are, they also uncover an obsession with decrepit, ruined space in contrast to maximized visual acuity, comfortable designer seating, carefully calibrated lighting, and excellent sight lines. More than its neutralized predecessors, the Black Gate shared its aesthetic with theaters that turned to pornography in the 1970s. Stephenson describes San Francisco's Mini Adult as a place where

> viewing conditions here are the worst observed anywhere. Giant, hairy, bobbing insect shapes attack the on-screen fornicators, as gobs of crud and hair work their way through the never cleaned rat's nest projectors and jam in the film gate. The screen itself is nothing more than a battered sheet of plywood, while seating consists of rows of hard, old-fashioned wooden chairs that resemble church pews and might well date back to the 1940s.[70]

Stephenson strengthens cinephilia's connective strands between cinema and church, but in opposition to the godly implications of luxury. As Farber explains, the sentimentality of the underground is that "a shrunken, impoverished film is necessarily purer, more honest than a highly budgeted studio film."[71] Such virtue extends into the space of exhibition. This is no vaunted cathedral of filmgoing as

68. Manny Farber, "Experimental Films," in *Negative Space: Manny Farber on the Movies* (Cambridge: Da Capo Press, 1998), 246.
69. Ibid.
70. Stephenson, "Grindhouse and Beyond," 148.
71. Farber, "Experimental Films," 247.

perfection; instead, spirituality emerges in degradation. We are no longer among the wealth of bishops, the pristine gilt of papal garments. We are amongst the mystics and stigmatics whose torn robes belie their proximity to the divine.

Aldo Tambellini's Gate Theater opened in 1966 with two hundred seats at Second Avenue and Tenth Street, over forty blocks south of Cinema I & II. There, cliques of art enthusiasts could watch avant-garde and underground films projected seven days a week until midnight each night. To enter the Gate, Farber described, one first stepped into an old apartment entryway, then moved through a marbled hallway from the 1920s, then was totally absorbed into a marshy pit of blackness, "God help him."[72] Despite its connections to other theaters of the 1960s underground movement and porn industries, the Gate was more than a film theater, and showed experimental pieces unlikely to be found elsewhere. In 1967, Tambellini and Otto Piene expanded into the upstairs space to premiere the Black Gate—the first "electromedia" theater in New York. A wooden platform covered the floor, and Tambellini painted it black and added black cushions where spectators could sit, lie, or recline. The walls were painted white, and the space kept relatively open for a variety of installations and projections. Inside, Tambellini staged happenings and events by himself and other early video and media artists including Piene, Yayoi Kusama, Takehisa Kosugi, Takahiko Iimura, Nam June Paik, and Jud Yalkut.[73] In a release from 1967 describing Piene's *Proliferation of the Sun*, a "multi dimensional experience in changing imagery," and his own *Blackout*, an "experiment in simultaneity," Tambellini explained the theater's intentions:

> The Black Gate, a unique light theatre opens with a series of experiences in electric media. A new art form is being explored by artists from Germany, The United States, Korea and Japan. Electro Media Events must be experienced in terms of the totality of their live presentations. The experience of simultaneity—multi electric stimuli and shifting time-space relationships are one in the Electro Media Event.[74]

Although the Black Gate operated far on the fringes of exhibition, diverging extensively from the high-profile, high-profit world of elitist foreign imports shown at the glamorous art house theaters of the 1960s, Tambellini's investment in "simultaneity," multidimensionality, "totality," and "shifting time-space relationships" linked his work to earlier experimentation with wide and large screens and invisible architectural cinematic space. At the same time,

72. Ibid., 246.
73. Press release from the Black Gate, "Proliferation of the Sun and Blackout: Electro Media Theatre Events at the Black Gate," October 10, 1967, Theatres, US, NY, Black Gate, Billy Rose Theatre Collection of the New York Public Library.
74. Ibid.

his insistence on the productivity of blackness—even in naming his exhibition space and work after it—highlights what Noam Elcott has called the "artificial darkness" inherent to the cinema and avant-garde alike in the first few decades of the twentieth century. For Elcott, the avant-garde located the essence of theater in space and light. Yet it is through the plunge into darkness of the Wagnerian auditorium, changes in movie theater illumination, or the inky ballets of Oskar Schlemmer that an alternative *dispositif* unfolds. Following Elcott, Tambellini's Black Gate emerged, then, from the residue of figures such as Etienne-Jules Marey's photography and its "enlightenment through darkness."[75] The Black Gate was at once a product of the ruins of neutralization's utopian dimensions and a larger modernist impulse toward a spectatorship of deep dives into visual eradication.

*Blackout*, Tambellini's most famous piece, consisted of Tambellini's typical multimedia exercises, here focused on simultaneity (Insert 8). Describing *Blackout*, Tambellini wrote the following in 1966:

blackout

    astronauts do not walk on a two way street . . .

blackout

    there are no roadsigns between planets but light years

blackout

    how would man relate to a city if the buildings moved

blackout

    we do not see the star but the light which comes to us from the star

blackout

    atoms have become cezanne's apples

blackout

    pollock walked into the unknown

blackout

    man does not need his eyes but to function with 13 billion cells in his brain.[76]

Although Tambellini deliberately set his work against the mainstream, his written accompaniment to *Blackout* suggests investments in space, vision, scientific advances, and the possibilities of travel into the larger universe—with the added caveat that "man does not need his eyes but to function with 13 billion cells in his brain." Whereas the attentive visual structure of the

75. Noam Elcott, *Artificial Darkness: An Obscure History of Modern Art and Media* (Chicago: University of Chicago Press, 2016), 28.

76. Press release from the Black Gate, "Proliferation of the Sun and Blackout: Electro Media Theatre Events at the Black Gate," October 10, 1967, Theatres, US, NY, Black Gate, Billy Rose Theatre Collection of the New York Public Library.

transcineums relied on a disembodied vision extending outward into a directed nationalist project, Tambellini's reliance on the "unknown," "light years," and "astronauts" paired with the refusal of the eye for the sake of the brain argue for a shifted sense of vision directed only by the spectator. To participate in a blackout, the spectator succumbs to darkness, but not quite the darkness of a neutralized theater. Release into architectural and filmic immersion also indicated hegemonic ideologies: capitalism, the society of the spectacle, the exhibitionary complex. Resisting the aseptic nature of a faded functional space required an alternative to the streamlined walls of the modernist movie theater. Although certainly partially dictated by low budgets, the Black Gate Theater distinguished itself from such structures by being haphazard, eroded, a dilapidated ruin of a theater. To be in a "blackout" was to be an individual functioning with "13 billion cells in his brain," an astronaut shooting off into one's thought space. To be in a "blackout" was also to deny the authoritarianism of Hollywood cinema for the sake of an alternative pathway rising from the ruins of theatrical exhibition. Yet Tambellini's obstinate stance against mainstream exhibition and film ironically implied his link to the history of American cinema: an obsession with how the space of viewing coupled with the object itself separated moving imagery spectatorship from its ancestral aesthetic experiences. Although the Black Gate's clutter and filth seemed entirely opposed to the perfected optical conditions and blanked out space of the mid-century austere theater, his insistence on incorporation of spectator, space, and object reinforced a connection to endlessness, immersion, and integration. Even in the underground, the place of seeing netted together object and spectator, binding viewer to thing by filling in the surrounding space with instructions on the best way to look.

Blackout, however, bore additional historical resonances especially poignant for a 1960s audience. After World War II, "blackout" might also conjure up the dampening of city lights in the event of a bombing or attack by external forces. Paired with the "underground," "blackout" implied a public still experiencing a mid-century threat new to Americans after Hiroshima and Nagasaki: the hydrogen bomb. Although the 1950s were the decade most filled with the potential of air raids and drills, the influence of the atom bomb on popular American culture continued through the Cold War's cease at the end of the 1980s.[77] Experimental film such as Bruce Conner's *A Movie* (1958)

77. Such persistent fear centered on bombing emerged, per Anthony Vidler, "in fantasy in the 1880s, in more concrete terms after the First World War, and was reinforced by the technological advances used in the Second World War: quite simply, the anxiety about being bombed into oblivion." Vidler points to the de-urbanized garden-city movement as a direct response to the risk traditional urban space faced of being leveled by air raids after World War II. In response to this impulse, to construction of bomb shelters, and to the threat of nuclear annihilation came a postmodern "architecture of disillusion, produced out of the near certainty of total destruction; an architecture

similarly took up iconic images of mushroom-shaped clouds to comment on the postwar anxiety of the atomic age. Farber's war metaphors for the Black Gate, terms such as "bombed out," "blitzed," and "pock-marked terrain," thus evoked the sense of destruction and decay pervading much postwar popular culture. By the 1960s, "underground" could evoke notions of rarity, authenticity, intellectual challenge, and the thrill of the new, but also dirt, filth, sex, war, apocalypse, and ruin—always in the context of experiential space. Paired with the supposed death of modernism and birth of postmodernism, the rise of drive-in culture and subsequent suburbanizing movement of theaters from urban centers to malls, the blight of the American cityscape, and the general disillusionment of the youthful American populace, avant-garde cinephilic exhibition in the 1960s retained its investment in experiential space but moved increasingly toward fetishizing theaters as ruins. The ruined theater suggested the potential for American ruin. In looking toward the future in cinematic terms, the underground proposed an encroaching temporality of devastation and apocalypse.

Yet the underground's cinephilia also traded in idealized rhetoric. Typified by Jonas Mekas and Anthology Film Archives, experimental cinephilia balanced an archival impulse with an immersive one to articulate, as Michelson describes, "a prescriptively utopian and *redemptive* cinephilia" that, despite its resistance to established and politically fraught media ideologies, underscored a latent lineage traced from modernist spectatorship.[78] Underground filmmakers, exhibitors, and supporters (often the same people) established themselves in opposition to monetized and mainstream art, as well as the high modernism that, by the late 1960s, increasingly seemed an abject failure. As Michelson explains, however, their investment in formalist challenge as well as the inescapability of American mass-produced culture did as much to define the underground movement and its dedication to the redemptive power of art as did the concept of revolutionary art itself. While the neutralized cinema stood, in many ways, exactly for what artists such as Tambellini and Mekas resisted, that is, mainstream Hollywood movies shown in clinical profit-making environments, the two shared more than appeared at first glance. Both were dedicated to the utopian possibilities of film viewing, both promoted attentive contemplation, and both insisted on the importance of space for cinematic display. Although the underground celebrated the cavelike experience of secrecy and neutralization the power of whitewashed unobtrusiveness, both agreed upon the necessity of a specific place of viewing

that, after the realization of the enormity of what had happened in 1945 in Japan, inspired a sometimes unconsciously—but sometimes very consciously—negative response to the human condition." Anthony Vidler, "Air War and Architecture," in Hell and Schönle, *Ruins of Modernity*, 32, 36.

78. Michelson, "Gnosis and Iconoclasm," 9 (emphasis original).

to maximize the intended experience. In this sense, Tambellini and Mekas typified the moment of the "funeral of practice," per Elsaesser, or, the emergence of the apparatus's identification.[79] Their ostensible resistance to the ideological indoctrination of Hollywood cinema cements Baudry's understanding of mainstream film as a programmed capitalist system—one in which the neutralized cinema found companionship.[80] Yet their investment in the spatial dynamics of watching implies Pedullà's ethics of attentive spectatorship: one where immersion and contemplation are uneasy bedfellows for the spectator who repeatedly traverses the pathway between absorption and dialectics.[81] Like neutralization, the apparatus is a condition of ambivalent cinematic spectatorship, both entwined within theatrical bones and a sign of its own fragility.

Meanwhile, theaters dedicated to art film and European imports stood seemingly in direct contrast to the "perversity" of underground cinephilia. Where the underground cinema was a filthy bombed-out wasteland, the art house theater soared into a brighter future through high levels of illumination, extensive use of glass and shining metal, and elevations reaching far above the ground.[82] Where the Black Gate Theater was a lean-to shelter in a radioactive dystopia, Donald Rugoff's Cinema I & II was a glamorous spaceship propelling spectators into a crystalline vision of progress at once national, filmic, and economic. In addition to Cinema I & II, Rugoff's art cinema empire eventually included the Paris, Plaza, Sutton, Paramount, Beekman, Murray Hill, Gramercy, and Art theaters, all of which Rugoff fiercely maintained until losing control of the chain in 1979 after a bitter stock-trading battle.[83] Rugoff's approaches to making foreign and art house cinema both desirable and accessible to the New York City public included both elegance in design and unlikely exhibition practices; William Klein recalled exclusively showing *Eldridge Cleaver* at Cinema I & II, where Rugoff offered "Revolutionary Prices" of one dollar for admission and provided 50 percent of profits to the Black

79. Thomas Elsaesser, "What Is Left of the Cinematic Apparatus, or Why We Should Retain (and Return to) It," *Recherches Semiotiques/Semiotic Inquiry* 31, nos 1/2/3 (2011): 10.

80. Jean-Louis Baudry, "Ideological Effects of the Basic Cinematographic Apparatus," trans. Alan Williams, *Film Quarterly* 28, no. 2 (Winter 1974): 39–47.

81. Gabriele Pedullà, *In Broad Daylight: Movies and Spectators After the Cinema*, trans. Patricia Gaborik (London: Verso, 2012).

82. Building above ground was not, of course, limited to art house theaters. In 1965, the Evergreen 1 & 2 in Chicago was described as an "airborne" "ultra-modern" "theatre in the sky" rising fifty-seven feet above the ground on an elevated platform. Opened by Arthur Rubloff & Co., the theater obtained "air-rights" for the twin screen, double-curve seating patterned space. "A 'Theatre in The Sky' for Chicago," *Boxoffice*, May 17, 1965, *Modern Theatres* section, 6–7.

83. "Donald Rugoff, 62, Presided over Chain of Movie Theaters," Obituaries, *New York Times*, April 29, 1989.

Panthers.[84] For Daniel Talbot, founder and former owner of New Yorker Films, Rugoff presided over a golden age of exhibition in New York, booking "tough films" and forbidding the consumption of popcorn in his theaters.[85]

One of Rugoff's first theaters, the Paris, still the country's longest-operating art house and import theater, opened in 1948 under Pathé management. Ten years later, Rugoff took over the James J. Munro and Warner Leeds-designed theater at the onset of his New York empire. Of particular importance to Rugoff's reign as king of art exhibition in New York, the Paris's exclusive approach to sophisticated style, European film, and luxurious moviegoing undoubtedly influenced Rugoff's later efforts throughout the city, especially in the conceptualization of Cinema I & II. In architectural pastels of the Paris, modern exteriors with streamlined glass and an abstract art image combine with elegantly attired attendees and glossy streets reminiscent of the "wet-down" look in prestige film (Insert 9). The resulting image is of a glamorous filmgoing event where going to the movies is akin to being in the movies, a star of a momentary, fleeting night out. Sketches from inside the cinema are composed not in the same broad spectrum, but drawn instead on black board with white chalk lines; elegance, here, is restricted to the outside and lounge areas, while the auditorium is dedicated to the expected 1948 experience of a black-and-white film (Insert 10).

For Rugoff, and for his flagship theater Cinema I & II, the Paris inspired a kind of exclusive filmgoing experience, one linked indisputably to European refinement as well as more American approaches to class, but also to optics, sightlines, and immersive exhibition practice. By the early 1960s, when Rugoff's theaters were in full swing, sophisticated art house theaters like the Paris implied both architectural mystique and visual function. Prior to Cinema I & II's opening in July, Archer Winsten asked in the *New York Post*,

> You know those Rugoff theaters, the ones that appear all together, the seven of them, in a vertical advertisement, and are usually devoted to art films or foreign ones? Well, they're going to have a "flagship" theater, a sort of twin, called Cinema I and Cinema II. It's on Third Avenue opposite Bloomingdale's, and just now you can see steel beams there big enough to support Madison Square Garden audiences, but when it's finished it will appear to be an airy thing of glass on the outside. Inside it will be remarkable, being the first movie theater built in NYC from the ground up since the '30s. It will be three-dimensional and have great sight-lines with the screen 30 inches off the floor. People will see over

---

84. Apparently the Black Panthers would also sell magazines and records in the lobby during *Eldridge Cleaver*'s run; at the time, Nelson Rockefeller was trying the Panther 21 and sitting on the board of Cinema I & II. Jared Rapfogel and William Klein, "Mister Freedom: An Interview with William Klein," *Cineaste* 33, no. 4 (Fall 2008): 24–29.

85. Daniel Talbot, Letter to the Editor, *New York Times*, May 21, 1989.

heads only because the seats will rise steeply, and there will be more room for legs and feet and no center aisle. . . . The first picture to be shown at this Cinema I & II will be *Boccaccio '70*, which will be Italian-made and contains three widely advertised stories. The thought is, two theaters, three stories, three directors of world-class stature, stars without number, you're certainly going to get your money's worth of culture-convenience, aren't you?[86]

"Culture-convenience" perfectly encapsulated Donald Rugoff's plan for the theater, as well as his chain in general, which was, according to *Interiors*, the "latest in the Rugoff 'little cinemas' specializing in foreign and art films to the accompaniment of free coffee served in lounges that double as art galleries."[87] Inside Cinema I & II, either one popular art film would be shown on a staggered schedule in both auditoriums, or two films of varying interest would be shown at the same time. Patrons could catch one or two properly vetted films, enjoy coffee and socializing in the lounges, be seen from the street by passersby, admire rotating artwork in the theatrical gallery spaces, and, before or after, drop into Bloomingdales for a quick shopping trip. Joe Wolhandler's press release regarding the theater established that "Cinema I-Cinema II will be the first movie houses in America to devote as much of their space to permanent art works as will be occupied by those commissioned for the new project. . . . Completing this, Cinema I-Cinema II will be the first movie houses to offer their patrons a 'complete cultural experience,' as planned by the architects and circuit president Donald S. Rugoff."[88]

Winsten's note of the theater's proximity to Bloomingdales illustrated the extent to which Cinema I & II openly acknowledged its association with upper-class pleasures, efficient transportation, and purchasing power—all ideals in the era of Robert Moses's urban renewal. Designed to be an "airy thing of glass," the theater stood as the pinnacle of the soon-to-be-doomed Rugoff chain, as relational to the imposing skyscrapers of the city's skyline, and as a marker of the end of FDR Drive in Manhattan. Cinema I & II also included a glass corner on East Sixty-Sixth Street, ribbon windows on East Sixty-Fifth, a glass façade, and a "sloping streamlined lounge ceiling that refers stylistically back to the Moderne style of the 1930's."[89] Inside, Cinema I boasted the first continental seating plan in New York. Although Cinema II included a

86. Archer Winsten, "Rages and Outrages," *New York Post*, April 9, 1962.
87. "Two-in-One Art Movie," *Interiors Magazine*, November 1962, Abraham Geller Collection, Box 1:33, Files Large Projects, 1962, Avery Architectural and Fine Arts Library, Columbia University.
88. Press Release, Joe Wolhandler, Public Relations, 15 April 1962, Abraham Geller Collection, Box 3:1, Public Relations, 1961–1989, Avery Architectural and Fine Arts Library, Columbia University.
89. Robin Pogrebin, "In Preservation Wars, a Focus on Midcentury," *New York Times*, March 24, 2005.

more typical seating plan with a center aisle, marketing materials highlighted Cinema I's excellent optical conditions and reduced "interference created by patrons entering or leaving the theatre. This feature was incorporated here by Schlanger, as in the world-famed theatres he designed at reconstructed Colonial Williamsburg, Va."[90]

Rhetoric around both auditoriums emphasized the substantial benefits of sightlines and calculated seating patterns. The appearance of class embraced by Geller and realized in marble-sheathed windows, copper chandeliers, and blue Venetian tile slipped easily into the power of pristine vision within the auditorium. Six years prior, writers in *International Projectionist* argued that variations in standards required new approaches to showing foreign films. Different aspect ratios might cause heads, feet, or subtitles to be cut off by widescreen apertures, while the predominance of low-key lighting in moody European films could make widescreen projection impossible.[91] In 1966, Schlanger would also argue for specific approaches to screening art and foreign films, which, he pointed out, required relatively high projection points to accommodate subtitles. A high position paired with a lessened angle between spectator and image results in "the feeling of looking at a framed picture up on a wall. The art, despite this 'art' audience, is now destined to go far beyond the 'picture' concept towards the ability to recreate living experiences. The economic factors must be analyzed to determine if and for how long there will be more than one philosophy of presentation for motion pictures."[92] As such, viewing conditions were, at this point, both attuned to specific filmic product and indicative of theatrical investment expected by upper-class patrons accustomed to events in luxe surroundings.

For New York in the 1950s and 1960s, cinema had become indelibly entwined with the high-art world, visible in literal connections such as galleries with rotating objects in the theaters, moving image installations in high-art museums, and architectural references to opera houses exemplified by Cinema I & II's above-ground lobby structure.[93] In underscoring film's relationship to art, however, the art house represented a kind of return to an architecture of attractions, but with fewer joyrides and more broad spaces filled

90. Press Release, Joe Wolhandler, Public Relations, 15 April 1962, Abraham Geller Collection, Box 3:1, Folder Public Relations, 1961–1989, Avery Architectural and Fine Arts Library, Columbia University.

91. "Projecting Foreign Films," *International Projectionist* 31, no. 10 (October 1956): 5.

92. Ben Schlanger, "Criteria for Motion-Picture Viewing and for a New 70mm System: Its Process and Viewing Arrangements," *Journal of the Society of Motion Picture and Television Engineers* 75, no. 3 (March 1966): 163.

93. Such as, for example, Charles Dockum's Mobile Color Projectors, carried out at the Solomon R. Guggenheim Museum from 1952 to 1953. Amanda Brown, "Charles Dockum's Mobile Color Projector," Solomon R. Guggenheim Museum Library & Archives Findings Blog, November 18, 2010, https://www.guggenheim.org/blogs/findings/charles-dockums-mobile-color-projector.

with multiple media forms. Both the popular press and arts organizations celebrated Cinema I & II for its rotating galleries and architectural elegance.[94] Yet
it was also sold to the public as an entire experience, up to and including the
trappings of such an experience. Whereas designers of the neutralized house
of the 1930s deliberately disassociated their theaters from the lavish excesses
of the 1920s palace, owners of the high-class 1960s art house sought to provide a lush experience sharing some elements with the elaborate theaters of
the earlier parts of the century. As neutralization's essential points such as
better sightlines, demasked screens, lack of proscenia, and more intimate and
darker auditoriums were absorbed into mainstream theatrical structure, a
shifted sense of cinephilia began to emerge with the elegant art house that
proposed the usefulness of decorative surroundings for the promotion of
film. To be sure, such an impulse related to mid-century American wealth,
when conspicuous consumption and additional leisure time were more widely
available to the general populace. Wealth seemed closer within reach for more
Americans, and glamor more attractive than austerity. In the wake of critics
such as Agee, Farber, and Crowther, however, film was more widely considered
its own specific form.[95] Associating film with opera, as in the case of Cinema
I & II, no longer seemed either counterintuitive or necessary, but simply an
example of art and capital intertwining to seduce the populace into becoming
an audience.

Alongside a solid economy of growth and progress in the 1950s and early
1960s and the promise of the space race, the beguiling but accessible art house
theater signaled a general mid-century American optimism. The urbane art
house's architecture implied a forward and upward trajectory in terms of individual wealth growth, the increasing strength of the American economy,
and the new possibility of space travel. Earlier filmic utopia proposed by
the neutralized cinema of the 1930s through the 1950s suggested revelation through film: a disembodied projection toward a higher ground of aesthetic experience. The dream proposed by the art house theater, on the other
hand, presented an aspirational utopia encouraging the viewpoint that all
spectators, too, could participate in the new dawn of American wealth and
progress: economic liberation through taste. In contrast, underground movie

94. Cinema I & II received the following awards: 1963, Municipal Art Society of NY,
Certificate of Merit; 1964, New York State Associations of Architects Design Award;
1964, City Club of New York, Bard Award for Urban Architecture (Abraham Geller
Collection, Avery Architectural and Fine Arts Library, Columbia University, Box 2:51,
Photographs, Cinema I & II, Manhattan, NY, 5-D Master, 1962–1964). The theater
was also chosen for an exhibit at the American Museum of the Moving Image in 1988
as an example of world-class theatrical architecture ("Cinema I and II among Sites in
Museum Exhibit," *Variety*, November 16, 1988, Abraham Geller Collection, Box 3:2,
Avery Architectural and Fine Arts Library, Columbia University).

95. *Cahiers du Cinéma* has frequently been credited with ensuring film's status as
art with the publication in 1954 of François Truffaut's essay instantiating the auteur

houses—experimental houses such as the Black Gate and Anthology Film Archives—denied this turn, choosing instead to focus on the potential of dystopia and the unglamorous but "authentic" experience of the experimental. Where the art house reveled in a glistening rendition of corporate spectacle, the underground movement looked to degradation to separate art from capital. While the operatic art house celebrated an approach to cinephilia in some ways recalling the decadence of the movie palace, underground exhibition embraced a spirit of invention through disarray that evoked Kracauer's productive disintegration illuminating the failures of capitalism.

Although the New York press celebrated Cinema I & II for its innovative twin screen design, its position as the first ground-up theater construction in the city since the early 1930s, and its modernist serene beauty, the theater's sophisticated and upper-class status sequestered it from the edginess of the underground movement or alternative New York cinephilias of the 1970s. Exemplified by the Film Forum's opening in 1970 "in a dingy space with fifty folding chairs on the Upper West Side," the elite scene often found a more secure home in the forbidding filthiness of the underground than the aseptic cleanliness of the foreign house.[96] Underground cinemas frequently relied on reused or do-it-yourself spaces rather than expensive new theaters; the original location of downtown's Cinema Village (1962) was a converted firehouse, while the Film Forum eventually found a home in a repurposed garage.[97] Although optical perfection was secondary to simply providing access to the films, during Cinema Village's renovations in the late 1990s manager Ed Arentz "fussed over sight lines ('How important is the screen size when the head of the person sitting in front of you is blocking a third of it?')" and added Dolby sound wiring.[98] Film Forum's reopening in 1981 included a "jazzy Deco marquee" in its new locale.[99]

## THE AFTERLIFE OF ART

The late 1950s and 1960s could be considered a success story for neutralization. At a mid-century moment when functional modernist forms represented

theory, "Un certaine tendance du cinema français," *Cahiers du Cinéma* 6, no. 31 (January 1954): 15–29.

96. Kathy Davis, "The Return of Film Forum," *American Film*, September, 1981, 62.

97. "According to the employees of French Kisses, a poster and prints store below the theater, the pornographic films were part of a short-run gay festival that lasted only a few weeks and the theater has been closed ever since." Rachel D. Lendner, "Small Cinema Deaths Greatly Exaggerated," *West Side Spirit*, February 26, 1991.

98. Michael Atkinson, "It Takes a Cinema Village," *Village Voice*, December 15, 1998, 146.

99. Davis, "The Return of Film Forum."

the pinnacle of good taste, the well-funded art house was a crowning achievement that fully acknowledged Schlanger's approach as the progressive one.[100] At the same time, its undeniably aspirational attributes demonstrated the theater's interest in democratization through wealth—that filmic utopia was something achieved not just through proper vision but the markers of capital. Thus the neutralized cinema in the era of the art house completed both the cycle of transportation—automobilic and stratospheric, into higher orbits of class—and of indoctrination into the capitalist ideologies that underpin apparatus theory's reading of cinematic experience.

To return to Baudry: Schlanger's neutralized theaters sought out a "transcendental subject" in that their intention was to create bodiless eyes in motion that identified with the camera lens. This was most evident in the transcineum structures, with their fixation on screen integration via *Williamsburg: The Story of a Patriot*'s shooting and editing that mimicked perspective. Yet while the transcineums were site-specific buildings, Schlanger integrated many of their experimental features into his later art houses, including continental seating and, perhaps most strikingly, metal-covered walls that mirrored glass exteriors and reflected screen and auditorium light with a gentle, pristine glow. In opening up the front of house with multileveled glass lobbies floating above the city streets, Cinema I & II was a model for other art houses and twin theaters to take up the perfected display not only of films but of spectators themselves.

Here, then, the neutral theater performed two tasks: first, the decades-long goal of immersing the spectator into the film, and second, completing the transit of the desire to be a part of the spectacle. For a passerby on the street, the spectators were visible on the second level as plainly above him, framed by light and glass: the aspirational civilized shuttling upward into higher classes through the vector of film. He might then pause, yearning to be a sophisticate like these ethereal beings who drive on brand-new highways and shop at glamorous department stores and appreciate foreign films in exquisite settings; and he might consider how such a transformation could be achievable simply by purchasing a ticket at the street-level box office and ascending the elevators to the artichoke chandelier-lit second-floor lobby. It is, then, at that moment that the neutralized cinema most clearly achieves the status of apparatus, as the spectator identifies, per Baudry, "with what stages the spectacle": the reality function that underlies theatrical space and effaces difference for the sake of suture into capitalist ideology.[101] The spectator, too, "stages the spectacle" by becoming a part of its display. What on the one hand was the ultimate

---

100. For further reading on the American mid-century braiding of modern art, taste, and media forms, see Lynn Spigel, *TV by Design: Modern Art and the Rise of Network Television* (Chicago: The University of Chicago Press, 2009).

101. Baudry, "Ideological Effects," 45.

example of neutralization's mainstream success was also evidence of its decline into ruin: the spectacle-made spectator no longer fades into the dark but glows with self-evident confidence like the screen, framed like the image, available to be admired, desired, and witnessed. It is little wonder that the underground's response was to darken, to tunnel, and to hide; and it is also little wonder that the underground gained its fetishization of theatrical space from the very exhibition practices it understood to be degraded and impure.

By the late 1980s, a third auditorium had opened in Cinema I & II, transforming the structure into Cinema I, II & III. At the end of 1987 and beginning of 1988, extensive renovations overseen by Geller resulted in the reduction of Cinema I to 570 seats for better sightlines, the lobby reduced to a single entrance, and the double marquee reduced to one. The exterior gained a new patterned sidewalk, and black granite panels replaced the white marble on the arcade columns. Each auditorium was given a color scheme, with I decorated in red, II in blue, and III in gold; illuminated handrails were installed throughout for ease of seating.[102] Four of the original art pieces were restored, including the Bolotowsky mural. The renovations included new velvet curtains in each auditorium matching the new color schemes, a throwback of sorts to the luxury of the palace that maintained the art house theater's visual connections to filmic luxury. Given Schlanger's death in 1971, the renovation was completed solely on Geller's watch. Much of the work done added considerably to the already relatively decorated interiors and even the auditoriums, particularly in the case of illuminated handrails and curtains. Cinema I, II & III are still open, and art house theaters in general remain fixtures on the exhibition scene, though most are owned by major corporations such as Landmark and few retain the particular splendor of Cinema I, II & III or the Paris.

In Lincoln Center, where an entire performing and visual arts complex has long stood as a cultural touchstone for New York City, cinema as art continues to be well attended and well funded. Moving imagery in gallery and temporary exhibition spaces retains a link to the makeshift and fluctuating sites of the underground. In June of 2011, the new Elinor Bunin Munroe Film Center opened at Lincoln Center to house the Film Society's extensive programming (Insert 11). Designed by David Rockwell with consultation by the conceptual architectural firm Diller Scofidio + Renfro that oversaw the larger Lincoln Center renovation, the center is accessible from street level where 90 feet of glass display the titles of over 1,000 films shown at Lincoln Center and 160 in-ground lights "create a kind of welcome mat" for a building intended

---

102. Information from Architect's Office, Abraham Geller Collection, Box 3:2, Folder Renovation of Cinemas I, II, and III, Avery Architectural and Fine Arts Library, Columbia University.

to be open and democratic.[103] Made from the bones of an old parking garage and underutilized office space, the center recalls its spatial history through exposed ductwork, raw concrete columns, and an enormous garage door in the amphitheater. Each of the two theaters within the center boast sound-absorbing walls made of pleated, perforated metal ostensibly designed "to look like the curtains typically found in Italian opera houses of the 1920s," while the central auditorium seats 87 on tiered benches for lectures or other special events (Insert 12).[104] Although conceived of as a kind of temple for movies, Rockwell described the design process as "like doing a theater piece where the set is based on a narrative."[105] New York Film Festival selections screen mostly in the larger Walter Reade Theater, which seats 287, while the two smaller theaters in the center, seating 144 and 87 respectively, show a variety of repertory, new, and special-occasion films, often with question and answer sessions attended by directors, producers, stars, or others involved in the film's production. In addition to showing lesser-seen independent features and foreign imports, the center hosts a midnight movie series with cult classics such as *Eraserhead* and *Evil Dead*. Operating in the same complex as Julliard and the Metropolitan Opera, the Lincoln Center Film Society has long been a model for cinephilic exhibition and film preservation. Perhaps even more so than its compatriots at Anthology Film Archives or the Quad Cinema, the Elinor Bunin Munroe Film Center encapsulates the current trajectory of cinephilic exhibition as a combination of high and low forms, a legacy inherited from the 1960s and 1970s New York scene of Ingmar Bergman, Maya Deren, and Jean-Luc Godard as well as David Lynch, Bruce Conner, Jack Smith, John Waters, and Aldo Tambellini.

What is to be learned from the Elinor Bunin Munroe Film Center is not only the enduring appeal of high- and low-taste cultures brought crashing together. The center also illustrates a continuing insistence on theatrical space's use, even in an era of at-home entertainment. Such space owes a debt to the mid-century art house's linkages with transportation by car and with the class markers of high culture. And such space replays the circuits through which mainstream and underground film meet and cross one another, over and over again, in the auditorium. In glass-framed lightness or shredded, filthy darkness, the powers of the spectacle supplant repeated arguments that theatergoing has ended and that film has died. The memory of the neutralized cinema haunts the center, with its perforated metal walls and its sound-absorbing technologies, and reminds one that the streamlined auditorium has always held very different— if impossible—hopes for the movies than the palace ever did.

103. Quote by David Rockwell in Robin Pogrebin, "Renovations That Seek to Put Film Out Front," *New York Times*, May 15, 2011.

104. Ibid.

105. Ibid.

# Coda

On May 3, 1971, Ben Schlanger died at French Hospital in Manhattan at the age of 66. Schlanger had entered the hospital to provide blood for a transfusion for a family member; after going under general anesthesia, he never woke again. After his death, his fourth wife (and now widow) Marion Friedberg packed up his archival notes, drawings, and papers and sent them in the mail addressed simply to "Columbia University Library." They are, to anyone's knowledge, lost. The bulk of his work that still exists can be found instead in the vast number of studies and articles he wrote for numerous industrial periodicals, as well as scattered bits of ephemera and correspondence at Colonial Williamsburg or in the papers of other, more well-known architects like Abraham Geller and Wallace K. Harrison. Schlanger has both faded into time's ravages and shaped the course of exhibition history. Like an optical vacuum, his ideas are an invisible structuring force, a shadow that quietly articulates the conditions of cinema.

In a 1983 *SMPTE* article, William C. Shaw and J. Creighton Douglas described the ideal of IMAX and OMNIMAX systems as "involv[ing] the viewers with the motion picture and with each other in a way that puts everyone 'in the picture.' This strong sense of reality is achieved by reducing or eliminating the various 'clues' which normally remind the audience that they are watching a picture."[1] The authors observed that clients fell into one of two categories: those who preferred OMNIMAX, an awe-inspiring planetarium system with slightly poorer resolution but larger surround, and those who preferred IMAX's resolution and steadiness in a "large enough" image. "Perhaps," they concluded, "it is a distinction between the dreamers and the thinkers."[2]

1. William C. Shaw and J. Creighton Douglas, "IMAX and OMNIMAX Theatre Design," *Journal of the Society of Motion Picture and Television Engineers* 92, no. 3 (March 1983): 284.
2. Ibid., 290.

Such a set of compromises between reverie and analysis, between immersion and contemplation, or between disembodied abstraction and attentive inflexibility, reveals that the debates surrounding decoration and austerity, showmanship and revelation, and utopia and dystopia continued and still continue to be waged even after Schlanger's death and neutralization's dispersal. Neutralization was one of many moments in cinematic exhibition and technological history where theoretically and culturally informed debates found manifestation in the theater's architecture.

These debates were hardly unique to cinema, and suggest the power of moving imagery and how we view it for the larger implications of spectatorship in general: in film, in art, in theater, in buildings, in everyday experience. In a sense, the neutralized theater was always a cinematic ruin, hinting at film's radical potential for liberation paired with the impossibility of ever fully achieving an escape velocity from embodiment or from an ideological standpoint. Its space was an aporia: at once an every space, everywhere, and a no space, nowhere. To make a house for this still confusing and new thing of the cinema meant imagining its eventual demise.

Now, when the movie theater seems a vestigial reminder of older patterns in constant danger of disappearing completely, neutralization might seem a curiosity for the dustbin of history. Yet it is at this very moment that it begs to be more fully understood. Schlanger's obsessions with visual acuity and with scale speak to the governing properties of moving imagery; although once their ideological demands were confined to theatrical space, now they have infiltrated all aspects of everyday life, where screen proliferation and narrative expansion have neutralized many of the borders between body, eye, mind, and media object. While the spatial attributes of the apparatus have declined physically, in other ways they have been absorbed into our quotidian habits of looking, their political demands even further shrouded by virtue of their lack of identifiable and separate spaces.

But neutralization's story is not only that of the capitalist ideologies from which film and exhibition can never be fully disentangled. It is also a history of fraught transportation and transcendence. If its success over the course of the first two-thirds of the twentieth century speaks to discursive and sinister elements of cinematic transcendence, Schlanger's unceasing crusade hints as well at the (always failed) utopian dimensions of spectatorial desire: immersion and contemplation; industry and theory; cinephilia and discipline; indoctrination and transcendence; apparatus and vacuum. Schlanger's work stands as a reminder of these unsolvable conundrums at the heart of spectatorship, and how such fascinating dilemmas can be found not only in film's theoretical modes but its material and ephemeral histories.

If neutralization eventually faded, its arguments and pathways remain to be traced in the mysterious and invisible places of seeing that continue to be constructed in the search for aesthetic revelation. Studying its movement through time provides both a fuller view of American cinema and a deeper understanding of its frequently contradictory desires: both to construct and to liberate the spectator. Within the walls of the theater or the cocoon of the home, such dramas continue to play out across a multitude of screens, their glowing lights softening the borders of the darkened voids around them.

# INDEX

Note: Figures are indicated by an italic *f* following the page number.